IT WAS ALL
A DREAM

IT WAS ALL A DREAM

A NEW GENERATION CONFRONTS THE BROKEN PROMISE TO BLACK AMERICA

RENIQUA ALLEN

NEW YORK

Nation Books
116 East 16th Street, 8th Floor New York, NY 10003
www.nationbooks.org
@NationBooks

Printed in the United States of America
First Edition: January 2019
Published by Nation Books, an imprint of Perseus Books, LLC, a subsidiary of Hachette Book Group, Inc.

Nation Books is a co-publishing venture of the Nation Institute and the Perseus Books.
The Hachette Speakers Bureau provides a wide range of authors for speaking events. To find out more, go to www.hachettespeakersbureau.com or call (866) 376-6591.

The publisher is not responsible for websites (or their content) that are not owned by the publisher.

Print book interior design by Linda Mark

Library of Congress Cataloging-in-Publication Data

Names: Allen, Reniqua, author.
Title: It was all a dream : a new generation confronts the broken promise to Black America / Reniqua Allen.
Description: New York, NY : Nation Books, an imprint of Perseus Books, LLC, [2019] | Includes bibliographical references and index.
Identifiers: LCCN 2018028528| ISBN 9781568585864 (hardcover) | ISBN 9781568585871 (e-book)
Subjects: LCSH: African Americans—Economic conditions—21st century. | Race discrimination—Economic aspects—United States.
Classification: LCC E185.8 .A56 2019 | DDC 330.900896/073—dc23
LC record available at https://lccn.loc.gov/2018028528

LSC-C

10 9 8 7 6 5 4 3 2 1

For my Aunt Dee—
my American Dream

CONTENTS

Contents

INTRODUCTION

It was all a dream
I used to read Word Up! magazine
Salt'N'Pepa and Heavy D up in the limousine
Hangin' pictures on my wall
Every Saturday Rap Attack, Mr. Magic, Marley Marl
I let my tape rock 'til my tape pop
Smokin' weed and bamboo, sippin' on private stock
Way back, when I had the red and black lumberjack
With the hat to match

—The Notorious B.I.G, "Juicy"

My first version of the American Dream was simple, materialistic, and perhaps misguided from the jump. I remember it clearly, its conception around the time puberty was beginning to take hold of my body and I was captivated by all things adult. I would have a hot red Toyota Corolla, a perfect chocolate-brown husband with shimmering skin who looked like Blair Underwood, and darling Brown kids. I'd be some sort of professional, with a graduate degree and a well-paying corporate job, and I'd live in a fancy New York City condo. Oh, and I'd of course have a slick hourglass shape, flat stomach, and long straight hair with my edges *laid*.

It completely grosses me out looking back, but I understand now that it was the beginning of my quest to succeed and move up in class and social status. Back then, in the eighties and nineties, the world seemed to hold endless possibilities. People constantly told me that I could be anything I wanted to be, and I had no reason not to believe them. My own family had "moved on up" from the South to New York during the second wave of the Great Migration, and then fled the concrete jungle to the suburbs, claiming their own piece of the Dream. My mother, a baby boomer who came of age of during the Civil Rights era, had completed undergraduate and graduate school and owned her own home. Plus, there were a ton of Black middle-class shows on television, Oprah Winfrey was shattering all kinds of glass ceilings in the real world, and the words of Biggie's dreams realized lulled me to sleep every night. Sure, I was aware of the shitty sides of America: I gasped when riots broke in Los Angeles, cried when Phillip Pannell, a young Black man, was killed by cops in my own hood, and watched in horror as Anita Hill was attacked for speaking out against sexual harassment. But it seemed for a while that my generation of Black millennials would actually do better than our parents and prove that for Black Americans, dreams could come true. Looking back, I think perhaps I was just being young and naïve, having not fully understood what America often does to young Black kids with dreams of a better life.

As the world changed and I grew up, my dream evolved. It was no longer solely about material things; I wanted to make some kind of difference in the world, too.[1] A stint in a youth journalism program made me want to do social justice work as a journalist or in politics. The hairstyle I so loved—short on top, with a bump 'n' curl on the bottom—became played, the Corolla too boxy. I realized at some point I wanted to be like the fictionalized character Khadijah James on *Living Single*. She had a Black-ass-sounding name (like mine), ran her own magazine business, was not too girlie, remained down for the people, was loyal to her friends, and had a fine man at the end of the series. Plus, her real life portrayer, Dana Owens, better known as Queen Latifah, was from Jersey—just like me.

Today I laugh at my 1980s and 1990s notion of making it, yet at its core it never really changed. My American Dream was to not fuck up. My dream was to defy expectations. To be unpredictable, to do something better and something more than my ancestors. Perhaps I thought that if these dreams came true, I would finally be respected, embraced, so that America would recognize that I too existed and had a voice. In retrospect, I wonder why I even cared about any of that, because again and again America has shown it cares so little about people who look like me.

AS AMERICANS WE LOVE TO OBSESS ABOUT THE SO-CALLED AMERICAN Dream. We fight over whether it's attainable, whether it's dying, or whom it's even for, though we rarely talk about what it is or admit that we all have our different versions of it. The American Dream is one of the most enduring myths in America, yet it is also one of its most prominent falsehoods. The Dream, the idea that anyone can succeed and enjoy a prosperous life through hard work, has been around since the founding of the country. But despite the reality that the Dream applies only to a limited number of people, America never seems to grow weary of this idea. The Puritans and Pilgrims believed that they could build a kind of utopia in the new world; Benjamin Franklin and Abraham Lincoln rose from humble beginnings to shape our nation; and Horatio Alger popularized the rags-to-riches narrative for generations of young men.

The term itself was first coined by James Truslow Adams in 1931 during the Great Depression. He defined the American Dream as a "dream of a land in which life should be better and richer and fuller for everyone, with opportunity for each according to ability or achievement." Though he left the idea ambiguous, he was careful to clarify what it was not. It was not about community or material possessions, but about aspiration. The American Dream, Adams later wrote, was not only America's "most precious national possession but our only unique contribution to the civilization of the world."[2]

A 2017 survey by the Pew Research Center shows that if anything, the popularity and belief in the American Dream is growing, not shrinking—46 percent of Americans believe they are on their way to achieving it, and 36 percent think they have already achieved it. The reality is different. Wealth inequality is at a historically high level, wages have stagnated despite increases in productivity, and it is harder than ever for Americans at any level to move above the social strata they were born into. Yet millennials too fall into that same thinking. The same survey found that 61 percent of millennials think they're on their way to achieving the American Dream, though only 29 percent say their family has achieved it. And only 9 percent believe that the Dream is out of reach.[3]

More curious, perhaps, is that the myth continues even among communities whose economic and social standings in America have been repeatedly marginalized. Black and Latinx communities often believe in the Dream with more fervor than their White counterparts, a trend also noted by the Pew study. The report found that 62 percent of Blacks and 51 percent of Latinxs said they were on their way to achieving the Dream. In comparison, only 42 percent of Whites said they were on their way to achieving it, meaning that those who are most likely to be left out of the Dream are also the ones who believe in it the most.

Just because the American Dream is a falsehood for many does not mean the myth should totally be discounted.[4] Perhaps it means we need to engage with it even more. The idea of the American Dream in our society provides important clues into how Americans see themselves, how we view upward mobility, and what we believe the promise of America is.

For Black folk, who have consistently been oppressed and marginalized in this country, the Dream has always been complicated. It has meant not just economic opportunity but equality as well.[5] In a speech at Drew University in 1964, the Reverend Dr. Martin Luther King Jr.

noted that "America is essentially a dream, a dream yet unfulfilled." "On the one hand we have proudly professed the great principles of democracy," he continued. "On the other hand we have sadly practiced the very antithesis of those principles. Indeed, slavery and racial segregation are strange paradoxes in the nation founded on the principle that all men are created equal." The next year, novelist and social critic James Baldwin directly took on his disappointment with the American Dream in a live debate with conservative William F. Buckley. "It comes as a great shock around the age of 5, 6, or 7 to discover that the flag to which you have pledged allegiance, along with everybody else, has not pledged allegiance to you. It comes as a great shock to see Gary Cooper killing off the Indians, and although you are rooting for Gary Cooper, that the Indians are you." He noted that when you as a young Black person are becoming an adult, you start to realize that your place in America may not be what you thought. "You are 30 by now and nothing you have done has helped you escape the trap. But what is worse is that nothing you have done, and as far as you can tell nothing you *can* do, will save your son or your daughter from having the same disaster and from coming to the same end."[6]

Whether or not Black millennials today have children, we are still asking these questions for ourselves. What is our place in America? And how can we escape the trap?

IN THIS TRANSFORMATIVE MOMENT AT THE DAWN OF THE TRUMP era, millennials overall are struggling to create a new version of success for ourselves—one that often looks different than the postwar, middle-class, cookie-cutter success stories of our parents' generation. In this post–civil rights, post-Obama moment, I wanted to explore what the world looks like to young Black Americans and what aspiration and mobility means to us. I decided to focus on Black millennials because our experiences are different, the stakes higher, and the challenges unique. Yet so many don't understand our plight.

All too often the experience of the Black millennial gets ignored in favor of narratives about overeducated White hipsters drinking pricey coffee in Brooklyn. When we imagine the face of the generation that *Time* magazine reporter Joel Stein called "narcissistic, overconfident, entitled and lazy," we don't see the young Black sex worker, the charming Republican student, the protester jumping on cars, or the injured track star with a pile of student debt. A select few are trying to change this image, but it's been a hard one to shake.[7]

The media likes to note the diversity of the millennial generation—43 percent of all American millennials are non-White. But discussions about millennials and their ideas of "success" are often deeply rooted in the experiences of privileged White men and women—think more Lena Dunham than Issa Rae. What's more, this generation's diversity does not automatically mean we are better about issues of racism and inequality. Despite their degrees, interracial partners, and love of Beyoncé, White millennials think more like their parents than their fellow Black and Brown millennials. Research by Spencer Piston at Syracuse University found that 51 percent of young Whites think Blacks are lazier than Whites, while 43 percent said Black people are not as intelligent. Equally problematic is that 32 percent of White millennials believe that racism isn't a major problem compared to 24 percent of Asian Americans, 21 percent of Latinxs, and 12 percent of Black Americans.[8]

Superficially, however, it looks as if we're succeeding. Marvel's *Black Panther* broke all sorts of records; there's a crop of new television shows by creatives like Donald Glover, Lena Waithe, and Issa Rae; hilarious podcasts like *The Read* feature unabashedly Black views; Beyoncé is everything; young Black authors are winning awards; Serena is still dominating on the courts despite her haters; and a whole range of new activists and policymakers are running for office. I don't want to kill these much-needed moments of Black joy that I too revel in, but these wins are too few and far between for a people who have been here for over four centuries. Our stories are still misunderstood, our bodies taken advantage of, and our voices silenced in a world that shows little concern for our everyday struggles.

With the increasing cost of college, the proliferation of a low-wage, low-skilled work force, and a recession that wiped out the wealth of a generation, whatever dreams we once had are in grave danger of never becoming a reality. We see versions of Black millennial success in sports (alongside struggles against the White-dominated power structure, like Colin Kaepernick's protest kneel, which seems to have gotten him ostracized from the NFL), in popular culture, and in politics, yet these are the exceptions, not the rule. Success for young Black people is increasingly difficult to achieve, and while we are working harder than ever to try to make our dreams come true, to have our stories told, we may be fighting a losing battle.

But our stories matter. Young Black people have been trying to realize the promise of America for centuries and coping with the reality of its limitations for just as long. We have often been at the forefront of migrations and movements hoping to usher in change, but instead we are left with broken promises, devastated by broken dreams.

Reconstruction failed to deliver the equality that the end of slavery should have heralded, so young people moved to the North to escape Jim Crow. Segregation raged in much of the country, so young Black people helped spearhead many of the civil rights campaigns in the 1950s and 1960s, building groups like SNCC (The Student Nonviolent Coordinating Committee). When that progress was slow, young Black people embraced Black Power and became Black Panthers. The next generation turned to hip-hop to make sure their voices were told, then Barack Obama, hopeful that he would bring about change. When that too failed, when we realized we were still brutalized and battered, we let the world know that our Black Lives Mattered. And now, when technology allows videos of our pain and struggle to be broadcast to the world, we wonder what is next, as Donald Trump leads a country that feels more polarized than ever.

We're not being chased down by dogs, we don't have to fight to use the same restrooms and water fountains as people who don't look like us, but we're still tired of having to prove our humanity. So here we are, centuries later, another generation of young Black Americans trying to make sure that America makes good on its promise to us.

∽∽

INITIALLY, I THOUGHT THIS WOULD BE PRIMARILY A STORY OF downward mobility, of a community that just couldn't find its way. But as I talked with more young Black people, I realized that what had at first seemed like stories of failure—college dropouts, sex workers, moves away from cities to the slower-paced South, hustling in the entertainment industry—might also be stories of rejecting definitions of success imposed from the outside.

A lot of my peers seem to be eschewing traditional ideas of success and upward mobility, bucking the system, and creating happiness on their own terms. Because of technology and the Obama effect, they believe that change is possible, that their voices matter. But they are worried not just about a particular president or a movement, but that this change hasn't taken place yet. There is still discontent, but like so many generations past, there is also hope, creativity, and excitement about better days ahead. We are learning that we don't have to define our dreams in the same ways as our White counterparts, and we have adjusted accordingly.

Maybe we're tired of watching a system that failed our parents—that downsized and laid them off, pushed them out of their family homes, and left many struggling to survive. Maybe it's that we think playing by the previous generation's rules all but guarantees losing. Maybe it's the intersection of millennial entrepreneurial spirit, a generation of "wokeness," and individualism that's creating this new vibe. Or maybe it's all just an "F— you" to a country that never seemed to truly believe in young Black America.

I wanted to see what dreaming meant to folks who looked like me all around the country. I wanted to see what their strategies were for upward mobility, since it has become obvious that America's ideals weren't quite working for us the way it seemed to for all those families on TV. I wanted the answer to the question Jay-Z posed when he remixed Biggie's song, asking, "Was it all a dream?"

In order to find out, I spoke to over seventy-five Black millennials in cities and towns like New York; Los Angeles; Jackson; Chicago; Tampa; New Orleans; Bluefield, West Virginia; and Raeford, North Carolina. I found some people through friends, others through organizations, and others in stories I read online and elsewhere. Not everyone I spoke with appears in this book, but their voices and concerns are still articulated throughout these pages. I especially wanted to hear the voices of Black women because their stories—our stories—are often left out of the narrative of America. I also wanted to make sure the voices of queer Black millennials were represented because they, too, are excluded from these conversations.

Defining a generation can be challenging, and years don't always exactly correlate with people's experiences. In fact, it's so hard that the Census has given only one generation exact dates: the baby boomers, born between 1946 and 1964. Various researchers have defined millennials as being born anywhere from 1978 to 2004. Neil Howe and William Strauss, who are known for being the first to name a generation "millennial," include those born between 1982 and 2000 (later they amended it to 2004). *Time* used the years 1980 and 2000 to define the generation, as did the Obama administration in a report the White House issued in 2014. For this project, I defined a millennial as anyone born between 1980 and 2000, roughly anyone between the ages of eighteen and thirty-seven in 2018, though most of my interviewees line up with the Pew Research Center's new definition of a millennial as being born between 1981 and 1996. I was born in 1981, one of the earliest millennials. Sometimes I am grouped under generation X, or more commonly a micro-generation called the xennials, often identified as being born between 1977 and 1983. This microgeneration grew up in an analog world and came of age in a digital one. I agree in part with both assessments and hope that my experience gives me an understanding of the millennial generation as well as some distance from it in order to critically and honestly tell these stories.[9]

Each of this book's nine chapters incorporates a major aspect of Black millennial life as it relates to mobility and the American Dream. In some I focus on the standard sociological components to upward mobility, like education and homeownership, while in others I discuss different avenues to success and happiness like politics, migration, the entertainment industry, and even love and relationships. In between each chapter I have included "millennial moments": sections about significant trends and moments in young Black life that are raw and unfiltered and presented in an "as-told-to" voice. Taken along with the chapters, their stories—our stories—capture something about a new generation of young Black people that are once again trying to believe in America.

Black folk in America, especially Black youth, have always dreamed of a better life, of "moving on up," yet it's been a struggle to make those dreams reality. In fact, by most measures, Black millennials are doing worse than their millennial counterparts. While "The Dream" has become a clichéd reference to Black America's hope for a better way, it's still an apt concept for a group that has been fighting for equal opportunity since the days of slavery, who are still hoping that America will one day keep its promise to them.

Black millennials are figuring out how to pull themselves up in the best way possible, and because of their unique plight, they're trying myriad ways of doing so. But they can't do it alone. Today, as this new generation comes of age, I wonder what amazing things Black millennials could do if America learns to keep its promise. What if our dreams, from the days of Reconstruction, had been realized then? What would America look like for young Black people now? What might it look like if we actually try to make those dreams a reality?

chapter one

WE OUT

SIMPLY PUT, BELTON FELL IN LOVE WITH THE BEAT OF THE CITY. NEW YORK CITY represented everything to him as a twenty-year-old moving up from the South in 2006. He loved the excitement, the movement on the street, the food, the summertime, and that indescribable chorus that only New York City seems to have. It was a place like no other, where he could wander the streets and watch people draw or make jewelry, where art could come alive right before his eyes.

More than the quirky people and the "dope street edgy vibe," though, Belton loved the idea of possibility in New York. And back then, in the city where investment bankers rode in the same subway cars as homeless people, and you could spot celebrities on street corners, it felt as if anything was possible. Belton needed that feeling. So, like many others before him, the aspiring writer left the South after attending Morehouse College and headed to a city he thought represented everything he wanted and desired.

He had flirted with life in New York before, completing a few internships, including one at *Time* magazine, but this time it would be different. He'd become a permanent resident of the "epicenter of media"; he'd live, breathe, and walk the streets. It was the only way he believed he would be able to carry out his dream of being a magazine writer and developing a publication for African Americans. Or so he thought.

Belton wasn't completely naïve about his dream. He knew the move would be hard, and he'd have to make sacrifices. His plan to attend a top-notch graduate program at New York University meant going into a considerable amount of debt, and it also meant leaving friends and family behind. But he believed his dream was worth it, so he decided to take the risk. The City represented to him what it does for so many: freedom, hope, and opportunity—life. Belton remembers his first ride on the subway as if it were yesterday. "I felt like it was an adventure. I felt like the whole city was its own world and the subway was like my magic carpet to be able to access New York City. It was almost like the MetroCard was like the passport for it. I could go anywhere I wanted to go and explore anything I wanted to explore."

Anyone who has ever truly fallen in love with the City knows that pulse, that sound, that feeling, that vibration that moves you along, pushes you, embraces you, drags you, seduces you in seconds. It feeds your desires, or so it seems, in a way that nothing else can.

I too remember that beat Belton heard, that energy. New York was like a sky scattered with diamonds, filled with bright lights that I'd been gazing at since I was a young child. I don't remember stepping foot in the actual city until 1986 or 1987. I'd probably been driven through Manhattan or the Bronx before, most likely in my mom's teal Volvo, chauffeured around like some bratty suburban kid, but it was unremarkable until that day. I don't remember why I was there or for what reason, but this time it felt different. We'd taken a graffiti-covered subway train to Times Square. Grit, dirt really, was everywhere. The lights of the cars flashed on and off, smells of dollar pizza hung in the air, and the sight of all the people was at once intoxicating and overwhelming. It was such a difference from my quiet suburban streets across the river, and the noise of horns, sirens, and shouting was deafening. As I walked outside, what I remember most, though, is the break-dancers. I wish I could tell you what song they were playing, but I've forgotten. What I do remember is what these chocolate boys were wearing: red and black Adidas gear and some gold chains. All they had was a boom box and a bucket, but they were doing it big. A crowd surrounded them, and my six-year-old self stood there, eyes wide open. The kids were young, some perhaps not older than me. They were having fun as people threw coins and dollars in the hat they had laid out as they twisted their bodies, spun on their backs, and swerved on the ground. I want to say it was a Kangol, to complete my urban fantasy of yesteryear, but who really knows. Perhaps none of these details really matter, because what I absorbed that day was that this was a place where dreams could happen. At that very moment, clichéd or not, those four boys had begun to make their dreams come true.

In 2009, hip-hop stars and New York natives Jay-Z and Alicia Keys released a song called "Empire State of Mind." On it Keys sings about dreams being realized in New York. The City had a reputation like that, even in the eyes of young Black folk—despite what the City dished out to them. No matter how many of us were sent to jail as a result of the draconian Rockefeller laws that disproportionately targeted Black men and women, no matter how many of us protested, horrified, when the Central Park 5 were proclaimed rapists, no matter how many were tired of living in rat-infested housing, or frustrated with a stop-and-frisk policy that seemed to do everything but prevent crime, Black youth loved their city. Onika Maraj, Belcalis Almanzar, and other young Black girls who normally would be shunned by Madison Avenue and turned away from the modeling agencies in Midtown for having fat asses and thick lips, until some White girl would call it chic years later, still bled for the city, still shouted out their boroughs. Still gave their heart to the City.

In some ways it's understandable why young Blacks would be so dedicated to the City. It was the place where many of our families too believed their dreams could come true, and they worked hard to get here from the South, struggled to come from lands abroad. They believed in this city, believed opportunity was manifest, and did all they could to make it all happen. Starting in the days after slavery was abolished and having been disappointed by Reconstruction, one of the first of many promises that would be broken to Blacks in America, frustrated Blacks in the South began to see migration to the North as a way to make their dreams manifest, and young adults were the first to go.

Young Black people between the ages of fifteen and twenty-eight made up many of the first migrants to New York City. Scholar Marcy S. Sacks noted that it was those of the freeborn generation who were young and single, who had the "greatest ease of movement and the most intractable resentment about the broken promises of Reconstruction," that decided to make the move first. "The old people are used to their fare, and they never leave, but the children won't stand for the situation down there," she quotes one migrant to New York in 1907.[1]

Still, while New York has been the dream for many young African Americans looking to improve their lot in life, whether it was a physical escape from bondage in the eighteenth and nineteenth centuries or in the post-Reconstruction moment, it wasn't until the Great Migration that Blacks, 90 percent of whom lived in the South, decided en masse they were fed up with their treatment. Between 1910 and 1970, over six million African Americans fled the South in attempts to escape that bastard Jim Crow and his passive cousin Uncle Sam, who was freely bestowing loans and awards to help uplift White workers while Black sharecroppers toiled away broke. In New York, like other places in the North, Blacks believed they would have better work opportunities, experience less racial violence, and have a shot at education. So they did what so many of their ancestors had attempted to do from slavery to the present: they left. It was an extraordinary act of agency, and according to author Isabel Wilkerson, "it was the first big step the nation's servant class ever took without asking."[2]

The city was flooded with hundreds of thousands of migrants, and New York's Black population grew from 92,000 in 1910 to 1.7 million in 1970, as places like Harlem and Bedford-Stuyvesant boomed. People like musician Duke Ellington were enchanted by the city. He left for the Big Apple in 1923, from the District of Columbia, and said later, "Harlem, to our minds, did indeed have the world's most glamorous atmosphere. We had to go there. . . . It was New York that filled our imagination."[3]

Years later Belton too believed in New York. Following in the tradition of Ellington and millions of others, he was excited by his now home, and for awhile he was content. He lived in Brooklyn, the Bronx, Queens. He got a taste of different cultures. He lived that Dream. Made it a reality. Enjoyed the city. It was magical; it was musical. But soon reality struck.

By the time he finished his master's degree in journalism in 2008, the world had changed a bit more. The Great Recession of 2008, which would hit African American and Latinx communities the hardest, was in full swing, and Belton was unable to find a job. It's not surprising: statistics from the Bureau of Labor in 2008 found that nearly 4 percent of Black college graduates ages twenty-five and over were unemployed, compared to 2.4 percent of White graduates. But Belton, whose writing had been published in *Vibe* and *Upscale* magazines, wasn't a quitter and he continued to search for jobs as a writer. He found none. He blames the Recession, the rise of the internet, the fierce competition in the industry, or perhaps a combination of it all. It wasn't just him or the economy; the media industry as a whole was suffering, particularly for Black writers and journalists. A report in the *Columbia Journalism Review* found that Black journalists held just 5.5 percent of jobs at newspapers—that was at the peak of their employment in the industry, in 2006. In 2010 they held 4.7 percent of newspaper jobs.[4]

Belton took it all in stride and decided to try something new. He became a fashion copywriter for Bloomingdale's. He wrote all sorts of material for ads and catalogs, but he wasn't feeling fulfilled. So after a few years, he left, got another master's degree at the City University of New York and became a teacher at a charter school. He liked working in education, and life was good again.

After three years of teaching, he began to feel stressed and burned out. At first he wasn't sure exactly why—perhaps it was the job. Research has shown that Black male teachers, who account for less than 2 percent of the nation's teaching population, sometimes feel they have an "invisible tax" on them, which often means they are asked to deal with things like discipline or racial issues instead of focusing on their craft and subject area, and many end up leaving the field.[5]

But Belton realized it wasn't his teaching job—he wanted to stay in the field of education—but it was the city that was wearing on him. He began to feel more like a caged bird than one soaring through the air. "I felt like everything around me was moving so quickly that it was very hard for me to find balance and find energy." All he wanted to do was to go back to the South, drive a car, sit on a porch, and drink some sweet tea.

Belton knew his love affair was over when even his beloved subway rides became a chore. Walking to the subway became a laborious task. He began to resent the overheated cars and seats. He dreaded the people even more; he was annoyed that he had to deal with them, especially at five o'clock, when sweat rolling off the foreheads of exhausted workers would drip slowly onto him. He was even annoyed that he had to touch the railings, which now looked dirty, he said with wistful disgust. No longer did that magic carpet ride feel quite so magical. "Everything became more of an annoyance, the stuff I loved about it was the very things I started to hate." Within months he was gone, back in Atlanta, starting a new life.

Turns out, he wasn't alone.

A 2016 report by the Office of New York City Comptroller Scott Stringer found that Black millennials are leaving New York quicker than their White counterparts. From 2000 to 2014, there was a net increase of about 83,000 White millennials int the city's population in contrast to a decrease of about 42,000 Black millennials. Looking at the data even more broadly, it's not just New York that is losing its young Black population; it's the North overall, including cities like Chicago, Philadelphia, and Detroit.[6] While White millennials and other groups may move to places outside the North, it's not as rapid an exodus as Blacks are making from the region. I couldn't help but wonder, if Black parents and grandparents saw Northern cities as some sort of "promised land," do Black millennials now see the South that way?

Millennials are more likely to migrate to another state than older generations. Thirty percent of young adults ages eighteen to twenty-nine move every year. It makes sense; the older and more established you are in a home and a career, the less likely you are to move. Black millennials aren't any more likely to migrate than millennials of other races and ethnicities, but the places they move to are different. Among Black millennials who move, the South is by far the most popular region—44 percent move there. It's followed by the Midwest (22 percent), the West (20 percent), and the Northeast (14 percent). This a different pattern from millennial Whites and Asians, whose moving choices are more evenly divided.[7]

Of those migrating to the South, Black and Latinx millennials have the highest migration rates proportionate to their population, with 44 percent of Black and Latinx millennial migrants moving to the region. In 2016 alone, 73,000 Black millennial migrants moved to the South. Thirty-nine percent of those Black millennials who migrated to the South come from the Northeast, 37 percent from the Midwest, and 23 percent from the West. Black Millennials and Latinxs who come from abroad are also most likely to settle in the South, more so than White and Asian millennials from abroad.

TOP FIVE STATES BLACK MILLENNIALS MIGRATE TO COMPARED TO OTHER MAJOR RACIAL/ETHNIC GROUPS

BLACK		WHITE		HISPANIC		ASIAN	
State	**Interstate Migrants**	**State**	**Interstate Migrants**	**State**	**Interstate Migrants**	**State**	**Interstate Migrants**
California	16,480	California	93,680	Texas	31,580	California	9,760
Texas	11,840	Texas	65,980	Florida	24,320	Texas	5,330
Georgia	11,720	Florida	64,920	California	19,710	New York	2,990
Florida	8,950	Colorado	61,780	New York	11,630	Pennsylvania	1,880
Pennsylvania	7,860	New York	51,300	Pennsylvania	9,650	Washington	3,770

SOURCE: US Census Bureau, *American Community Survey*, 2016 Public Use Microdata Sample (PUMS), 2017.

Further research shows that the top five states Black millennials are moving to are California, Texas, Georgia, Florida, and Pennsylvania. While all groups seem to want to migrate to California, the other states vary by race and ethnicity.[8]

While the South has often been affiliated with the traumas of Jim Crow and slavery, it also has been touted as *the* place for young Black Americans since the end of the Second Great Migration in the late 1960s and early 1970s. On July 21, 1970, an article in the *Baltimore Afro-American* newspaper explained, "Most of the young Blacks in the South cite the difference in cost of living, the better environment, and a bright and dynamic economic future as chief reasons for returning." "The North is stagnant now," Morris Keye, a thirty-one-year-old college-educated deputy sheriff and New Jersey native is quoted as saying at the time. "You just don't see growth. They're building on top of each other, but I don't call that growth." Nearly fifty years later, young Blacks are giving many of those same reasons for leaving the North, increasing their exodus, and continuing the trend of the "reverse migration," something that demographers said began in the seventies and continues to increase today.

At first scholars who study the reverse migration, like University of California, Berkeley, professor Carol Stack, described it as "a call to home" for earlier migrants who had missed the South. But others I spoke to, like Sabrina Pendergrass, an assistant professor at the University of Virginia who studies the reverse migration of the twenty-first century, believes there's more at play. She explained that Black migration is usually about more than economics. For Black folks, she said, sometimes migration is about defining who you are as a person, about moving away from where you were raised just to prove you can make it on your own without your parents. It can also be about finding your Black identity. The Black media plays a role, too. Pendergrass sees it as parallel to the way the *Chicago Defender*, during the Great Migration, portrayed the Midwestern city as "good for Black people."[9]

I asked a handful of millennials who were leaving or had left New York why they had decided to move. They all said the same thing: New York used to be a place where dreams are made. But they've had to sacrifice those dreams for practicality, mobility, and a sort of freedom that they believe is missing in New York and other Northern cities.

Thing is, the North, including New York City, as several scholars show, was never as hospitable as it was made to be. It was never the "promised land." Sure, slavery was abolished there in 1827, and Blacks were able to publish newspapers, engage in politics, and start schools, but racism was still pervasive. Property ownership requirements virtually ensured that Black men were disenfranchised from voting. And in 1863, race riots broke out over the draft, leaving anywhere between 74 and 1,200 Blacks and White allies dead. As Black people began to arrive in even greater numbers during the Great Migration, Whites prevented them from joining unions to avoid competition in the workforce, forcing them into low-wage and low-skilled jobs. Even during the Civil Rights Movement, despite New York being home to one of the largest protests, people worried about racism so much that an article on the front page of the *New York Times* noted, "For the Negro in the North, segregation is as much a fact of life as it is in the South. Almost invariably the color of his skin determines where he lives, where he goes to school and how he makes his living." Today, over sixty years after the US Supreme Court decision in *Brown v. Board of Education,* New York State has the most segregated schools in the nation, mainly because of intense segregation in New York City schools.

New York City was also home to a police program known as "stop and frisk," which disproportionately targeted Black and Latinx citizens—who were overwhelmingly innocent—until it was ruled that the city's implementation of the program was unconstitutional, with the judge calling it "a form of racial profiling" of Black and Brown men.[10]

It's not just New York City that is seeing an exodus of Black people. It's many states in the North, and it started as Jim Crow laws began to loosen in the 1970s. Today, 55 percent of Blacks live in the land of Dixie, while cities like New York, Chicago, Detroit, and Philadelphia are losing their Black population and places like Atlanta, DC, Raleigh, and Dallas are gaining them—especially young college Black graduates who cite the appeal of cheaper costs of living, warm weather, a better quality of life, and an emerging Black middle class. In the postrecession world, where young Black millennials struggle to keep up with their counterparts, New York and other enclaves become expensive and besieged with gentrifiers, and inequality and discrimination persist, it seems we may be at another tipping point.

In some ways, I understand the pull of the South. Apart from the DC[11] area, the Southern states enjoy a lower cost of living and higher Black employment rates than those in the North. And despite common wisdom suggesting the North is the more liberal, culturally progressive place, the movement of college-educated and professional Blacks means that a progressive Black elite has established itself in the South. Atlanta, for example, hasn't had a White mayor since 1969. Some of these places have always had Black elite communities, thanks perhaps to employment with the federal government in Washington, DC, and to the historically Black colleges and universities that pepper the South, but in recent decades, those numbers have risen. In fact, Washington, DC, Raleigh, and Atlanta now have the most educated Blacks in the United States, and Washington, DC, Baltimore, and Atlanta have the highest number of top-earning Blacks in the country.[12] Whether the South has provided a true place of opportunity for young Blacks—and whether it can provide Black millennials with what they're looking for—remains to be seen.

In 2016, Jasmine made an offer for a nine-hundred-foot co-op in Harlem. It wasn't the Bronx assistant district attorney's first choice, but she decided she had to make do. The space was small and in an underperforming school district, so she'd have to pay for private school for her six-year-old son, but at $170,000 for a mortgage and $810 a month for maintenance, the apartment was a pretty good deal. She had been living in New York for almost eight years, after spending over four years looking, unsuccessfully, for a job in the South. She decided that despite the smaller apartments and the expense of school for her son, she would somehow make the city work. She was fairly happy as a lawyer and had a great group of friends to rely on. But still, something felt off, and she was perpetually uneasy. "I was doing well, but at any moment something could've gone wrong."

Jasmine was born and raised in South Carolina and had gone to law school in Louisiana. She moved to New York because she wanted to experience one simple thing: a city that had public transportation. She liked the ability to walk around without a car, so after law school she applied to jobs in Chicago, Boston, Philly, and every single borough in NYC. She ended up being hired in New York. She was excited and scared when she first arrived, and everything was a shock, especially the rent. But life was good, and for the most part, she enjoyed it. In 2010, though, when her son was born, the single mom realized it might be time to leave. Not only could she be closer to her child's father, but she had more support networks in the South. Plus it seemed to her that opportunities for Blacks were on the rise there. "When you come down here, you have a better quality of life, as in: you get more money; you get more bang for your buck. You can actually put your child in a public school that is a really good school. You can actually own something and build something here as opposed to New York. I had the sense that I was basically living check to check." She cites increasing costs of living in all of the boroughs and gentrification as major barriers to upward mobility in New York, noting that even in her old neighborhood off the Grand Concourse in the South Bronx, a notoriously cheap neighborhood, housing costs were rising.

Like the other people I spoke to, Jasmine said the lure of the South was not just economic but also cultural. She was attracted to the large Black professional population and Atlanta's reputation as a "Black mecca," something she believes New York never has been despite its large Black population. "A Black mecca in my opinion would be a location where you know that wherever you go, you can find people that look like you, that have the same experiences, that have the same background," she said. "You don't have to go out of your way to try to find people that look like you and have your same experiences because you know that they're there." It's quite the contrast from New York, a city she thinks is not as welcoming to African Americans. She described the city as segregated and ethnically cliquey, with people sticking to the people they know and what neighborhood they're from. "Even though I feel like New York is culturally diverse, it's still very segregated in how people interact." She said people would always assume she was Dominican and seemed disappointed when they found out she wasn't. Plus, she said, unity among the Black population was just lacking.

So when, while waiting to hear about her apartment bid, she got a call from the district attorney's office in Clayton County, Georgia, with a job offer, she decided it was definitely time to go. "I knew that it was best for my son to leave. I could've stayed, but I just knew it was better for him if we came down here." Instead of a cramped co-op, she has just moved into a spacious four-bedroom townhome that cost her $200,000.

LAST WINTER WHILE WAITING FOR FRIENDS TO VISIT A TONY ART exhibit on Manhattan's Upper East Side, I felt a strangeness, a discomfort really, as I walked in and out of the high-end boutiques lining Madison Avenue. I saw eyes following me as I meandered in and out of the stores, rocking a big afro, hoop earrings, and an even bigger book bag. Again and again, I was met with the same condescending glare as I bumbled through the shops looking for some unknown item.

I wanted to casually stroll through the stores, yet at that moment, nervous that my brown skin and youthful look would deem me guilty for something and cause a ruckus, I ended my voyage and went to get a cup of coffee. I wondered, as I walked down Madison Ave, if I was being paranoid, or if those eyes were really following me. I honestly wasn't sure, but the unease I felt that day reminded me of a time when I was driving through the mountains of West Virginia and came across several homes and shops covered in the Confederate flag. I didn't exactly feel hate, but a strange uneasiness, as if I didn't quite belong. These things were on my mind as I entered an espresso café ready to recharge. The shop was full of White men and women laughing and chatting over afternoon coffee. Unsurprised and nonplussed, I took a seat at the counter and began scribbling down a quote from Claude Browne's book *Manchild in the Promised Land*: "Where does one run to when he's already in the promised land?"

The barista walked over to me and asked for my order.

"An espresso," I replied. Yet he didn't budge.

"Are you sure you want a cup of espresso?"

"Yes," I said emphatically and now confused.

He went behind the counter and grabbed one of the cups. "Are you sure?" he asked again. "Do you know that it comes in this small cup?"

"Yes," I said, angry and embarrassed. Why would the waiter ask me if I knew what a cup of espresso looked like when I intentionally walked into an espresso bar? I watched as other customers, who didn't share my skin tone, streamed in and out, ordering tiny little cups of espresso, without being met with even a raised eyebrow.

Racism, I thought. Or at least a racial microaggression at its finest.

I didn't know how to respond, so I did what so many millennials do and fired off a complaint on Twitter. I realized once again that New York is never as progressive as it's made out to be, and often it's downright lonely to be young and Black here.

I remembered being at one of New York City's oldest bars on Election Day 2016, as a bunch of Donald Trump supporters gathered near me talking about how their candidate was the change the country really needed. I exchanged looks with two of my friends wearing Hillary shirts, amazed that young guys in the city were actually excited at the prospect of a Trump presidency. As they peered in our direction, I felt that same unease that I'd felt in West Virginia surrounded by Confederate flags, and I wondered how many other Trump supporters packed the room. As my friends and I—a diverse group of Black, Brown, and White women—left the bar when Hillary Clinton's upending seemed likely, the men shouted at us that they were going to "Make America Great Again." I sighed and ignored them as I walked out into the night.

Perhaps this is the reason that so many young Black people are leaving the New York area in search of opportunity elsewhere. Years after the 2016 election, in a country that still feels divided, I can't tell if the red state/blue state differences even matter still. Hatred, fear, and resentment seem to flow through the land.

It's still hard for me to walk into Baumgarts, a local ice cream parlor in my hometown of Englewood, New Jersey, though it has the best ice cream I've ever tasted. My mom told me they discriminated against Black people when she was growing up in the 1950s. I would be surprised if I *wasn't* followed today as I walk through Barney's in Manhattan. And I still remain horrified that a school district less than thirty miles away in New Jersey recently assigned and then proudly displayed pictures of a slave auction that their fifth-grade students drew. I remember my sadness walking around the slave memorials in lower Manhattan, the sheer terror watching Eric Garner mumble the words "I can't breathe" over and over on that street in Staten Island, and the fear I felt when a young Black man was killed by a White police officer steps from where my great-aunt lived and where I currently reside.

The Southern Poverty Law Center reports that New York has more hate groups than Georgia, Alabama, Mississippi, or Virginia. The Center for the Study of Hate and Extremism at California State University, San Bernardino, found that more than 1,000 hate crimes were reported in nine major cities in 2016. New York City had 380 incidents, the highest nationwide. These incidents, many fueled by Trump's election, included swastikas in Philadelphia, two Indian men being killed in Kansas after being reportedly told to get out of the country, the murder of a Black man in New York by someone frustrated over interracial dating, and a Sikh in Washington State being shot and also told to "leave"—places far from a good glass of sweet tea.[13]

~~

Kiyma had never been to Atlanta before she decided to move there. She was in her twenties with a kid and felt she wasn't really making any progress as a medical secretary in the New York suburb of Hackensack, New Jersey. She was ready for a change. When her aunt, who lived there, told her of the opportunities the area had, she decided to give it a chance. "I did my research, and I figured, you know, I'm young. If I can get the same money and pay cheaper rent, why not?" Within two months she and her young daughter had moved in with her aunt in the suburb of Alpharetta. Kiyma started going door to door looking for jobs doing secretarial or billing work in the medical field. She found a job at a neurosurgeon's office. It was different for sure, and the self-described "city girl" had to adjust to the slow pace of the region, but it didn't take long for her to enjoy the country way of life. Soon she fell in love with the South. When she moved out of her aunt's crib and into a two-bedroom apartment in Roswell, she was shocked. She was paying $625 a month, and the amenities were "incredible" compared to what she was used to in the New York area: wall-to-wall carpet, pool, barbeque, gym, and a walking path. She was elated. She was making around $18 dollars an hour as a secretary, and she finally felt comfortable. For the first time she didn't have to struggle so much. "I had so much money in my pocket, and I was doing so much overtime. I was good!"

She'd travel back up North time to time, and her daughter would even stay there with relatives for the summer, but Atlanta had become home. She had come to love the peace and open space, plus it was brimming with choices for young Black people: "It is a really big mountain top with a lot of opportunities." She saw other young Black people there doing well, and she wanted to be around that. "African American people are taking over down there, and I want to be around successful people. I want to be around people that are making money, with houses. Just living their life and not struggling." But, she said, you have to have some kind of career already established. "You can't really go down there working at Publix or Kroger and think, 'Oh, I'm about to come up.'"

When she lost her job, though she had years of experience doing administrative work in the medical field, Atlanta began to test her. She was denied unemployment benefits and then lost her car, something essential for a city, she said, where public transportation is known to be unreliable and inefficient at times. To add to that, her daughter was starting to complain about missing friends up North. But Kiyma was determined. She worked a temporary job at a tax office, even though the commute on the bus was less than pleasant; when that gig ended, she tried to find other work. Unable to secure another administrative job, she became a stripper. "I had to do that to survive. I hated it." She avoided the traps of the life, like drugs, and stayed focused on finding a new occupation. Every guy she came across as a dancer told her it looked as if she didn't want to be there. It was true. She didn't. She would dance all night and then get up in the morning and go to the unemployment office to fax out résumés and call jobs. But she wasn't having any luck.

One day, after returning to Atlanta from a quick trip to New Jersey, she stepped through the door of her apartment into darkness. Her lights had been cut off. Suddenly Kiyma was overwhelmed. She had recently learned she was pregnant and didn't know how she was going to make ends meet. She decided that this was a sign that it was time to leave. So she packed up her bags and headed back North, where she could live with her grandmother and find jobs more easily without a car.

But coming back was hard, and her circumstances today only remind her of how good life was in Atlanta. She now has a job in a cardiologist's office, but her days of struggling have returned. She just left a small two-bedroom apartment near her family, where she was paying $1,600 a month, for a larger three-bedroom apartment in Newark that is about $250 dollars cheaper. It's farther from her children's school and her job, but she's happy to have more space for her two kids and new baby, a cutie who was born needing a pacemaker. She's not thrilled with the neighborhood or the gunshots she can hear in the distance at night, but she's okay for now. She waves a friendly hi and bye to her neighbors and "keeps it moving."

Atlanta, though, is never far from her mind. "It's just disgusting. I'm looking on Trulia and Zillow and all those apartment apps, I was looking at the prices [in Atlanta], and you just get so much bang for your buck out there. You really do. The way my credit is, I mean, I'm working on it now, but I would never be able to afford a house up here. Down there, I could definitely, probably, get two or three houses!" On top of everything, she has lupus and can't afford the $250 health care payments that would be deducted out of each check. She's doing okay at the moment and relies on Medicaid support, but her frustration is clear.

More than anything, although she's happy around her friends and family, a sense of inertia hovers over her, as if her life is not going anywhere. She is barely getting by. She's tired of that, so she's planning on moving back to Atlanta the week after her daughter graduates high school in 2018. She plans to get a rental for a year, then start saving up for a house, because she wants something for her kids to have, someplace, she said, that they can call home. Kiyma said she feels she can make more progress down South and is working to convince her kids to move with her. Her teenage son, who is a star basketball player, is ambivalent, and she still isn't sure what her older daughter will do. At age thirty-four, she's ready for a change and also wants to get training in stenography and ultrasound. She thinks that opportunity lies in the South. "I was doing things! Not once did I ever call anyone to borrow anything. Up here, every week, it's 'Can I just borrow $20 until I get paid?,'" she said. "You know, it's always something."

OVER THE LAST FEW YEARS I'VE BEEN TRYING TO FIND THE "NEW South" that young Black millennials like me are moving to. That Black Mecca of upwardly mobile Black folk that is so prominent in the Black imagination. But I can't. I look for it every time I visit the South. I look for it in the stories of Belton, Jasmine, and Kiyma. Instead of a feeling of freedom and comfort, all I feel is the weight of a past that doesn't feel so distant. I want to love places like Charlotte, Charleston, Memphis, and of course Atlanta, the place the SNL writer Michael Che called the "Blackest" city in America, but it's been hard. It's been even harder after Trump became our president and I see Klan and Nazi rallies and White power signs peppering the region.

I feel guilty for my bewilderment because so many of my beloved friends and family adore the region. I love the gracious Southern hospitality, the grits, the sweet tea, the plethora of HBCUs, and the warm weather, but still, something about the South feels different to me. Perhaps it's the pain when I see statues dedicated to the Confederacy, read about laws that won't let transgender people use the bathroom (since 2013 over half of transgender victims of fatal violence lived in the South[14]), hear about government officials actively fighting against memorials recognizing slavery, or ride past homes draped in Confederate flags. It's painful and hurtful, and I don't know how to react to the many markers of oppression, slavery, and Jim Crow that are on full display in so many areas of a sometimes unapologetic South. It feels anything but liberating or free. It's as if the chains of bondage remain shackled to me, and I find freedom as stifling as the air in the Carolina heat.

It's personal, too. In some ways, much of my identity is tied to the South. It is perhaps the painful memories often shared by my relatives that make me want to stay away. I always want to understand the stories better, but whenever I asked my now deceased great-aunt why she left Manning, South Carolina, during the Great Migration (after explaining to her what the Great Migration was and that she was a part of it) she said it was for better jobs, that there was nothing there for her to go back to. Recently, when I was afforded the opportunity to visit her hometown, I felt a sense of pride as I tried to find pieces of her South, overwhelmed when I learned that *Brown v. Board of Education* was started by a case in her county, and near tears when I found Meesha a young educated millennial woman who may be my cousin. I was frustrated to learn of the vandalizing that occurred a few years ago at Meesha's church, Bigger's African Methodist Episcopal: someone kept removing the first letter of the name and replacing it with an *N*. And I felt saddened when I heard that two White men affiliated with the Ku Klux Klan burned a Black church down there—in 1995.

Because my grandmother and great-aunt did follow some sort of American Dream narrative and achieved those traditional monikers of success in the North (buying a home, getting married, owning their own businesses, putting their kid through college), their tales of the South stung even more. The North, most likely by sheer luck and also because of their hard work, was good to them. But in reality, it was also good to many of my relatives in the South who did not move North.

If you Google "the South sucks" you get plenty of material about rednecks, failing school systems, opioids, and Jesus, but that's not my beef with the region. I've found that folks in the South are no less educated or "backwards" than people who live in my part of the country. In particular, the Black folk I know in the South are super educated. Most people I know have gone to college, bought homes, and are fairly happily raising their families. Meesha has two degrees and is the director of the county archives. And there is that sense of home. In the last presidential election season in particular, Black folk in states like North Carolina and Georgia played a significant role. Art, music, and other markers of American culture remain to flourish in the region.

For me, in such polarized times, when White privilege, nativist sentiment, and xenophobia have been clearly visible, the South, with its racial past and unwillingness by so many to renounce it, have especially frustrated me. When states like Mississippi refuse to remove the Confederate flag from their state flag or signs that urge to "Keep America White" are displayed so openly on the streets, I'm horrified in ways that I'm not up North. The public and bold way that Southern Whites cling to the flag and memorabilia is frightening, but it's more than just the flag and statues. It's about a history that so many in the region are unwilling to let go of, a past they seem to yearn for—an America of yesteryear. And while that sentiment has crept up nearly everywhere in the nation, the South always seems to lead the charge.

There are signs of progress. South Carolina removed a Confederate flag after a racially motivated killing in a church in 2015 (and sentenced the killer to death). In New Orleans, a city I love, they have just removed the last monument dedicated to the Confederacy off of public property. A movement to take down additional monuments to the Confederacy has spread, despite the president's lamentation of the trend. Nevertheless, the solid hold Donald Trump seems to have on the region makes me wonder if it really is a place that would welcome me.

Yet no sooner had I proclaimed myself a Northern Yankee snob than I found a fairly recent report that confirmed my thoughts: the South is still dealing with race in ways other places aren't. The research came about in the aftermath of the Supreme Court ruling on Section 5 of the

Voting Rights Act, when chief Justice John Roberts blatantly asked, "Is it the government's submission that the citizens in the South are more racist than citizens in the North?"

The lawyers in the case didn't seem to want to deal with that question (the government's lawyer replied, "It is not, and I do not know the answer to that, Your Honor"), but two law professors, Christopher Elmendorf of the University of California, Davis, and Douglas Spencer of the University of Connecticut, figured out the answer to that question. They proved that the South—specifically those states cited in the Voting Rights Act—correlated with research of non-Black residents who have "exceptionally negative stereotypes" of Black people. Plain and simple, it seemed: the study confirmed that people in the South do seem to have more anti-Black prejudice than other regions of the country.[15] Other reports I read contradicted that a bit, with one specifically noting that the research about whether the South was more "racist" has been inconclusive.

I was left trying to figure out if the South was really that great for Black millennials and whether upward mobility—economical, spiritual, cultural, or all of the above—looked different in this region. I began to question my generalizations and simplistic understandings of an entire geographic area and decided to reach out to Jessica Barron, a sociologist and demographer. She thinks that race and racism play out in different ways historically and contemporarily in the South. She noted that the South's particularly harsh regulation of and brutality toward Black bodies was horrific, but doesn't discount policies like redlining that also damaged Black communities in Northern cities like Chicago. She explained, "The South is an easy scapegoat. After the Civil Rights Movement, when the country wanted to rewrite the narrative of this color-blind racial utopia, somebody has to be the villain. Somebody has to be the antagonist."

For a while I wondered if the South, and particularly Atlanta, was a good metaphor for the upwardly mobile Black experience. Popular culture has certainly hyped up the South as the place to be for upwardly mobile Black folk with television shows like Donald Glover's award-winning *Atlanta,* a range of Tyler Perry films, and Beyoncé's stunning visual project *Lemonade* firmly rooted there. Recently, many Black coming-of-age stories seem to be set away from New York City, while it still remains the place for several White coming-of-age stories like *Girls* and *Broad City*. Even mainstream media outlets have picked up on the trend. *Forbes* said the South had become in many ways "the new promised land" for Blacks. The *New York Times* called Atlanta the epicenter of the Black "glitterati."[16]

I couldn't help thinking about the other side of the South, especially that more working-class Atlanta, that Glover portrays in his popular series. Was that too the promised land? In 2013, the Brookings Institute released a report that found that the city's wealthiest residents had twenty times more than the poorest that year, and a few years later, the Federal Reserve chief of Atlanta noted the city was "one of the worst" in terms of economic mobility. Of course this disproportionately affects the city's Black residents, and the gap between White and Black households is high. In 2016, the median income for White families in the Atlanta metro area was $78,000 a year, compared to $50,000 for Black households. And a report by Clark Atlanta University professors in 2010 also found Blacks were unemployed at twice the rates of their White counterparts (reflecting a longstanding national trend), that there were fewer supermarkets in Black neighborhoods and less access to public transportation in these same communities. For all its positives, the idea of a "Black Mecca," it concluded, was more "public relations and image management" than reality.[17]

There are some other statistics to consider when looking at the South as a region. While Black millennials who live in the South have the highest rates of employment in the country, at 68.9 percent, they also earn the lowest (making about $22,000 in median wages)[18] and have the lowest levels of educational attainment of millennials in other parts of the country.

Jasmine said these statistics reflect the reality, and while she loves it, she wouldn't move to Atlanta without securing a job first. "I think a lot of people move here because they see Black people thinking that it is the mecca for Black people and they don't properly prepare and then they're in for a rude awakening. There are opportunities, but it may not be the opportunity that you particularly want. You may have to try something different."

I DON'T KNOW WHAT TO MAKE OF ATLANTA AND MANY OF THE other parts of the South. The data seems to show that the realities of Black life there, like other parts of the country, can be tough and it certainly appears to be no utopia or promised land for Black folk. But there still seems to be something to this idea of the city as a Black Mecca, which people hold near and dear to their heart. It seems to be something not always solely measurable by the usual markers of success and economic well-being, but by happiness and work-life balance.

I feel so betrayed by America, by those on the right, by White women, that maybe it doesn't even matter where I live. I still want to believe in America. Believe that things can be better. America of late is making it hard. Perhaps the South is this place of my American Dream, even in a land where the hope of 2008 seems elusive and change a joke. Perhaps getting out of blue-state liberal land, which is never quite as ocean blue as I dream of, is the answer to me finding that slippery American Dream. Perhaps it is my future.

Jessica Barron, the sociologist, reminded me of the importance of a visible humanity that often draws young people to the South. Its slower, less competitive, and more communal pace can often feel like a needed respite for a generation that's tired of working twice as hard in their personal and professional lives. "People want to move away from this grind and this constantly trying to vouch for your humanity and dignity," she said. Black people can go to a place where Blackness is seen as valuable because of the large Black population and is held to some kind of standard, even if it does have roots in slavery. "This is still a place that is somewhere that I want to be because I will be seen as Jessica XYZ versus the Black girl here doing XYZ. I think people underestimate that."

After our conversation, I began to see the South in a different light, as a mystical, mythical, complicated mess of pain and beauty. Maybe the Black millennials who choose to live there have it right.

In the spring of 2017, I stood in the sticky hot heat watching the removal of a statue of Confederate General Robert E. Lee in New Orleans. As workers, allegedly clad in bulletproof vests, chiseled loudly away at the over-hundred-year-old statue, I couldn't help but feel that progress was being made despite the previous night's protest over the removal. In that moment I ignored the few Confederate flags in the crowd. I was overjoyed to be part of a diverse group of people watching Lee be evicted from his perch over the city, waiting anxiously to erase a blighted history. I was pleased when two Black men gave out some Powerade to the crowd. It was a comforting moment, and I thought, despite whatever mess was going on in Washington, maybe change could happen.

But then some folks came up arguing about how the statue deserved to stay, which somehow devolved into a conversation about "those people" who apparently get "plenty," and once again, I was disappointed in the region. As the statue popped off the structure, secured only by cords and rope, it looked ironically as if a lynching was occurring.

The next day I headed to Hattiesburg, Mississippi, to visit a church created for LGBTQ members, where I was greeted by a tattoo-covered, nose-ring-wearing lesbian minister, and once again I noticed the emergence of a different (yet still complicated) South.

As Belton settles in and Kiyma works toward a future in the South, I head to New York City again and try to hear the beat that was once so loud to me. I stand on 125th Street after a conversation with a twenty-something Bronx native who has decided that she definitely won't be coming back after years living in Florida. In the background steel drums are blaring in front of The Clinton Foundation's former Harlem office, but the sound is fleeting. After about a half hour, they are silenced, and only sirens can be heard in the distance.

MILLENNIAL MOMENT: **KATRINA**

It's been over a decade since Hurricane Katrina destroyed New Orleans, left more than 1,800 people dead, and displaced tens of thousands of residents. A study of Black youth ages ten to sixteen conducted between 2012 and 2014 found that nearly one in five participants exhibited signs of post-traumatic stress—a rate four times higher than the national average.[19] They were depressed, stressed, and concerned about violence. A psychiatrist said the data was consistent with surveys taken after Katrina, meaning that Black youth were still grappling with the trauma from the event. Dr. Ansel Augustine, the former director of the New Orleans archdiocese's Office of Black Catholic Ministries, is not surprised Black youth remain traumatized by Katrina. "Home is not home anymore."

JHAMAL, AGE 24, SIXTH WARD/TREME

You had to evacuate.

They tell you to evacuate, but evacuation is expensive. Storms hit here all the time. You have to pay for a hotel at least three days or two days. Me and all my family went to Waco, Texas. We were like, "It will be all right." You had to evacuate. [I was] fussing with my mom about that. We ended up sitting in twenty-seven hours of traffic. Twenty-seven hours of traffic. You take out a few things like your major documents. Your birth certificate, your social security card. You only have clothes for a few days. I thought it was cool. New Orleans is hit with a storm every year. You get used to it. It's kind of like earthquakes in California. When you feel the earth shaking, you stand up, and then it's over with.

Once we got to Waco, that's when everything came down about how bad it was. We stayed there for a good two or three days. My parrain stayed in Atlanta. Parrain's another word for godfather. Once it came back that we can't go back home, we went out there by them. They had a nice crib. Every family had their own room at their house. It worked out fine. You were around your cousins all day. You got a chance [to] play football. I ended up getting registered for class. At this point we didn't know what our house looked like. All [we knew] is, we can't come back to the city right now.

All of a sudden, my father's job called and said, "We're going to pay for your housing; we're going to pay for your food; we'll pay for everything. You just have to go to Houston." He worked in the mailroom for Hibernia Bank. He was a supervisor for them, so they needed help. Me and my mom had to literally leave to go to Houston. I remember bawling, crying in my room. I didn't know anybody in Houston. I'd just lost everything. Imagine not knowing whether your best friend is still alive. My mom was depressed. I was depressed. But you don't really know you depressed.

When we got to Houston, it was a transition process. I went to school. You had a lot of New Orleanians that was in the school. At this point and time they started bussing people out to Houston. I'm not going lie; at first Houston was kind of a cool place to be. We stayed in a hotel. We had food. It was decent.

I remember going to the Goodwill and shopping. I didn't have any clothes. That was one of the most humbling things I've ever done out there. I was around a majority of Hispanics. I wasn't around Blacks.

New Orleans is a major city, so we're going to have high crime. When the city floods, the crime is going to leave. It got to a point where everything that happened was [blamed on the kids from] New Orleans. The kids hearing their parents say stuff, so the kids would say stuff. You had Houston versus New Orleans fights. Depending on what school you went to depended on how many fights you got into. If you went to a rougher school and you was already rough yourself, y'all going to bump heads automatically. It was a lot. It was one point and time, it's me in the class: I'm cursing out everybody. I'm standing on the desk. I didn't care. I remember later on I started hanging with the New Orleans crowd. That was who I hung with. We were just terrorizing people. Like terror-

izing. Being from New Orleans, you don't care. We throwing oranges up, and they hitting people. One dude was like, 'I'm going to get my brother, and he's going to . . .' I was like, 'Go ahead.' We had situations like that.

How can you express how you feel when you don't know how you feel? You are a kid. You know how it feels to be a kid. You just living life. It was just different.

My mom was like, "We're moving back." In the midst of that we're trying to build back the house. We had four feet of water. Everything all on the ground was pretty much done. I don't know how to describe it. The National Guard kicked the French doors in because they were looking to see if people was inside. That's one of the things they had to do. They had to kick everybody house in. Maybe you could save them. Maybe they were dead. The refrigerator had floated to a point, and it turned itself around. That was on the ground. They had a stool that was in the den. It floated all the way to the dining room. It was crazy stuff that happened.

It's not really about loss; it's the mindset of the person. One of the biggest regrets I had, my middle-school stuff, all that's gone. I threw all of that away. Everything else in my room, I just tossed it. It was a frustration type of thing, but you don't know you frustrated. I just tossed everything. I got rid of all that. My mom got rid of a lot stuff she regretted. We got rid of a lot of stuff. Some stuff you could save, but it's frustrating. You have to go through the whole house and try to salvage what you can.

You still run into people you haven't seen for a while. Certain people from a lot of different places. Like I said, it's a major city and we still have large poverty. You have people who have found better lives elsewhere all the way up to Arizona. Certain people stayed. If it worked out for you, I support it. That changed other places too. You ever had Hot Sausage before? Hot Sausage moved to Houston. Maybe it's in Atlanta now, I'm not quite sure. They started importing that over there.

New Orleans is probably one of the best places to grow up just because of the cool family aspect. We have a lot of wonderful things to offer. Katrina did affect us to this day. In my mind, we all can survive anywhere. Anywhere. You just tough it out.

chapter two

DON'T DOUBLE DOWN ON STUPID

AFTER A VIDEO WAS POSTED ONLINE ABOUT MICHAEL'S[1] UNDERGRADUATE STUDENT debt, people were upset at his decision to take out more loans to go to graduate school. He already owed $75,000 for his bachelor's degree, and his full-time job working at a nonprofit only paid $22,000 a year, hardly enough to pay his bills. But Michael *had* to go to graduate school. There was really no other option in his mind. He felt, like so many other young Black people trying to get to that "next level" of success, that higher education is practically mandatory for Black youth, who have to still constantly prove their worth in society. For Black kids, who have to work twice as hard, he said a bachelor's degree is just the minimum requirement for even a sliver of the stability that his White peers have, and even that only happens to a lucky few.

As I listened to Michael talk about his college experience with his deep, confident voice, all I could do was think about the line from the children's novels by Lemony Snicket about an "ersatz" elevator. "If we wait until we're ready," the character Violet says, "we'll be waiting for the rest of our lives."[2] Indeed, patience is something that young Black people hear about a lot. Wait your turn for this. Wait your turn for that. After his story was publicized, Michael was told over and over again online that he shouldn't go to graduate school to get a "useless" master's degree in Africana studies. That he should wait until he has more money or more job experience and not be "stupid" about his decisions. But Michael is done waiting. He's ignoring the comments urging him to quit, and instead he's focusing on finishing up his first semester of graduate school. He'll fight to get through grad school, just the way he fought to get through college, because he feels his time is now.

Michael knows the statistics. Whites are so privileged in our society that the median wealth among White high school dropouts is significantly larger, at $51,300, than Black families headed by someone with a college degree ($25,900), according to a 2014 study by the think tank Demos. Most of us don't have intergenerational wealth to rely on, partially because we have systematically been denied any opportunity to accumulate it. We weren't able to retain wealth from our labor on the plantations because it was put in the hands of companies like Aetna, JP Morgan Chase, and USA Today, which still operate today. In the twentieth century, when FHA loans and the GI Bill helped usher in a new educated and homeowning White middle class, redlining and predatory lending prevented many Blacks from accumulating wealth. Affirmative action and other programs to increase diversity helped Black people for a bit: they entered higher-paying professional jobs in the seventies and eighties, and for a while they were making progress. But after the 2008 financial recession and housing crisis, Black families saw 31 percent of their wealth evaporate (compared with 11 percent for Whites), which was already far behind Whites. Today, White families are recovering from the recession, but a report published in 2018 by the Center for American Progress found that the median wealth for a Black family was $17,600. White families by comparison had $171,000 in wealth.[3]

So what are we supposed to do to make our dreams come true? Education, we are told, coupled with hard work, will solve all our problems. Or at least that's the fantasy pushed on young kids today. But attending college isn't the same as it was for our parents, when college costs were much lower. For example, tuition and fees at public and private nonprofit four-year colleges has increased 247 percent since 1975.[4]

College tuition has become a challenge for millennials of all ethnicities, who have 300 percent more debt than our parents, but for Brown and Black millennials, who often don't have the same amount of wealth or security as their White counterparts, the cost can be prohibitive.

Young Black people have been patiently waiting for their shot in this country for nearly four hundred years, and it feels as if the time will never come. White men get to do what they want. They aren't told to be patient, they aren't told to wait for the perfect time, and yet they end up making more money, living longer, getting better jobs, and retaining the most power. Black kids, meanwhile, don't believe they can have dreams. Or at least, they can't have dreams in the way White kids do. But the thing that many fail to realize is that all too often, even when we are allowed to have dreams, our dreams are tempered by reality.

The fucked-up thing about being young and Black in America is that we can't just be free—we can't just have dreams. Michael is ready to change that narrative. Michael has a lot of student debt—almost $100,000 at this point—and he's trying to free himself from it in the only way he can see: getting another degree.

Education has always been a liberating force for young Black people, a key component to achieving upward mobility, but in today's economy, a bachelor's degree seems to be the bare minimum requirement in order to earn a decent wage. All too often we don't have the financial resources or parental support to pay for college or graduate degrees. So debt becomes our family, our inheritance checks, our stock and oil money, and we try to borrow our way into a dream of education that we've been sold. We aren't going into debt buying rims or paying for expensive weaves; we're going into debt to pay for education. We know that we're held to a higher standard in ways that other young people aren't. We know that we can't host reality shows and then become president. We have to be top of our class; we have to be the head of the *Harvard Law Review*. We can't be C students; As are a must. We have to be exceptional, good-looking, "articulate," "clean," charming, intelligent—superhuman, really. One of the ways that we best know how to do this is through education.

It's certainly the way Michael was raised. He was born in 1992, during what he called the "last of the good days" for industrial workers in a town in northeastern Ohio, where he said only steel, football, and God mattered—in that order. His dad, an electrical engineer with Delphi, a subsidiary of GM, was making good money and, despite the fact that he divorced Michael's mom when Michael was three, had ensured a pretty solidly middle-class lifestyle for his family. He worked hard as one of the first Black steel tradesmen to graduate from his program and dedicated his life to his craft. Yet the old man, with his crippled fingers and weary heart, didn't want the same for his young son and drilled into his head that college wasn't an option—it was mandatory for survival.

It's a narrative a lot of us have heard before. To some degree, it is true: educated Blacks make more money when you look at their socioeconomic position relative to Blacks with a high school education.[5] A study by the Young Invincibles, an advocacy group for millennials, found that in order to gain the same job prospects as a White male who didn't *finish* high school, a Black man would have to take at least some college classes. Overall it found that Black millennials have to "earn two educational levels higher" than their White counterparts to have the same job prospects. However, they found that at higher degree levels, Blacks and Whites "have nearly equal probabilities of employment." The same group says a professional degree offers a young Black male a 146 percent larger effect on employment opportunities than a White male; Black millennial women have similar but less dramatic patterns. In terms of money the group found that a bachelor degree means that Black men make about $10,000 a year more than if they had an associate degree, and an advanced degree would make them $21,000 more a year. The same can be said for White men, though a degree is clearly less important to their salary. Having a postbaccalaureate degree, for example, only gives White men $15,100 more a year.

This would all seem like no big surprise, except when wealth is taken into account, the argument for college becomes more complicated. A study in 2015 by the Federal Reserve Bank of St. Louis found that college doesn't do much to eliminate the racial gap in our society, proclaiming that "higher education alone cannot level the playing field." One of the authors of the report, William R. Emmons, told the *New York Times* that the trends make it clear that White and Asian college grads do "much better" than their peers who don't have degrees, while college-educated Blacks and Latinxs do "much worse proportionately." For Blacks and Latinxs, Emmons said, "there was almost of a reversal of the college effect." Black college graduates lost 59.7 percent of their wealth between 2007 and 2013, while Blacks without higher education only lost 37.3 percent of their net wealth. Compare that to Whites with four-year degrees. They lost 16 percent of their wealth during that same period, but Whites without degrees lost 32.9 percent of their wealth. The data for the long-term impact of college degrees was equally as disturbing. The report found that from 1992 to 2013 Blacks who finished college saw their median net worth drop 56 percent, while Whites with college degrees saw their median net worth *increase* by 86 percent during that same period.[6]

Nevertheless, Michael's dad was focused at the time on the one thing he thought would help ensure his children's success: education. He taught Michael and his younger sister how to read at an early age, and he was constantly making Michael watch videos of great speeches from people like Martin Luther King Jr. and John F. Kennedy. He pushed him harder than his sister, he told Michael because he thought as a young Black man in America he might find things a bit more difficult. And for a while Michael's father was right.

Michael began acting out during his elementary and middle school years. He was bullied and beaten up every day in school, and his stability at home began to deteriorate. First, his mother, who was dealing with drug and alcohol addictions, kept breaking promises to meet up and spend time with him. His father was trying hard, but it was tough. His father had found new relationships with other women, and that soon became problematic. According to Michael, he was sexually abused twice, by his dad's girlfriends. He didn't tell anyone of those encounters at the time, or of another similar experience by a neighborhood bully, but anger was building. He was lost and had a hard time connecting to a world that seemed increasingly unfriendly. On top of all that, after Michael's grandmother died, his grief-stricken father, who was a recovering addict, relapsed.

But his dad remained committed to his family, and his work ethic enabled him to power through the day even when he was high. He would get up every day at five a.m., drop Michael and his sister off with the babysitter, work not just one shift but two, get high as a kite, sleep, and then repeat it all the next day. Michael knew something was off and was unhappy. Plus Michael missed his mother. "My dad was trying all he could, giving me all the love he had, and I just wanted to know why she wouldn't love me. If you take that with growing up in my father's household, with the juxtaposition of the hood with the world outside of it, it was kind of like Kendrick Lamar, 'good kid, M.A.D.D. city.' All of the factors around me, everything was pulling me in a different direction," Michael told me. He was trying every way he could to cope. Back then, he said, he would "spazz out," "shout," or throw things across the room at school at the drop of a dime. He once even broke a table. He said he was mimicking his surroundings, a community he said that was filled with violence, and trying to prove himself as a young man. In his everyday world, violence along with "physical dominance" was how you proved yourself. He didn't have anyone to talk to about what was really happening in his life, so he played into that narrative, with even his own aunt telling his father that Michael was "violent and crazy." "It was really the definition of being misunderstood. Folks had no idea," Michael said. In his own words, though, he wasn't crazy; he was just an "angry kid" trying to make sense of the world we live in.

His life changed when one substitute teacher, Mr. K, sat down and asked him what was going on. He realized that no one had actually ever asked him before; instead he was usually just suspended or shuffled off to detention. Mr. K was different from the other adults at school, and Michael said the teacher really listened to the challenges he was dealing with. They started off talking sports and then worked their way to family life, and Michael slowly opened up. Mr. K didn't treat the conversation like an extended after-school special: when it was over, the teacher simply told him to get back to work. But it was the prefix Mr. K used in front of Michael's name that got his attention.

"'Okay, Doctor, well, let's get back to class,'" Michael glowingly recalled. "Doctor." Michael hadn't really thought of becoming any type of doctor, but he liked the sound of it, and the name stuck. From then on and throughout high school, Mr. K. referred to Michael as "Doctor," and Michael decided he was actually going to live up to that moniker, though he didn't exactly know how. "I think for me he saw a young Black man with potential who just had some circumstances that made it difficult for him to function. With that, he was really able to take a chance on me." Michael was also put into gifted and talented classes because he scored so well on tests, though initially they wanted to give him an Individualized Education Plan (typically created for students with special needs) and put him in classes for kids with behavioral problems. He had also just begun to participate in track and field, and finally it seemed, things were looking up.

Michael's father had been a star football player in high school and in college. He played for a while but left when he needed to make money, noting that, as a Black man in America in the 1960s, getting a good job with benefits always took precedence. Eventually the years of first working in a car factory, then a steel factory, took a toll. He had made good money, enough to raise his family, but his body started to decline.

Michael witnessed the change over the years and watched his dad's body slowly give out, as carpal tunnel in his fingers left him barely able to hold a coffee mug. At that point, Michael knew factory life wasn't for him and decided he needed to do something different, though he wasn't exactly sure what. His dad, too, saw the industry shift as his own future at the company became less secure. He was forced to retire and, concerned about what kind of future his son would have, started saving up for Michael's college education.

Jobs had been leaving Michael's city for decades, ever since Bill Clinton signed the North American Free Trade Agreement in December 1993 that removed tariffs between Canada, the United States, and Mexico and created one of the largest free trade zones in the world. Add in advances in automation and globalization, and places like his community seemed to enter a free fall. Though often portrayed as a White working- and middle-class issue, the loss of manufacturing hit Black families like Michael's hard. According to Robert Scott, the director of trade and manufacturing policy for the Economic Policy Institute, Blacks lost 281,000 high-paying manufacturing jobs between 2001 and 2011, with 25 percent of people of color being affected by trade with China, losing more than $2.5 million in wages. As factories and steel mills continued to close, the population shrank to a fraction of what it was, and by 2009, the year Michael began high school, a reporter for the Associated Press said the city, now with a declining population of 43,000, was "littered with abandoned dreams." Yet by the time he was ready for college, Michael wasn't worried about what he would do with his future or his father's shrinking checks. His destiny had become clear. He would become an all-American athlete.

~

Michael's tangential interest in athletics began during middle school as a way to alleviate some anger, release some steam. At some point along the way, he realized not only was he feeling better mentally but he was enjoying the games, and soon sports became a full-time obsession for him. In his freshman year he lettered varsity in track and field and dressed varsity for football, something that was rare at his high school, which is home to nine state championships. He was doing well, though he wasn't perfect. During his sophomore year, feeling the high of being a varsity track player, he began to skip classes. Despite the fact that he had a good year in track, he was put on academic probation. Devastated but not deterred he became the water boy for the football team, just to stay near the sport. He got his act together and was back on the team the next year. By senior year he was being recruited by several Big 10 schools in the Midwest for track and field.

For Michael, sports was a verifiable way out of what seemed to be a predetermined life in the factories. It was the only path he saw. His grades were above average but nothing spectacular, and with a father with a solid middle-class job, he wouldn't be considered poor enough to qualify for the best financial aid packages to college, yet his family still didn't have enough to pay for him to go. So sports, he decided, had to be his future. Besides, sports was what his town lived and breathed, and he too wanted to be a part of that legendary group of men and women from his community that people talked about for decades.

Michael admitted that for Black youth, sports sometimes seem to be the more reachable path to success: "The way our society is set up, it's an easy grab." But, it's not as easy as it seems. One study found that the average high school basketball player has a .003 percent chance of making it to the pros. A 2017 study from the *Undefeated* found that the number of athletes who come from poor families without degrees (known as "first-gens") have decreased. More student athletes are coming from middle-class backgrounds, meaning that sports as a way out for this generation's underprivileged is also not as accessible as it was in the past.[7]

Even *making it* can take its toll, and Michael knew he was playing by different rules. "I had to work when my teammates wouldn't work. Show up early. Leave late. It was a grind. I had to make a lot of sacrifices." It wasn't easy, Michael said, and his body, much like his father's, is still paying the cost for his dreams. He's in a perpetual state of pain: his knees hurt; his back hurts; his shoulders hurt. He has arthritis, and he has trouble walking and moving and even sometimes thinking as a result of complications he believes are from concussions. Back in high school, however, Michael was flying high.

Several college recruiters were after him, but only two mattered in his mind. If you were from his school, the unspoken rule was that the best athletes went to Michigan or Ohio State. His teammate was going to Michigan, and it seemed almost manifest that Michael should go to Ohio. His cousin was there as a running back, and he had been recruited by the track and field team and given the opportunity to walk on the football team. But after a few visits to Ohio State, Michael started to second-guess his choice. Whenever he visited, it seemed the students he met would only be running or partying, and he saw little else. "They treat athletes like gods there, and I felt like I wouldn't have gotten out of college what I should have." After a visit to another large public university, the school choice of many of his family members, as well as his father, he decided that despite the fact that they weren't in a top five conference, it was the best place for him. They had top-notch academics, and he received a full scholarship—a rarity for track and field players. Recruiters swooped down even more when Michael placed in a top time for the hurdles, and his coach urged him to hold out for other offers. But Michael's mind was made up. With that decision complete, Michael finished senior year on a high. He had a dope-ass prom, a high school sweetheart he was happy with, and his team had just brought home the state championship for track and field—the first ever for the school. It was a good ending to his high school career.

~

MICHAEL'S LIFE AS A COLLEGE ATHLETE STARTED OFF WELL. SURE, there were a few stumbling blocks along the way, like the unanticipated expense of toiletries and the heavier clothing he needed to buy for the colder weather in his new college town, which weren't covered by his scholarship nor the $5,000 that his dad, now fully retired, had saved up for him. He didn't think much of it; he took a small loan of about $2,000 and focused on his athletic career. The more rigorous world of collegiate sports was initially tough on him, but he adjusted, and freshman year started to breeze by.

He ran through part of the indoor season until he injured his back and was unable to run hurdles anymore. His coaches urged him to go on and push through the pain, disagreeing with him about the "validity or severity" of his ailments, but he couldn't. He tried harder and eventually learned to work through some of the discomfort, but his season was shot. The school reduced his scholarship, which was based on his performance in track, and the next year Michael had to take out more loans.

Fired up and feeling better, he had a promising start to his sophomore season, but then the stomach pains began. He started to throw up during practices, and he couldn't figure out why. He had never been ill during track except once when he ate too close to a practice. So the coach sent him to the team doctor for cold or stomach virus symptoms. It didn't help. Practices were getting harder for Michael; he was regularly fatigued and bloated and experienced jabbing pains in his stomach. He was frustrated by his body, but mostly he was sick. Eventually he saw a specialist and was diagnosed with H. Pylori, a bacteria in the lining of the stomach that can cause ulcers, irritable bowel syndrome, and even stomach cancer. Once again, he tried to work through the pain, but he found it increasingly difficult. Things only became worse when he injured his quad muscle during practice. He was going to miss another season of outdoor running.

By the end of the year, his coach sat him down and told him the bad news: they wouldn't be able to bring him back on a scholarship the next year. In fact, they couldn't even cover his books. His coach asked if he wanted to compete in tournaments with the team to see if he could earn his scholarship back, but Michael now had to get real. If he was going to complete his education, he'd have to find a job. With the addition now of medical bills, he knew things were about to get tight, so he decided to end his career as an athlete. "We had that conversation, and that was that," he said with a sigh. He never looked back.

~

According to the NCAA, the organization that deals with competitive intercollegiate sports, many athletic scholarships, like academic ones, are given to students for one year. This means that college athletes can get scholarships reduced or not renewed and be forced to pay for their own health care after sustaining injuries while playing for their school. It's an issue that students, athletes, and the NCAA itself have taken up, with many, including the NCAA, advocating that students need more protections from things like illness and injury. A representative for the NCAA noted that in 2015, the year Michael graduated, sixty-five schools in the Big 10, Big 12, and several other conferences passed a rule that schools can't cancel scholarships for "athletics reasons," which include injury, but it is up to the individual institution as to whether it chooses to follow that rule. The NCAA also pointed out that Division I schools (Michael's school is one) have been allowed to give out multiyear grants since 2012 and that in many cases it's the coach who determines who will or won't receive a scholarship and whether it can be renewed.[8] Michael's school has a policy of not speaking to media about specific individuals but stated in June 2018 that it offers one-year athletic scholarships that are renewable at the end of each academic year.

For a while Michael wondered what he should do. His dad told him he could come back home and work, but he knew going home was a death sentence, in both the metaphorical and perhaps physical sense. The neighborhood where he grew up was changing; there were new dope boys around, ones who may not have sheltered him from the streets and urged him to go to college, the way the guys did when he was coming up. Michael felt it would have been dangerous to go back. "I either would not reach my potential, I would become frustrated and burnt out, or I would become a product of my environment and get involved in illegal activities or just be a bystander."

So he borrowed more money, about $18,000 that year, and pushed ahead. He had become involved in student leadership and decided to pursue that further. Some of those activities, like being a part of the Black United Students Executive Board and eventually becoming student body president, made up for scholarship money he had lost, but he was starting to struggle financially. When I asked him if he'd been worried about his mounting debt, he bluntly answered that it was a mode of survival: "Really I didn't care. I needed to finish school. This was something I set out to do. This was something that someone said that I couldn't do, so any way to make that possible I was going to do it. Taking out the additional loan money—I knew what it was, I knew that it was going to put me in a nice sizable amount of debt, but I was going to graduate, and that was really it."

Things were tight for a while, and Michael had no backup when things didn't go his way. He noticed this was especially a problem for many Black students who didn't have parents to rely on for extra cash. Students, he said, contrary to public opinion, that were doing whatever they could just to stay in college. Some were homeless and slept on different couches every week; others never had enough for food. He was in the latter camp and had to learn how to take food so he wouldn't go hungry. "I stole food all five years that I was in school from our cafeterias. Whether it was sliding past the cashier without them noticing or knowing somebody that worked at an eatery on campus that would do the fake card swipe." Even with that, Michael said, he didn't eat the most balanced meals. And by the time he graduated, his blood pressure was astronomical from all the cheap food he was putting in his body. "I had issues with my blood sugar out of stress because you know you can only get so far on eating ramen, spam, Vienna sausage, and cans of tuna. I did what I could."

It was a different world from his White friends, who he said live a completely different life from him and his Black cohorts. "Most of my

[White] peers, they were middle class. They would have all these nice expensive things. They didn't have an idea of what it was like to know that hey, I'm going to go home and I'm probably not going to eat today. Or I'm going to sleep in my office because I don't have a car, and my place is so far away, and I worked so late into the night that it's not worth it for me to walk the hour and fifteen minutes it is to my apartment. They didn't have a concept of those things. It was clear at the most basic level that there was disagreement and separation among us just because I lived a life that they would never understand."

Michael took jobs wherever he could, on campus, off campus at a barbeque restaurant, working up to three jobs at a time just so he could make ends meet. Racial tensions were flaring on campus, and the police shooting of Tamir Rice happened not too far from the school; he went through a breakup and soon realized he would need an extra year to finish. Exhausted, worn out, and depressed, he began drinking every day. But he was determined not to leave and pushed on. It wasn't all bad, he tells me, making sure I understood that college wasn't entirely disastrous—he had some good moments too.

Michael refused to fail his family and especially his father, so he worked hard to keep going. He said this kind of pressure is something unique to Black millennials who are trying to deal with getting good grades, financial difficulties, and race: "Black students have to exhibit a great deal of triumph in dealing with the pressures of college and being able to finish. It's no small thing for a Black kid to graduate from college these days."

In 2015, with $76,000 worth of debt, he graduated. He turned down corporate internships to work in the nonprofit sector, as a marketing and advertising coordinator with a nonprofit in Atlanta. A few months later, determined to continue with his studies and become "Doctor," he enrolled in a master's program. The program cost a little less than $20,000 a year, and his new job paid him just $2,000 more than that—before taxes—meaning Michael would have to take out more loans. He knew that by the time he finished his master's degree in Africana studies, he would be over $100,000 in debt, but higher education is important to him.

Like other studies noted earlier, a report by Brookings found that graduate degrees, while often a riskier option for Blacks, who have more student debt than their White counterparts after getting a bachelor's degree (in the 2008 cohort Black graduates had $52,726 dollars in debt versus $28,000 for Whites), still "confer large returns" on the job market for all groups, including Blacks.

Michael seems to draw the line, however, at a master's degree. He said he already plans to apply to doctoral programs but will only enroll if it is a fully funded degree. Ultimately he hopes that when he finishes up his studies, he can get into a debt forgiveness program that would eliminate some of his loans after working in a nonprofit or government job for five years.

Michael knows the amount of money he has borrowed is staggering to some people, but he seems genuinely unbothered because he believes his loans helped get him through school and set him up for success. "I think any decision I would have made with my loans would have affected me somewhere else. If I would have taken out less loan money, I would have had to work more. You think about different places where you wasted a dollar here and there, I would take some of those things back, but then again I probably wouldn't because I try to live my life with no regret. I think long and hard about decisions before I make them. Every decision I've ever made in my life I made it for a reason, so I wouldn't take any of it back. I don't regret any of it. I would do it all again if I had to." Still Michael said any kids he has in the future won't be taking out loans for college. He's already started financial planning and is trying to teach more Black folk about financial literacy. "You can't just blindly sign a paper, which is what most of us do. We have to be able to be smart about it. If you're going to take out student loans and have a stack of refund money, do something smart with it. Either keep it to pay tuition in the future so that you don't have to take out as much money or use it to open an IRA. Use it to attain something that you can build again.

Use it to attain an asset. There are ways that we can use student debt to be successful and not take out so much. I think there were times that if I would have been okay with struggling a little more, I could have taken out a little less money. A thousand here, a thousand here. Before you know it you've taken out 10,000 less dollars, and it makes a difference."

Michael hopes to one day become a professor in cultural and Africana studies so that he can support students the way people helped him. For now he will continue to work in the nonprofit sector, where he is passionate about assisting young people to make positive changes in their lives. "My story is not a sob story. I just happen to have a lot of debt. I'm doing great; I've done things that people dream about doing. I've done a lot of things in my twenty-four years that a lot of people don't do in their entire lifespan. By no means do I pity myself, do I feel sorry for where I am. I made some choices, and I got to pay some people the money back."

STATISTICS SHOW COLLEGE ATTENDANCE AMONG BLACK YOUTH is up, but because of the lack of wealth most Black folks have, the decision to go to college is not to be taken lightly. A study by Harvard's Institute of Politics at the Kennedy School found that for more than half of Black millennials surveyed, debt played a role in the decision to go to college, while only 38 percent of White millennials said the same. And though the number of loans Black students have taken out over the past decade has increased, with 81 percent of Blacks with bachelor's degrees having debt upon graduation (compared to 64 percent of White students), debt is still the main reason Black people drop out of college. Sixty-nine percent of Black students leave school because of debt, whereas only 43 percent of Whites say the same.[9]

On paper, the millennial generation, including Black millennials, are the most educated generation ever. But with less money to begin with and fewer chances of employment after, many Black youth are beginning to wonder if the debt is worth it. We have come to see student debt as a millennial problem, but it's also a racial problem, in that it disproportionately affects young Blacks.

After hearing Michael's story, I wonder if his $100,000 in loans made sense. In 2011, during a speech on economic inequality, President Obama told a crowd in Osawatomie, Kansas, that higher education is the "surest route to the middle class." In 2015, he repeated the same sentiments, while acknowledging the increase in cost: "Today, a college degree is the surest ticket to the middle class and beyond, but it has also never been more expensive." Blacks have heeded this call, despite the price.

Obama is right in some ways, but it obscures the reality that it may just not be practical for some, and emphasizing that approach makes it harder for those millennials who challenge the idea that education is the only path to success. It shouldn't be. While I believe in the importance of education, it remains available only to the privileged few—a third of Americans age twenty-five and over have a bachelor's degree—and there should be other avenues that lead to success.[10]

I COMPLETED MY UNDERGRADUATE AND MASTER'S DEGREES WELL over ten years ago, and I'm at the end of a doctoral program. I have doubts about whether these degrees are essential to career development. Yet nearly every student I interviewed for this book seemed to believe degrees were worthwhile. And while I'm probably just annoyed at having to still pay off loans, they're probably right in the long run. While Black and Latinx students don't see the same benefits of having a degree as White millennials, not having one spells even more trouble. The unemployment rate for Black *college* graduates is the same as for White *high school* graduates, and the wealth of a Black college graduate equals what the average White high school dropout has.

It seems for many, you're damned if you do and damned if you don't. We're taking on higher rates of debt not because we want to, but because it is both an economic necessity and another part of that idea of "twice as good"—a way to prove that we are worthy in a world that privileges mediocre White folks over well-deserving Blacks.

It may seem "stupid" for people to take on so much debt, but in a world that treats you as if you're nothing, you have to use every tool in your arsenal. While learning was important to many of the smart Black millennials I met, many of them spoke of their desire to go against a narrative of White entitlement. Higher education was important to them because it gave them a seat at the table; it proved to the world that they deserved to be there. It was, in their eyes, mandatory in a world that looks down at Blackness, that thinks of us as inferior. While taking on student debt is often characterized as irresponsible, so many of these young folk are trying to do the right thing, not so much because they want to, but because they have to do so to excel in America.

I know this was the case when I was growing up in a middle-class household, with above-average grades and above-average extracurricular activities. I never felt that what I did was enough; I had to be so much more just to get the one lonely seat reserved at the table for "us." I can admit: I wasn't a superstar. I didn't qualify for those big awards and grants given to folks who could do long division by the age of six, and I didn't have an athletic bone in my body. I understand that, at least in theory, no one wants to support mediocrity, but it seems that in reality no one wants to support *Black* mediocrity. White mediocrity is everywhere—one can just look at presidents 43 and 45 to attest to that. I'm tired of seeing mediocre White people who squeaked through college get good jobs, while Black people often feel compelled to get more degrees and certificates just so they can prove they deserve a shot. All too often, to be Black and successful you have to be a superstar, which is an impossible burden for anyone to bear. I look at my Black professional friends, and they are the exceptions. They had multiple internships in college and in high school, worked their asses off, had amazing grades. By their own admission, many of my White friends and peers were average students. They got Cs. Partied their way through college. Had 2.0 GPAs and were unfocused or confused about their majors, when so many of my Black friends had been preparing for their careers since the day they stepped foot on campus. Recently, I had to explain to an upper-middle-class White colleague who is getting a PhD from the same university as I am why I thought so much inequality existed, when I, in her words, had so many traditional markers of "success." It took all my power not to scratch her eyes out.

I'll be honest. My mom is still paying for my BA and MA programs even though I'm thirty-six. She said it was her gift to me, and I'll take it, though I do feel a bit spoiled. Despite the fact I still had student loans from my undergraduate and master's programs, in 2008, when I thought the media world was imploding, I left my $70,000-a-year job and went to graduate school to get a PhD. Like Michael, I wanted to gain a deeper knowledge of my culture that I felt was lacking. I liked the coursework, but after two years full-time, as a single woman with a condo bought during the recession, I was struggling with a teaching assistant gig that paid $24,000 a year, and I wondered if I'd really find a tenure-track job after finishing. I refused to take out a loan to pay for the program, so I got a job on the side, violating the terms of my stipend agreement, since you're not allowed to have a teaching assistantship and work part-time, even at a bookstore. I probably could have managed things better, but I decided to become a part-time student. Still, it was hard to focus on both a PhD and a demanding TV job. The year I turned thirty-five, I decided that I had to finish. I took out a loan of $20,000 to pay for my remaining credits. Instead of finishing, all I did was spend it worrying about how much more money it would cost to truly finish. So now I still don't have my PhD, though most of my courses are paid for, and I am struggling to complete a dissertation. What I do have is $50,000 in student debt, two degrees, and preparation for a career in an industry I may never get a job in.

Perhaps I've become too afraid of debt, but I see my friends—some who, like Michael ended up with over $100,000 to get their PhDs, others who had rich families—still struggling to find jobs. I don't feel a rush to create more debt. I worry about stability and family in the future and how student debt has the potential to cripple my entire lifestyle and provide very little return. Maybe I worry too much.

But even for those far smarter and savvier than I have been in the past, finances can become a problem. Even when you do everything the theoretically "right way" and have that picturesque middle-class family, you can still become mired in student debt. Such is the case with Joelle. I met the twenty-three-year-old on an unusually warm winter's morning at a fancy Swedish coffee shop on the very posh Lexington Avenue. Joelle, with her warm smile, long Black and gray braids, and stylish scarf, was getting her second cup of coffee and eating a muffin by the time I rushed in fifteen minutes late, with my hair askew and stained underarms, the result of a delayed train. She noted when we were setting the date that she usually prepares for things and is early, and of course on that day, she had already dropped off her lunch at her office after taking the long train ride into Manhattan from the Bed-Stuy area of Brooklyn. Not one hair seemed out of place, not one piece of clothing awry. This girl, I thought, was together. Prepared. As I fumbled for my tape recorder in my purse filled with tissues, books, notepads, and random unknown crap, I felt bad because I just knew her bag was orderly, and here I was in my thirties an absolute mess. This young thing was showing me up. But that's the thing about so many young Black millennials I met. While some were horribly prepared and had no idea how to get to college or why it was important, many more were ready for the future and just weren't quite able to achieve their goals because of financial needs.

Joelle was one of those folks who did everything right. Her family followed that quintessential path that conservatives love to tell Black people is the way to upward mobility. She had, she said, "literally, the kind of family that you have in a little kid's play set." Her parents, both military veterans, never went to college, struggled to work their way out of poverty, and did. Her mom was a nursery school teacher and her dad a police officer for the Los Angeles Police Department. Together they made too much money for her to qualify for full aid, and she wasn't eligible for Pell Grants. Her family worked hard, and yet they still didn't have enough money to pay for her or her sister to go to college. When she got into her dream schools, like the University of Chicago and Georgetown, Joelle was proud. But she had to turn them down because their financial aid packages were too weak. She tried everything to make her dreams happen, including negotiating with the folks at Chicago. In the end, they offered her $2,000 more in grants, but that wasn't anywhere near the money she needed. Frustrated, she turned down her top choices and headed to UCLA, a more affordable state school where she was able to get more funding.

Like Michael, she needed loans to pay for seemingly small things—books, living expenses, things she thought she could pay off but she hadn't planned for. She was annoyed by people who would ask why she didn't get a job: she worked the whole time, including a stint at a parking garage, but that wasn't enough to keep up with the expenses of college. Still, she was making it somehow, until her mother fell ill and had to stop working. Her middle-class family was suddenly thrown into crisis mode. Her supportive parents could no longer help her out. In fact, she had to give them a few thousand dollars when they filed for bankruptcy, and once again she worried about money. "It was like we technically did everything right. My parents didn't go to college, but they got good jobs. Middle-class family, we had medical debt, and then on top of that both me and my sister were going to UCs, and we didn't have enough money to pay for that, so me and my sister were taking on debt, my parents were taking on debt, and then they filed for bankruptcy, so then I had to take on more debt."

Ironically, it was a lack of degrees that caused some of her grief. Her mom, because of a lack of college, was limited in the number of teaching jobs, especially high-paying ones, she could take, and her dad, who has been on the force for twenty-six years, was unable to be promoted to a lieutenant from a sergeant because he doesn't have a college diploma. She understands these sorts of barriers but said if this is going to be such an impediment to a middle-class life, then everyone needs to truly have an equal opportunity to education. I asked her what I imagine she, like Michael, had heard from many others: Why take out all these loans? Why not work, save, and finish up later? Her answer made me think for weeks.

"I'm allowed to have dreams, right?"

"I don't know. Are you?" I replied, genuinely baffled by the question.

"My gut reaction to that is always, 'So I'm not supposed to try to take risks to achieve something higher than what the opportunities were for my parents? Sorry, at the time I wanted to be a lawyer. To be a lawyer you have to go to school. They don't just let you walk into a courtroom. So am I not allowed to be a lawyer?'"

She continues with a story about a family road trip when she was young. They stopped in front of CNN headquarters where her dad told her she could be a news anchor and on television. "He was trying so hard to prepare me to fit into White power spaces so that I could have some power, so that I could have some agency over my own life." It was an important moment, she said, because she grew up dreaming. She grew up thinking that she could work at CNN, that those "spaces" were for her.

After graduating in 2012, she went to work for a think tank, where she now runs a youth program. Her interest in economic policy, a specialty of the organization, means that it's mandatory that she will have to go back to school. Mandatory, because she is a young Black woman. "No one's going to listen to me if I don't have a degree that tells them that I know about economic policy." She said that it's sad that in this society Black and Brown people like her still have to prove themselves to other people. She tells me about a few conversations she had with professionals when she was beginning to decide if she needed an MBA/MPA or a PhD. She asked a bunch of economists in the Northeast what degree was best. The men told her not to bother with a doctorate if she didn't want to teach. All of the women, Black, White, or whatever, said that if she wanted to get any kind of respect, she would need that higher degree. "Especially for a field that's very old and very male and very White, it matters a lot that some other institution tells them that you're "smart" because they're not going to just believe you based off what you're saying." Exasperated, she understood what she had to do.

THERE'S A GROUP OF AMERICANS WHO BELIEVE THAT GETTING an education automatically means you are on the path to upward mobility. While higher education does mean that Blacks sometimes have more economic leeway than they would without a degree, the reality that education isn't the great equalizer should be alarming. In addition, attitudes that Blacks receive an unfair advantage also must be quashed. In 1989 Donald Trump said education, particularly for Blacks, was powerful and claimed that educated Blacks had more advantages than Whites: "A well-educated Black has a tremendous advantage over a well-educated White in terms of the job market. And, I think, sometimes a Black may think that they don't really have the advantage or this or that but in actuality today, currently, it's, uh, it's a, it's a great. I've said on occasion, even about myself, if I were starting off today I would love to be a well-educated Black because I really believe they do have an actual advantage today." There is no evidence that his thinking has changed. In fact, it reflects the sentiment of others who believe that affirmative action and other diversity tools are propelling Blacks to the top of the pool.

Yet research remains to show just how big of a burden education is on Black households. In late 2017, the US Department of Education released the results of its first long-term study on student borrowing. It found that Black students who entered college twelve years ago and borrowed money for an undergraduate degree now owed more on their federal loans than they borrowed, with half defaulting on their loans altogether.[11]

Michael ended up leaving graduate school during his third semester in the fall of 2016. He had fallen out with one his professors, and just wasn't getting the education he signed up for. When his dad got sick back in Ohio, he decided that it was time to go, and by December, he had left Atlanta to start a new job as coordinator for a youth program. He also began taking courses as a guest student back at his former university and plans to apply for its Master of Library and Information Science degree program. He's paying for it all out of pocket and said he's "not going further into debt."

MILLENNIAL MOMENT: **TWO LIVES**

GENEI, AGE 24, PATERSON, NJ

When the local newspaper asked sixteen-year-old Genei to describe himself in one word on a summer day in 2010, the shy teen confidently said one word: "Amazing." Genei wanted to be an architect, loved cars and playing basketball, loved his community even more, and decided if he won the lottery, he would give back to his neighborhood and start his own dog kennel. Almost ten years later, instead of finishing up architecture school, Genei is an inmate at Northern State Prison in Newark, New Jersey. He has been incarcerated since 2013 after being arrested on two counts of armed robbery. He was two months away from release when we exchanged email messages.

My experience is a little different than most, I was enrolled in schools outside of the community I lived in, for the majority of my educational journey. The smaller settings, arguably, allowed me to succeed, academically. Behaviorally is another story. I don't know what caused me to "act out" in my younger years but I know once I started to get older, the realization of going to a "private" school made me uncomfortable. On top of me being embarrassed of getting on a little yellow bus to go to a far away school while all my associates walked to the public school, I didn't relate to any of the other students in the private schools.

I was born and raised in New Jersey. Growing up I was always told by my teachers that I was very advanced for my age so with that in mind I always felt like I could do whatever and be good at it, but the thing is at a early age I learned how to manipulate, I knew what to say or do to make my mom or my teachers happy. Basically, I did and said things that I knew they perceived as "good" as to what I actually believed or found of interest. Fast forward a little bit, I think the big transition in my life happened in 8th grade, I started selling drugs not out of necessity but more so because that's what others my age was doing. That whole lifestyle made me start to live for the moment. I wasn't entertaining thoughts of the future. I actually was living two different lives. I was going to private school, fake socializing with kids that ain't never seen struggle then I'd get off the bus and go right to the block where the kids my age wasn't even going to school.

The main thing I was concerned about was the view others in the hood had of me though, so I finally got my mother to put me back in public school when it was time for high school. Sophomore year I was sent from public to an alternative 'till I told my mother to sign me out completely so I can get my G.E.D. *At age 16, I was done with school. I passed the* G.E.D *exam on the first try. A couple months later I was locked up facing 20 yrs.*

I was lost and didn't know my place in the world, had some goals but didn't know how to properly go about obtaining them. Me and my mother didn't see eye to eye and it came to the point where I didn't care about anything. As a result of moving without a purpose or care I eventually got caught. In fact, at the time I didn't even care about getting caught. I figured it couldn't get any worse.

At the time, I wasn't getting proper mental support or receiving the important thing to a teen—material items I wanted—so I choose to get it how I saw others getting theirs.

Selling drugs is just like any other business, you build a clientele and supply a product. The New Jack City *way is for the bottom feeders and they are the ones at extreme risk. Nowadays the "smarter" dealers don't stand on corners or in buildings. They communicate with their established clientele however they see fit and make transactions. Unfortunately, many don't properly invest. As quick as it come the quicker it's gone.*

Today, boys grow up socialized to "chase the bag" meaning get it how you see fit and girls the same. Boys resort to some sort of "criminal" activity and girls either cling to the criminals or the smarter ones use their looks to advance. They market themselves on Instagram and gain big followings and make money. That's how it is in the urban community. That's our culture. We attracted to it because that's what we are exposed to 24/7, any other type of exposure ain't sufficient.

I knew of people that was locked up but I never really gave incarceration much thought. I had the mindset like "I ain't never gonna get locked up." In hindsight and from being in this setting for the last seven years the stories people hear in the hood about prison is a reflection of what actually goes on when you're home. Most come in and out because the things they indulge in out there can be accomplished in here. I said that to say that subconsciously that might of had an affect on my "don't give a fuck" mentality.

For the last seven years, all I've been doing is reading and educating myself. I never regretted any of this because I made my experience positive. The authorities only had limited control.

I'm looking forward to my release because I now have a purpose, I won't just be living day to day, I'm going to actually enjoy the best thing life has to offer, freedom. I look forward to exercising all of my freedoms, even the ones they try to hide. I plan on jumping right into the fall semester so ain't gonna be too much relaxation. The first thing Imma do is take a long hot shower maybe even soak in the tub lol, then I just want to chill with my lil' bro and shop online. I'm looking forward to some homemade lasagna, baked ziti, and garlic bread. There's some anxiety because I know it's gonna be many temptations in every aspect, but I promised myself that I will not give any energy to anything or anyone that isn't worthy.

chapter three

SURVIVAL

ON THE SURFACE, TROY[1] IS THE KIND OF MILLENNIAL WHOM THINK PIECES ARE made of. He's arrogant, self-centered, and constantly worried about his image. He is convinced he is smarter than people give him credit for, despite a report card that would indicate otherwise. His favorite topics of conversation are girls, sneakers, and cars—not a surprise for an eighteen-year-old. But his mannerisms also reveal the patterns of someone who is troubled, scared, and unsure of the future.

On one bright day in Paterson, New Jersey, he throws a dark hoodie over his head, which hangs low as he talks about death and the fear that something may happen to him. Troy's been waking up angry and going to sleep with the same frustration in his stomach, though he's not sure why. Maybe it's personal: a recent betrayal by a close friend. Maybe it's bigger than that: the news stories at night that show Ferguson, Baltimore, and other urban communities like his own on fire. Maybe he's scared of the cops after seeing so many videos of brutality online. Or maybe it's just White people overall—he said he doesn't like them, because they don't like him. Or maybe it's none of that. Maybe it's all about his drug business that just came crashing down after a recent arrest.

Troy embodies many of the positive qualities this generation is known for: an entrepreneurial spirit, an independent streak, and a dedication to his parents. He believes in hard work and has tried gigs in both the licit and the underground economies just to get ahead, but he hasn't found his way and still dances between both worlds. Right now he's employed as a golf caddy for a local country club just beyond the borders of his community. He goes there every afternoon after school to try to make at least a hundred dollars a day carrying bags for rich men and women who may not care about his existence. Before that, he sold sneakers on Facebook—a big thing in the hood, he said, until White boys from the 'burbs with access to more cash and better products took over. He even tried selling candy bars and water bottles, since it's one of the safest ways you can make money, but he wasn't making enough to help his family or save up for a car anytime soon. He sees how hard his immigrant mother from Jamaica works and how little she gets back in return, and he vows to take a different path, though he doesn't know what it will be.

Troy started dealing drugs a few years ago, after sneaker sales fell flat, but he got caught and is now figuring his next steps. Troy's story isn't some New Jack tale of the 1980s. He isn't in the drug business because without the extra income his family will starve. And gang leaders didn't pressure him into the trade. His story is different, and it could only belong to a millennial. It could only happen at a time when America is crawling out of a recession but largely leaving young Black men, regardless of income or family history, out of that recovery[2] and incarcerating them in record numbers; when college tuition fees have massively outpaced inflation; and when so many adults took jobs they were overqualified for since the crash in 2008 that it's tough for a teenager to get entry-level work.

Troy knows he's largely shut out of work in the formal economy, so he and his peers have found opportunities outside it. But he also knows he needs a way out of this life. "I just got anger in my heart. I'm not scared of nothing. Something missing. Every morning, I get up, every night when I go to sleep, or when I get up, I feel angry. I'm not angry at nobody. I'm angry at stuff." He dreams of affording a car, not only to "get out" in a metaphorical sense but also to use as a safer space to sell drugs from and eventually to transport him to a better place. To him, that means Atlanta. He has it all planned out: he's going to save all his money from his part-time job as a golf caddy and then proudly walk into the dealership on Tenth Avenue and buy a used BMW. According to him, this will take about four months. He leaves out, initially, the part about not having a license or his recent troubles with the law. Troy moved to the United States when he was twelve, but he's already shaping his own version of the American Dream.

Shawn Grey,[3] the former director of the youth organization where I met Troy, has made a career working with boys like Troy. At thirty-three, he's on the other end of the millennial generation. He says dreams are different for Black kids, partially because of the lack of available jobs, partially because of discrimination, and partially because of the low self-esteem and insecurity that come from being seen as thugs and criminals. "If jobs were more readily accessible to kids, they wouldn't have time [to get into trouble]. Sit down and ask if they want a job: they'll say, 'Hell yes, I want a job.' They love the idea of having their own."

Still, he said that young kids just don't understand that "you can't be a boss at sixteen." Even when this group has the skills and vision of a young Mark Zuckerberg, young Black Americans are less likely to be taken seriously as business leaders or rewarded for the kind of brash arrogance that propelled Zuckerberg to the top of a multibillion-dollar company. That fact is not lost on these kids, though when you ask them about their future they know what they're supposed to say. They'll talk about college and full-time jobs, doing the "right" things, making some money, even if they know that the reality may be different. The difference, he said, at least for young Black millennials, is "not aspiration but access." It's the precariousness of that sense of possibility Grey is worried about. He wonders about what feels possible for the Black boys who turn on the TV and see themselves not only in Jay-Z or even Obama, but in Trayvon Martin and Mike Brown.

In a country where money equals power, quick money, at least for a while, often gives these young Black men and women a sense of control over their lives. Troy said that anyone who wants fast money has to deal in "heroin and lou [marijuana]," but he mainly did it because he wants a better life. "I want to take my family outside. They got money, but don't have it like *that*. Rent and stuff is a struggle. I want to take 'em to a quiet area, no crime. I wanted to have money on my own. I wanted to save money to get a car. I want to live a good life. I was greedy, and I got caught," he said with a sigh. Yet Troy still believes in the American Dream and, despite his recent arrest, believes that he can still move up. "You come to America—you start all over again. I am young; I just wanted more money. I didn't want to be a rapper. I didn't like rap. I didn't want to sit down and be broke. I was trying to get money and have a good life."

I ask what he means by a "good life." "A good life is . . . you just feel like you made it. No worries about anything." He pauses. "I don't know."

I don't know if Troy's dreams came true. He disappeared from the program he was involved in for troubled youth, and it seems he has slipped through the cracks. It's not a surprise; this happens to workers like him. It's hard to know how many Black millennials are in the underground economy, since by nature these jobs are unreported. But looking at research from the Federal Bank of Boston about the 44 percent of people who work in the informal economy, we can extrapolate the data to assume that there are as many as 3.9 million Black millennials working in the underground economy—legally or illegally.[4]

ARTICLES ON MILLENNIALS LOVE TO FOCUS ON THE LEGAL SIDE OF the underground economy. Not all of the informal economy is illegal or is even about survival. Some of it is about joy, particularly the side hustle—a gig that brings in supplemental income, in addition to a primary job. Side hustles can range from a college student making jewelry on Etsy to a production assistant brewing craft beer on the side to a mom working for Uber to make extra cash. There are a number of young Black millennials who are working on their own side projects, developing cool web apps, film scripts, or podcasts all on their own, doing it for love and passion. Among my own friends is one who writes comedy scripts after her day job during the week and another who has a jewelry-making business while attending law school. Many have managed to have successful side hustles and sometimes turn that success into a full-time gig. Heck, even I started writing magazine articles on the side while working a day job in television. However, it doesn't mean that the experiences of Black and White millennials are equal: Black people's side hustles aren't always turned into big projects or financed by venture capitalists looking for the next project (according to one study, just 1 percent of VC funding goes to Black entrepreneurs).[5] Perhaps more importantly, often these side projects are necessary as supplemental income for a group that's already underpaid and underemployed.

When it comes to Black women, who make less than their male counterparts, this seems even more relevant. Historically, Black women have always played the role of caretakers in their family, in part because of the discrimination in the employment market against Black men, and studies today show life is no different. Eighty percent of Black women are breadwinners in their homes, and they often take care of not only young kids but also older relatives. Nevertheless, while they have one of the highest rates of employment out of any racial or ethnic group, at 60 percent labor force participation, they, along with Latinx women, receive the lowest wages. A 2017 study from the Institute for Women's Policy Research found that while unemployment for women of all races and ethnicities peaked during and after the Great Recession, the rates for Black women were particularly high. It found that Black women and girls had the highest unemployment rate among all groups, including those with college degrees. Even as unemployment started to fall, in 2016 the unemployment rate for Black women was higher than White women's unemployment at the peak in 2010. This includes Black millennial women.[6] Add in higher rates of imprisonment, poverty, and lack of health care, and the reality that Black women face becomes clearer.

In *Sex Workers, Psychics, and Numbers Runners* scholar LaShawn Harris looks at Black women who worked in the underground economy in early twentieth-century New York. She found that women saw the informal economy as a way to gain some agency in their lives, "transforming their socioeconomic status and personal lives," when they often had no ability to do so elsewhere. The underground economy, she said, "opened the door for Black women to radically disrupt, violate and push pass the limits of conventional and acceptable public behavior and performances for Black women." She said she sees the same thing happening today with Black women who are still often left behind and have to fend for themselves, and while she sees the informal economy as a "complex blend of opportunity and oppression,"[7] Black women often have to use what resources they have at their disposal to get by.

One of the resources some women engage in is sex work. According to the World Health Organization, sex work is defined as the selling of sexual services for money or goods. It includes legal activities like dancing, stripping, and performing in pornographic films, as well as prostitution, which is illegal in much of the United States. Regardless of legality, this kind of work is not valued by society, and workers often face harsh criticism, violence, police brutality, and health risks as they take up this very unregulated field.

Still, for a range of Black millennials I've met, especially those who were trying to "move on up," sex work was a top choice, regardless of education, income, or sexual orientation. Some did it because they felt locked out of the mainstream workforce, or because they couldn't get by with a "vanilla" job. Others did it because they enjoyed the work and didn't see it as any different from working for a sleazy corporation, for bosses who are just legalized pimps.

Recently, young Black celebrities Amber Rose and Cardi B—both strippers before they became famous—have spoken positively of their previous positions. Cardi, who is in theory living the quintessential American Dream and whose 2017 track *Bodak Yellow* broke records, said that her time as a Bronx stripper was empowering because it saved her from a bad relationship after she was fired from a job. Entertainer Amber Rose said she began stripping at age fifteen because her family didn't have much money. "I was very young and I did what I had to, to survive at that time." Yet Amber also acknowledged the disparity in the industry. She told one website of a time in Milan watching a strip show with millionaires and billionaires. "Dita Von Teese [who is White] gets on stage and she gets buck naked and she spins around in a big martini glass and everyone *clapped* for her. And it's bullshit. It's not fair that it's OK for her to do it because she doing it for rich white people but you know I was in like, the hood, and I did what I had to do to survive . . . and I constantly get ridiculed."[8]

Since sex work has become a part of the public conversation and had become an option for a number of people, I went to Chicago to meet with a few women who worked in the industry. Their stories were all different, just like their relationship to the work, but when it came down to it, they weren't unlike other millennials. They all talked about the Black tax, feeling degraded by White folk and underappreciated for their work, and sometimes they wanted to talk to me about their dreams.

IT ALL STARTED WITH A WOMEN'S STUDIES CLASS DURING Lauren's[9] junior year of college. She decided to take it as an elective for her biology major; it was nothing she'd really thought much about, though it ended up changing her entire life. Up until then, Lauren had been having a rough year. She'd gotten pregnant and decided to have an abortion, then got caught up in a different relationship that had turned abusive, and she wasn't able to slip away easily. Everything changed when she started learning about gender, race, and sexuality. She eagerly absorbed the works of Judith Butler and bell hooks, and soon began to think about privilege and power on a new, deeper level. She couldn't get enough of the scholarship, so the next summer she decided to switch her major from biology to women's studies. She had been accepted into a bevy of programs to receive training to become a physician's assistant after college, but she decided to enroll in the sole women's studies graduate program she had applied to.

Lauren's upper-middle-class parents, to put it lightly, were angry and threatened to cut off all of their financial support. They were immigrants from Ghana—the family had moved to North Carolina when she was twelve—and wanted her to succeed. They didn't believe they had come all the way to the United States for her to study "women." But she insisted on enrolling, and they made good on their threat. They completely cut her off. They stopped paying for her tuition and living expenses, and suddenly Lauren was completely on her own. She was shocked, shaken up, and unsure about what to do next.

She was jobless and broke, but she was ready to excel in her new academic endeavor—with the assistance of a "shit ton" of loans. One day, as she was walking to her car in the parking lot of a mall in Durham, an old White guy catcalled her and said, "You're so beautiful." Confused, she muttered, "I'm what?" as he handed her his business card and suggested they hang out. She kept the card for a while, even told her friends about the odd scene. They got a good laugh about it and asked her if she planned to see him. She told them she probably wouldn't. Eventually, though, she changed her mind and decided to take the man up on his offer for a date. At the end of the evening, to her surprise, he gave her money. Lauren was genuinely perplexed, but given her financial situation, she didn't protest either. She was happy to get a few hundred dollars and a free meal, and the relationship continued for a while. They went out to dinner, talked, began having sex, and the money continued. Eventually, he was sustaining her life in the most minimal of ways, and for a while she was okay with the situation. She had always been body and sex positive and the arrangement was easy. The far bigger problem was that his life was a mess. He was a drug addict married to a Jamaican woman who needed to get citizenship, and on top of all that his fledgling business seemed to be in the red more than not. "It was super nice, but I'd have to suck his wrinkly dick for $200. I was just like, 'Ugh.' I was just not attracted to this person." But still, the money helped, so the arrangement continued, until he became too much of a liability. His checks were bouncing, causing her rent checks to bounce, and Lauren knew she couldn't actually sustain *him*.

When she told other people about what happened, they mentioned a classified website named Backpage. Backpage, created by founders of the *Village Voice* in 2012, was a classified website that had a popular adult section, which was said to be frequented by sex workers advertising their services. Lauren soon started responding to advertisements by men looking for "friends." It wasn't easy at first, and she had complicated thoughts about getting into such explicit sex work. She had to balance concerns about a profession that some people called "heathenism" with the newfound access to money, but eventually she decided to pursue her new endeavor. It wasn't a lot, but it helped. "I'd maybe have them pay my electric bill. Or someone pays some of my rent versus not having anything at all. It was not a lavish lifestyle."

One day she responded to an ad placed by someone who was looking for a dominatrix they could have a submissive relationship with. She didn't know anything about it, but she responded and met up with the guy. He wanted her to hit him. Choke him. Make him feel pain. She carried on with the whole routine for a while, until, after a few more sessions, he flat out told her she wasn't cut out for the job. His words stung, but it also made her decide to become a success at it. She refused to have some rich guy tell her that she couldn't do something. So, in that moment, she decided she was going to be the best dominatrix ever. She watched videos, found other doms to get advice from, and learned as much as she could about the world of domination and submission. The more she learned about the niche industry in the sex work world, the more she was attracted to it. She liked the idea that power was flipped on its head, but even more, she felt that this scenario allowed her to set boundaries with clients in a way she couldn't in the world of escorting and penetrative sex work. But first she had to figure out who she was, what her style was, and how she could make people submit.

Her home life was settling down, and she had already excitedly begun her graduate school classes in August 2014. Her loans covered her living expenses, and though it wasn't a lot, she could survive. She had also began dating, a guy she described as half-White, half-Lebanese who was working on a nursing degree, and fell in love. They had an open relationship, and he was very accepting of her life as a sex worker. After a year in the industry, Lauren was increasingly becoming more comfortable in her own skin, so much so that when she was asked what she did for a living on some paperwork for grad school the next year, she plainly and boldly wrote, "DOMINATRIX." She had finally arrived. Her business was growing, she was working in hotels and getting a few clients every week, and finally she was making more money.

It's harder in some ways to be a dom, Lauren told me. It's very niche, and "most people are looking to fuck," she said as she nibbled a fancy slice of pizza on Chicago's Millionaire Mile. Some doms engage in penetrative sex, she said, but Lauren won't anymore. As a dom, she feels she has more control during each session than she has in her other sex work, and she soon realized she just didn't like penetrative sex with her clients. "I don't like being fucked by these old men. I would rather be broke than do it. There's no judgment on it." Lauren thinks about the money she is missing, because she could make a lot more as an escort, but doesn't regret it.

Just as soon as she was getting comfortable with her life as a dominatrix and grad student in North Carolina, her partner (now her husband) got into a nurse practitioner program in Chicago, and they decided to relocate while she finished her program online. Being a sex worker in the Chi was much different from in North Carolina, and it took her more time to establish herself.

She also became a lot more worried about the police in Chicago. In North Carolina, the dom community was small. She knew of only two dungeons (places where doms often practice), and there was no threat of getting raided. In Chicago there were a multitude of dungeons, and they weren't immune to police raids. Cook County Sheriff Thomas Dart, whose jurisdiction includes Chicago, had also been cracking down on sex work and sex trafficking for years. He first sued Craigslist, trying to get the company to remove its erotic services section, calling the site the "single largest source of prostitution in the nation." Craigslist modified the page, but his work continued, and in 2015 he sent a letter to MasterCard and Visa urging them to stop allowing their cards to be used on Backpage.com. It worked. Sex workers were shaken: a major way for them to conduct their business had been shut off.[10]

While Dart focused on pimps and johns—those who are buying rather than the men and women workers—she was nervous. The energy in the city seemed anxious, and she didn't want to become one of the more than forty-three thousand women arrested for prostitution each year.[11]

But Lauren put all of that out of her mind. It was a whole new world for her, and she was determined to make it work. When she arrived at one of the dungeons for a job, they told her she'd have to up her game: create a flashy website, advertise more, and come up with a catchy name. Ready to take the Windy City by storm, Miss V was born. She was anxious about building a website—though she had been in the business for years, her parents didn't know, and the website would make secrecy harder. At first, she didn't show pictures on the site, but as she increasingly became comfortable with her persona, she began to reveal herself bit by bit. She's a little less worried if her parents find out now, because she thinks she can talk her way around it, using some excuse that her website is a project for school. She had to test that scenario out recently when a cousin from Ghana saw an article that Lauren was featured in and shared it on social media. Lauren thought she had blocked her family from seeing her account, but someone else had tagged her in a post, and her relative saw it. He asked her right away if she was a stripper. She cried and cried to her partner, thinking her life was over, but since her cousin doesn't speak English well, her excuse that it was for a school assignment seemed to work, though she is sure he is skeptical. Her sister is the only family member who knows about her true line of work, and she doesn't care.

On the day I met her, her natural locs were in a hot pink twist-out and her natural underarm hair long. It's sometimes dyed the color of her hair, but that day it was a natural dark brown. Her skin looks soft, and the moniker, Miss V, a reference to her smooth skin, seems appropriate. She wore a multicolored dress and a big chunky necklace, but her style was low-key. As she delicately sipped a glass of wine and continued eating the fancy pizza, I asked about a word she used earlier in our conversation: "healing." As a Black woman, she said being a dom had been healing, and I realized I had no idea what that actually meant. "I'm a Black feminist who beats up White men, and that shit is so cute," she said with a smile. "I like parading around this character of getting reparations and getting a lot of money from White CEOs that kiss my feet." When I ask if she's doing systemic work, she shrugs it off, since the root of much of her work as a dom, she said, is a problematic fetishization of Black women, of Africanness. "I think that healing doesn't have to be on a systemic level. Society expects so much labor from Black women. Just like, what can you do to take care of yourself? This could be a way for some people. It has been a way for me." She knows that her clients are there because they have a particular desire for Black women, and she tries to get past that in the best way she can. "My feelings about them is that they suck. Some of them are cheating on their wives with me. They're all scummy. I hate them. I would never interact with them. They're CEOs and capitalists, and I'm anticapitalist. I can get money from them and also cause them pain, even if it is overall pleasure, to crack that whip," she said with a smile. "Especially a whip—I use that when I'm most cynical because it's like a really painful thing. I'll be thinking of slavery and being like, 'This is for the ancestors.'" *Crack. Pop.* "I just leave there with this glow every time." The sessions are hard, she said, and she's often exhausted afterward, but when she's able to crack that whip, that ethereal glow just radiates from her body. As she walks out the door with a wad of cash, she justifies it all by telling herself that she is living "the best life" she can at the moment.

Ms. V's satisfaction, though, is not only about the whip. As a dominatrix, she also demands that her clients read essays from feminist literature, particularly those from Patricia Hill Collins, and makes her "slaves" write essays about it.

Miss V knows that her methods may be untraditional, but she thinks that in some small way she can help White folk understand more about the Black experience in America. She said the essays they write aren't great, and they often complain, but she hopes that she can get through to them, even if it's just a little bit. For example, she helps them understand the intersections between race and class. "Every new person almost every time says, 'You're not ratchet.' Or 'I've seen other Black doms, but they're all ghetto.'" It makes her double down even harder. "When I make them do theoretical work, we talk about valuing all Black women across classes. They're not going to only like me because I'm going to get my PhD and talk shit about a South Side dom that they met that maybe doesn't speak the way I speak," she said with a sigh. "I don't know if it really sticks, but I fucking drill that into them and will beat them for it. Punish them for it." Her lessons have helped at least one of her clients see Black women in a different light. He told her he started a foundation for single Black homeless women because of their sessions and his work with her. She was "blown away."

Miss V wrestles with the fact that most of her clients are White men. She identifies as queer and is in a lot of Black queer spaces, where everyone is "super cute, super lit and it's all just great," but she remains unsure what people in the Ghanaian or African American community think of her. She's attracted to non-cis White men, but in the past she's had to try to figure out how to navigate that. "I've slept with a lot of people. I'm such a ho. I love it, but I have not been with a lot of Black people. That's something I still struggle with." She seems to think hard about her next words. "I think partly it's that I was around a lot more White people. I think partly it's that I had a lot of internalized things. Then maybe the way that I feel valued in sexual or romantic relationships exists in a certain way that is a specific thing about Whiteness."

She faces other pressures as a Black queer woman in these spaces. There is pressure to be hyper-feminine, in ways that she believes White doms don't have to be. They have more space to be more creative. Miss V tries to push back and reject those restrictive labels, letting her true self come through, which means sometimes she wears combat boots, and sometime she wears heels, but she hates the notion that she has to constantly reify her femininity. White doms can be "super femme" or "hard femme," which is more in line with her persona, but she can't always do that: she is already losing people because of racism.

Miss V has no qualms saying that she believes that her clients in general are racist—as she said, that's why they're looking for a Black dom. She knows she is being fetishized and exoticized, often by people who have never been intimate with a Black woman. She tries to work with it and be understanding, but sometimes people take it too far. Like last week, when someone messaged her and said they wanted to be "dommed or controlled by a N-word bitch ape." She realized they weren't necessarily calling her an ape, but she found the language problematic and even more so because they thought she would be okay with that language. "Fuck you," she wrote back, and blocked them. There's only so much she can do, she said with another sigh.

She worries about repercussions and violence when it comes to dealing with certain clients. And though she has been fairly lucky when it comes to violence, though not immune to it, she still has her concerns. Her voice lowered as she told me a story about a new client she met the week before our meeting.

His previous Black dom had died ten years ago, and he was finally looking for a new person. But Miss V, in the interim, said he had lost some of his training. He wouldn't follow her commands. She'd tell him to get on his knees, and he'd boldly say, "No, I don't want to." He made excuses over and over for forty minutes and refused to submit to her, until she, annoyed, finally ended the session for the lack of his obedience. He was upset, and the look he gave her put fear into her eyes. Sensing a bad vibe and feeling that something was about to happen, she texted her husband, who was nearby at a coffee shop. She thought he was going to take the money he left on the table, and at that point she didn't care. He wasn't getting what he paid $700 for. She was scared as she realized that if he wanted to, he could hit her right there. He left without any incident, but Miss V was shaken. "It was a reminder about how unsafe the work is."

And the work is unsafe. According to a report by the Sex Workers Outreach Project USA, a sex worker advocacy group, of the over forty million sex workers around the world, 45 to 75 percent have a chance of encountering sexual violence in their careers, and 32 to 55 percent are likely to experience violence any given year. In the United States, over 30 percent of street-based workers in Miami said they had violent encounters with a client in the past ninety days. In New York, over 80 percent of street-based workers said they had experienced violence. The numbers for indoor sex workers aren't much better: in New York 46 percent said they were forced to do something they didn't want to do. Accurate data is hard to come by because of the underground nature of the industry, a lack of peer review, and author bias, according to one former sex worker.[12]

If you look at the rates for trans workers, especially Black trans workers, the amount of violence is even more frightening. In the trans community, where work is already hard to come by because of the harsh stigma they face, sex work is often the only option that people can turn to for cash. In 2015, ten of the reported twelve trans sex workers who died were Black, according to the National LGBTQ Taskforce, though data on this is shaky and the likelihood of accurate reporting of these cases is low. In all likelihood the numbers are even higher, as the federal government doesn't collect homicide data based on gender. Additionally police departments may misgender victims based on their birth names.[13]

Despite the negatives, Miss V believes that Black millennials have a lot of access to things that Black people hadn't had before: "We can own ourselves, and we could love whoever we want, queer or not, Black or not, in ways that we haven't been able to do." Also she said they can dare to dream. She has an idea of the American Dream—a White picket fence, financial stability, and living in the suburbs or a brownstone—yet it comes with a caveat. She said the Dream is rooted in racism, and therefore something that Black folk, even if they are middle class, don't have access to. Specifically, she said the dream is anti-Black. "I would say that for people of color and specifically for Black people, specifically Black people in the US, the American Dream is just like living. I don't think we've even been granted the right to be alive and much less have access to that picket fence. A Black family can occupy a house with that picket fence; it doesn't mean that we are inherently part of that." Instead, Miss V has her own idea of what success looks like in her life. "When I think about what I'm trying to accomplish in life, which is mainly just to be able to take care of myself and avoid being homeless and avoid being in an abusive relationship and being able to eat, my mind doesn't go towards the American Dream. It goes towards survival under White supremacy and then also liberation. I think that both of those things come in a lot of different ways. It's like why I am very okay with being a dom. Got to do what you got to do to take care of yourself to have money because it is so hard to work."

~

In May 2017, Miss V completed her graduate program and earned a master's degree. Her father didn't attend the graduation, and her mother barely acknowledged it, but she seems proud of her accomplishment. She used her experience as a sex worker in some of her graduate papers and included in her thesis chapters on BDSM as healing. She cherishes the ability to think critically about her work and generally, with the exception of her family, to be open and free about what she does. She's privileged, she said, because she can leave if she wants, and she gets to do the type of work she wants in a safe space that she pays for.

Right now sex work is sustaining her and also her partner. He stopped working once she was established so he could focus on school. As a Black woman, though, even one who is privileged, she knows she is making less than others in her field. She sees other doms online charging $1,000 an hour and knows she can't do that. Her base rate is $200 an hour, with tiers. In order to make three or four grand a month, she said, she has to work every day. It's about the same amount, she said, as she'd earn if she were working at a nonprofit. She knows that other Black women, especially Black trans women, make a lot less. It's not a lot of money, and she said it can be demoralizing. "We're not middle class," she emphasized. "It is so much labor. It is hard work. You use your body so much. You provide so much emotional labor for these people."

She wishes that there were more positive stories about sex workers and also less conflation with sex trafficking. She thinks that there is too much of a focus on the illegal sex trade, a complaint I've heard over and over. Instead of pathologizing sex work, she wants people to see it for what it is: a job. It's not always about someone's trauma, or by the same token, it's not always empowering, especially if you're poor and just doing it to get by. For her, the work has been fueling some of her academic research, and more importantly it's been a source of some of her healing. "It's been a source of my growth. I've grown with myself sexually. I've learned a lot about what I like and don't like based on what I do." She's thinking about switching over to working in the nonprofit sector and has three job offers related to sex education but is not sure what she's going to do. The prospective salaries of the job offers are more than she earns now, but not by that much, but the pay is at least steady. Ultimately, she doesn't think Miss V is going anywhere anytime soon. "I don't know what the future for Miss V holds. I'm going to keep doing it until I feel like I don't want to do it anymore. There is no expiration date at the moment."

~

Plenty of detractors criticize sex work. Often they say that sex work exploits women, denies them any agency, and reifies men's power, leaving women defenseless and vulnerable. And there are those who simply think it's immoral. It can be easy to paint a good empowering picture of sex work or a negative one, but many of the young workers said it's so much more nuanced than it appears to be.[14]

As Miss V alluded to, many of the stories about young Black sex workers don't feel so empowering—in large part because of the violence they disproportionately face. One story that stood out to me was that of twenty-four-year-old Alisha. I had been trying to reach out to Alisha for months, but she was hard to get a hold of. She has been in jail in Illinois, for nearly four years for the murder of a client she said tried to attack her. The State of Illinois has treated Alisha as if she is a dangerous criminal who killed a client during a skirmish over money, but her advocates maintain that, like so many other incarcerated sex workers, she is in jail for defending herself at work.

Alisha was raised in a predominantly White community in Ohio, by her grandparents and single mom in the early nineties, until her mom got pregnant by the man she was in love with and decided she was going to get married. The man happened to be Black, and Alisha's Papaw kicked them all out of his house. He had tolerated her mother's indiscretion with another Black man, which had led to Alisha's birth, but he drew the line at marriage. He wanted to keep their Italian bloodline free of any intermingling with "Negroes" and believed strongly in "staying within the race." But her mom, who was always a rebel and seemed to have a thing for Black men (more impolitely she was known as a "nigger lover" in the town), wasn't having any of that. So she picked up her things and moved to be with her man in Akron, a larger city a few miles from their home, but a world away in reality. Back in her small community, as a biracial child, Alisha was an outsider. People didn't know what to make of her; some even thought she was an albino because of her light skin color. Everyone there subscribed to the idea that racism didn't exist, and that false reality permeated her reality. Still, it was home.

When she relocated to Akron, things changed quickly. They moved in with her new stepdad, his twin brother, his sister, and all of their kids in a house across from the projects. It was like going from the "upper class to like fuckin' *Straight Outta Compton*," she said, laughing. Her mom felt she was finally at home and encouraged Alisha to explore the neighborhood, though it took her a little more time to adjust.

Alisha remembers riding her bike through the projects and getting beaten up by this big-ass eighth grader—bloody nose, two black eyes, busted lip, pee streaming down her legs—because she, as a new fourth grader in the area, had infringed on the girl's turf. It was, she said, a big wakeup call. Her new stepdad, who is Black and Puerto Rican, took her over to her cousin's house for a lesson. Her cousin was a serious type of dude, and was eager to teach Alisha how to fight. She learned quickly and learned well. Plus, her cousin told her, he would "beat her ass" if anyone beat her ass. She hasn't lost a fight since.

Despite these rocky beginnings, Alisha learned to adapt, she learned to love her new city, and it soon felt like home. They moved to a different house down the street, and her mom gave birth to a little girl and then a boy. They were starting to settle down. But it soon became apparent that her mom was addicted to more than just Black men. She was addicted to crack. Her mom began to disappear from the house, slipping in and out as she descended into the world of drugs. Her stepfather disappeared too, though his body lingered. He went to work, paid the rent and utilities, and was home every night. But he wasn't really present; he had become a ghost. Her mom was the one who had held the house together, and without her it was falling apart, and fast. Alisha knew she needed to step in. Her sister was seven, and her brother was going on two. She decided her life and her dreams had to be sacrificed for theirs.

She learned to cook and clean and take care of two young kids. She tried to make do with what they had, but often they were missing "little things" that they needed. The water that ran through their apartment was cold, and the food stamps were never enough, so she learned how to steal. She was stressed and angry at the life she was living. It wasn't the life she envisioned for herself.

On an average school day she would wake up and have to clean up the pee from the bed her sister had wet the night before. Her sister was terrified of the room she lived in, worried that monsters and ghosts would get her, so she peed the bed to cope. Alisha understood. The room did look creepy. But she still resented that she was the one stuck cleaning up pee, changing the plastic bed mat that they had to put down for her scared sister, and throwing her clothes in the washer. She was tired of waiting on those mornings for the pot of hot water to heat so her baby sister could take a bath, and argued with her the whole time she was dressing her, because she was irritated that she had to do any of it. She would realize at some point that the house always smelled like pee—it's hard to get that smell out of the air—and that she was simply tired. She had given up on her education. Her school bus left fifteen minutes before her little sister's, so she was often absent from school. Instead, after she got her sister out of the house, she woke up her brother, and got him dressed for the day. Sometimes she'd take him to nursery school. Other times she'd keep him with her. She didn't want to stay in the house—it was boring, depressing, and lonely, plus she was worried truant officers might find her. So she wandered the streets until it was time for her sister to come home. Sometimes she'd steal if she had to, putting the goods in her brother's shirt, but mainly she was just roaming.

During those lonely days, Alisha began to relish her freedom. "I wasn't bad. I wasn't having sex; I wasn't doing drugs. I just wanted to run and see what the world was." However, running around in the streets, eventually got her caught up in street life, and soon her friend's dad asked her to start helping him with his "work." Stressed and tired, she was glad for an adult mentor, and he started taking her to the store and buying groceries for the family. He watched out for her, and she didn't have to steal anymore. Looking back, she can see that she was being molded for something bigger, but back then she couldn't really see past the next day. Her friend's dad was high up in his "crew" and wanted a new protégé. She didn't specify exactly what type of crew it was, but it was clear she was being trained to run drugs. She said she was naïve at the time and didn't fully understand what was going on, though she wasn't stupid either. "I didn't see a future at that point," she told me. "When I was younger, I wanted to be a backup dancer. I love dancing, period. That was my dream before. Then it was just like all that stopped. It didn't matter what I was anymore, as long as I got to the next day. That's what was important," she said. She was just doing what she had to do to keep her family together.

Eventually her mom came home and decided to get clean. Her stepdad followed and slowly came back to life. Alisha hoped there would be some peace again. But then the parenting began. All of a sudden Alisha had to deal with rules and curfews. It was hard for the teen, who had been on her own for two years, and they all began to butt heads. Everyone was frustrated and annoyed, and Alisha's mom finally decided to give temporary guardianship of her daughter to the new mentor, the man she continued to work and swing for. She was his "main." Anything he needed done, she was doing, and life began to feel good again. She was now sixteen and on her own, living in a new apartment with a new car and making decent money. She was on top, and she felt "gangster" for the first time. She admits that her drugs weren't the best around, but she liked the feeling it all gave her. The power. "I'm a little sixteen-year-old girl having all the drug dealers in my city having to call my phone to get what they want." Her head was gassed up. "I finally felt like I ran something. Like I finally had control over something."

It had only been a few months, really a summer, but once again things started to fall apart. Her mentor/boss developed a crush on her and became jealous when she had a boyfriend over. Plus, she was making a lot of money as a dealer—she was a good student and he seemed mad that she was doing so well. He told Alisha his supply had dried up, but Alisha, having learned the game, found a new supplier and continued to deal. This enraged her mentor even more, and she knew that she was going to have to start fending for herself. "It was fun while it lasted. Fast money, it comes and it goes." She began to crave more of what that lifestyle brought. When her best friend suggested that she find work at the local strip club and deal there, she jumped at the thought. "I'm like, that's the perfect idea. Money on top of money."

Her friend helped secure a fake ID for the underage Alisha, and she was hired quickly. Stripping came easy to her. She was a natural at it, perhaps because of her love of dance, and was having fun. But when her drug-dealing ex-mentor found out about her new gig, he ratted her out to her mom. The strip club was raided shortly after that, while Alisha was working—a setup, she believes, by her mother. It was a month before she turned seventeen.

Alisha was put on probation for a year and decided it was time to go on the straight and narrow path. She had to go to classes, so she signed up to get her GED, but she also needed to make money, so she got a job at Wendy's working three days a week. It wasn't enough to make ends meet, so she got a job helping out a friend's family clean offices late at night from nine thirty p.m. to two a.m. for $25 dollars a night. That still wasn't enough, so she got another job as a telemarketer. All those nights at the strip club taught her how to stay up and not sleep. She passed the GED exam in two months but was feeling pressure because of all of her jobs. She quit Wendy's because it was too far away. Then she quit the cleaning gig because the pay was too low. She kept her job as a telemarketer, maintained a low profile, and stayed out of trouble.

A month before her eighteenth birthday she was let off probation. A month after that, on her actual birthday, realizing that she didn't have to act "good" anymore, she quit her job as a telemarketer. She was going back to the club. She bought some "stripper heels and a stripper outfit," auditioned at a few clubs, and got a job right away. She was pumped. It would be the last time, she said, that she had a "real job."

She loved it. She was at a strip club in Youngstown. It was right at a truck stop, and every night the clientele was different. It was upscale, she said, and mainly a place for lonely men to have some companionship. On her first night back she felt alive and free, as if she didn't need to pretend anymore. On top of that, her income surged. She was earning the same amount stripping in one night as she had been making in one week—even with three jobs. It motivated her to keep working. She wasn't into drugs or alcohol; she wanted to be able to "go shopping and have my own car and my own place to live, that stuff, my cell phone, my hair and my nails. I like to look good." Alisha said she was not the "baddest bitch ever" at the club, but she was friendly and had a quality that men found attractive: innocence.

∾∾

FIVE MONTHS LATER, HER COUSIN, THE ONE WHO HAD FIRST helped her learn to fight, asked her to make a run for him to Chicago. She had never left Ohio, so, excitedly, she said yes. While she was there, she met a guy named Cheddar.[15] He told her she was pretty and asked what she did. When she said she was a dancer, he asked her how much she made. He told her, "The girls up here make like $2,000, $3,000 a night." She admitted to making only $700 or $800 a night. "They don't have girls that look like you up here," Cheddar replied, and offered to sponsor a weekend trip for her. He promised her she could pay him back with the money she made the first night. She agreed. It would be the worst decision she had ever made.

A week later, she and two of her friends went back to Chicago to see Cheddar. They happily chatted with him as he drove them around the city, but soon their excitement faded. They found out that most clubs don't let newcomers work on weekends, plus Cheddar's connects weren't coming through the way he had said they would. Alisha became frustrated with their lack of work and was worried about spending all their money for this big trip. After ditching Cheddar and driving around for what seemed like hours, Alisha pulled over to the side of the street and hopped out of her car to smoke a blunt on the West Side of Chicago. All Alisha could think about was what a bust the trip was as she took drag after drag on the joint. Suddenly, a tall guy with a Coogi sweater came over and asked her what was up. She told him of their ordeal, and he introduced them to a friend of his who ran a strip club. After asking what the ethnicity of the other girls in her crew were (an Indian and a "Barbie," she told him), he told her to come back an hour before midnight.

When they arrived at the spot a few hours later, Alisha panicked. It was a raunchy club in the hood next to a gas station, and she wasn't sure about it. But there was a line down the street of eager patrons, so Alisha and her friends forged ahead. They called their contact, and he came out with a "big fat grizzly fucking burly man" with sweat stains everywhere. He told them to make sure their valuables were locked up in their car and told them to double check it was locked. Then he asked them do a model spin. Satisfied, he directed them in. As they walked past the line, someone grabbed Alisha's hand. Multiple people touched her ass. It was like being thrown into a jungle, she said. They were told about the house fees ($50 dollars every time they entered), cautioned about the VIP room downstairs where it was anything goes, and left to themselves.

It was an illegal after-hours spot known as a lockdown, where girls are "working," fucking, stripping. Fucking on the dance floor. Anything, it seemed, went. It was a far cry from her gas station stop full of lonely truckers. Alisha was shocked even more as she walked into the dressing room, which was really just a room with a few haphazardly strung curtains to change in, two benches, and some lockers without locks. It was funky and chaotic, but she was green and determined they were going to make it that night. They had a routine and a plan. They were gonna do some girl-on-girl action and some moves they had planned at home.

Alisha recalled, "Girl, I walk up the fucking stairs, and it's just asses on fire. She's twerking with it, on fire. This other bitch has a candle in her asshole lit." She was flabbergasted. "These bitches like doing handstands and fucking splits in mid air." One woman, she told me, still in disbelief all these years later, "her face was hanging upside down by her pinky toe." Alisha and her crew were freaked out and nervous. None of them had ever seen anything like this.

But they got through it. As the new girls they were a hot commodity, and people seemed to enjoy their work. They made okay money just dancing—about $1,500 between the three of them, and Alisha was satisfied. As she was waiting around for the "Barbie," watching the other member of their trio work the pole, bored and now tired, Alisha walked over to the bar to grab a shot. Somewhere along the way, a guy grabbed her arm, and she said, with the gusto one can only have for love at first sight, that "fire just went through my veins. It was love at first touch." When he looked at her, she knew right away that she would have given him any and everything. Her voice softened: "That's when I met That Guy." She left her friends for him that night without looking back, holding him as tightly as she could. To this day, she doesn't know what came over her, but from that moment she was under his spell.

Alisha was in love and in lust and happy to just be around him. But That Guy—let's call him B—it turned out would be many things, more than just her love. He became her pimp. Her man. Her everything. She learned a lot from him—he taught her everything she knew, she said. It was a love thing and a business thing, though I get the feeling it changes on what day you ask her. She ended up moving to Chicago and in a house with other girls who worked for him. At first she was just dancing, but then seeing all the money the other girls were making, she decided to get into the penetrative sex game. It was a competition, she said, but she also acknowledges the control he had over her. "During them two years that I was underneath his thumb, he had complete and utter control over me. I was brainwashed. I betrayed everybody and anybody for him. I would've jumped off a bridge if he told me he was at the bottom to catch me."

It seemed as if he loved her and cared for her, and soon he didn't want to share her. He hooked her up for her escort work, but eventually he didn't want her sleeping with clients, so she would just go on dinner dates and do "high end" overnights for $3,000 a night, maybe give a hand job. She was doing well for herself, but she was also becoming cold.

She had been naïve. She said she didn't even know pimps existed outside of Hollywood until she met him, and in some ways he didn't fit the stereotype. He didn't force her to do anything, and he always had her back. He wasn't like the other monsters she had seen, dudes who punished girls by forcing them to crawl on leashes or who would drop gumballs on their head. Still, she said, she had no freedom. She was under his thumb, and he was a very jealous man. Outside of the girls she lived in the house with—her work crew—she didn't have any other friends, and he had to know where she was every second of the day. Even when she visited her family back in Ohio, he would be there in a hotel around the corner. Soon she began to long for the freedom she had when she first left home at sixteen or when she was dancing in Youngstown at eighteen. "Those were only two times. . . . I never really had freedom, and I just always wanted more. I felt like happiness was more." She felt stuck and angry, but also determined to make it, and she proposed a grander vision than the life they were living. She wanted to take what they were doing and use the money to open a legal business, but no one cared. No one wanted to see her vision. Instead, she said, there was more jealousy and infighting.

It wasn't all bad. When it was good, it could be great. She'd go shopping, have her hair and nails done. Plus, they traveled. But that joy wore off too, when she realized she was not having fun. When they'd go to someplace like New Orleans or Las Vegas, she couldn't really enjoy it. When they went out, people would know who she was, and she had to pretend to be a certain way. Even simple things closer to home, like going to the Taste of Chicago, she never really had time to indulge in. Eventually that inertia took hold of her again, and she was done with the life.

Plus her relationship was stressed. She was barely twenty and mentally drained.

So one day when he left the house, she bounced. Took another girl from the house with her and left for Ohio. "We ran wild," she said. She moved back in with her mom. They made up and worked on their relationship. Her mom has had her back ever since. Her mom, she realized, was just twenty-one when she first became a parent, and Alisha could only imagine the pressures of a young mother. Plus, when Alisha herself was twenty-one, she said, she was "sucking dick," and therefore didn't want to judge anyone.

For eight months Alisha and her friend went shopping, partied, got massages, and enjoyed their freedom. And though she admits she still loved B to death, she also loved her independence. She was escorting on her own, posting her own ads. "I could finally do what I wanted to do." Eventually she got back together with him, though she kept living in Ohio and traveled back and forth to see him.

In January 2014, they had to drive to Chicago for a court date. Alisha had been caught with three ecstasy pills in 2012, though she swears that police officers put them in her purse. Her charges would be knocked down to a misdemeanor from a felony, she said, if she agreed to go to drug court. On the way, she stopped off to do some work in Pittsburgh. Then B, who was driving a car associated with her name, was arrested. She didn't have enough money to post his $10,000 bond, and he had the keys to her car (they had been in separate cars). They had been fighting, and while she still paid for his lawyer, she continued on to Chicago alone.

She made it to her court date, but then something happened. She and another woman decided to take a quick job in a wealthy Chicago suburb, Orland Park, and got into a fight with the client. During a videotaped discussion that was played in court, Alisha said she, her colleague, and her client got into a fight over a fee, and he threatened them while brandishing a knife. She'd had sex with this client before, making a little over a thousand dollars from him, and thought he was a "sweet" guy. That night, things were off, she said, and he got "weird," telling her he didn't trust her.[16]

According to the *Chicago Tribune*, the client took back some of money he had given them and told the two women that he was going to shoot them. He grabbed a knife, and Alisha managed to take it away from him, stabbing him multiple times.[17] As she tells it, she left his place thinking he was just hurt. She drove to Fort Wayne, Indiana, to pick up some more work. She made up with B, and a few nights later, while they were talking in her hotel room, high on love, a hotel staffer called and told her that another car had backed into her vehicle. Upset, they walked out of the room, and instead of a damaged car, she found a group of officers, who arrested her on the spot.

Initially she thought it was for prostitution in Fort Wayne. She kept asking what was going on, but she said they wouldn't tell her anything. They kept throwing the words "Orland Park" around, but since she got around by GPS, she had no clue where that was. Alisha soon realized she might have been arrested because of the fight with the man, and she was angry. She knew he probably hadn't told the police how he'd tried to rape her, or how he'd fought her. Thinking she had nothing to lose, she told them everything, exactly how it went down. As soon as she finished telling her story—how he was drunk, how he demanded unprotected sex and lunged at them—they told her the client, sixty-one-year-old Alan Filan, was dead.

"My whole world shattered," she told me. "I never would have imagined that in a million years, not even in my worst dreams, that's what they were going to fucking tell me." As she heard the words "first degree murder," she couldn't process it. She was in shock. In that moment, she wasn't even angry with herself. She was just sad and sick to her stomach and trying to keep it together. "What do you do with that? Can you imagine? What are you supposed to think with that?" She has been in jail ever since.

~~

ALISHA TOLD ME HER STORY OVER THE COURSE OF SEVERAL EXtended phone calls, emails, and a visit from a correctional facility. She didn't go into much detail about that night—her legal team has advised her against talking about it anymore, she said. According to Alisha and her defense team at the trial, when her colleague showed up, Filan became upset that her partner didn't look like the picture in the advertisement. He then became even more enraged when he requested unprotected sex and was denied it. Drunk and agitated, he refused to pay. An argument ensued, and Filan produced a kitchen knife, though he also threatened to shoot her. He punched her in her face and swung a blade at her. Alisha was able to fend him off and stabbed him fourteen times. As she ran away, she alleged, Filan "hurled expletives" at her.[18]

In a video statement that had been taken after her arrest, Alisha told officers about the attack. "He was cussing me out, saying, 'You stupid bitch. I can't believe you,'" she said. "Once I saw he had a knife, my adrenaline kicked in. I was not going to let that happen to me." Alisha was five-foot-nine and 170 pounds, while Filan was five-foot-five and weighed 138 pounds. Her defense attorney pointed out that the wounds to Filan were "fairly superficial," and most of the cuts were less than a fraction of an inch deep, which, he argued, is more indicative of self-defense than murder. He also pointed out that nothing was stolen from the house, and Alisha left immediately after the attack. In his closing argument, he went so far as to note that money wasn't her main motivation. "She doesn't have to pull a knife to get money," he said. "All she's gotta do is take off her clothes." He acknowledged that the whole incident was unfortunate. "But what's the other side of the coin? That could've been Alisha there dead."[19]

Prosecutors argued that things happened quite differently and cast Alisha as a liar and a "master manipulator." The assistant state attorney, James Papa, argued that someone who was trying to defend themselves wouldn't leave someone to die or not call for help. He believed that Alisha's breakdown after her arrest when they told her the man had died was "an act." Papa dismissed the idea that the wounds were superficial. "Superficial wounds? Really?," he asked. "The guy is dead. [She jabbed] the heart, the liver, the kidney, the spleen. I mean—what other organs are there?"[20]

After six hours of deliberation, a jury found the then twenty-two-year-old guilty of second degree murder. Her mom ran out of the room, screaming in the hallway, "She's just a baby." Alisha quietly sobbed. Alisha's attorney later told the press, "This is not a victory or a defeat. This is the end of a tragedy."[21]

During her sentencing hearing, Alisha apologized to Filan's family for the act. "I am so sorry this happened. . . . I pray to God for forgiveness everyday. It was bad on both [of our] parts. I shouldn't have been selling myself. . . . A fight broke out. It caught me by surprise. . . . I hope you find it in yourself to forgive me in your heart. If not, I completely understand. . . . I had no right to play God." Filan's family was active in Chicago politics and remains so. His sister is a Cook County judge, his cousin a former state budget director, and his brother a prominent lobbyist. They said they weren't ready to forgive her.

Judge James Obbish said that Alisha "came from a broken home," noting that her mom had "her own issues" and her real father wasn't in her life. Things that didn't "set her up for success." The judge also scolded Alisha for what he described as her "dangerous" lifestyle, noting her previous convictions for prostitution and drugs, and for her loyalty to a pimp. Obbish concluded that if Alisha hadn't been worried about pleasing a pimp, Filan would be alive. "She wasn't walking out of there without her money, and that's why we're here today."[22] He sentenced her to fifteen years.

ALISHA RECOGNIZES THAT THINGS MAY HAVE BEEN DIFFERENT IF she was a "little tiny White girl" and it was her first time doing sex work. Or if she was a Black woman fighting her abusive boyfriend. But people judge sex workers. If sex work was regulated, she told me, if it was treated like a real job and workers had a safe and controlled environment, the industry would be far better. Without it, Alisha said, the murder, rape, assault, and robbery rates are just going to go up.

Today Alisha is thinking about the future. She wants to run a business, and she wants to show young girls that even someone in her situation can feel powerful. She thinks she has four years left—since in Illinois defendants often don't serve the whole time they were sentenced to—and she will be out before she is thirty. She envisions going to school, working a job, maybe doing a little escorting but mainly spending time with her family. Her little sister had a baby, is working at Walmart, and is going to get her GED, and her brother just started high school. She misses them dearly. It's expensive for them to visit her from Ohio. Her mom doesn't work, so she can watch the baby, and her stepdad suffers from ulcers. They're making it, but Alisha's income was helping them get by, and without it money is tight. They rely on donations to occasionally rent a car to drive to visit Alisha, but it's been more than a year since she has seen them. She usually talks to her mom on the phone, but on one of the days I spoke with Alisha, her mom's phone had been shut off.

She wants to help her family out, but even when she is released, it's going to be hard. "Who is gonna go want to hire a prostitute-murderer?" she muttered. I'm not even sure she realized I was still on the phone.

IN APRIL 2018 BACKPAGE WAS SEIZED BY THE GOVERNMENT AND shuttered for good. It was accused of facilitating sex trafficking, particularly of minors, and helping to encourage sex work. The seizure was praised by politicians on the Left and the Right, but once again sex workers are worried that what little layer of protection the site offered them, by allowing them to screen clients and talk with other workers about customers, would make them even more vulnerable to violent offenders. Alisha too was devastated when she heard the news. "When I was out and working, that was my avenue to work from. It was safe and gave me the freedom to pick and choose who I wanted to see. I can only imagine now how workers are gonna have to reduce themselves to some harsh environments to be able to survive." She said it's a major blow to the sex worker community, but if anything, she said, like herself, she has learned that sex workers are resilient.

MILLENNIAL MOMENT: **AUTHENTICALLY ME**

JASMYN, AGE 25, CULTURE EDITOR

I was born and raised in Michigan, a small town called Jackson. My home lifestyle was super, super Black. All of those different aspects of Black culture, whether it's around hip-hop culture, R&B, cinema, were just a big part of my life.

I went to predominantly White schools from kindergarten to seventh grade and then public schools from eighth grade throughout high school. In terms of Black culture being mixed in, I went to school with braids in my hair, beads in my hair. Whenever we had days we were not wearing our uniform, I wore my Sean John, Rocawear coats and my Baby Phat jeans. When I switched to public school and I started hanging around more Black people [I was] teased for certain things, [like] how I talked.

[I went in] just trying to survive mode and was more "performative" in my Blackness. For me it was just more so like saying extra slang words or cursing more than I would usually or wearing my hair in different ways. Just trying to be what people thought Black is.

I think a lot of people who've ever been teased in terms of the "not being Black enough" go through that. I think that for me, it wasn't long-lived. I've seen a lot of people deal with it for life. I'm like, "Damn you're still holding on to that? You still think that skiing is something to be sad about?" I can't relate, I just can't. After a while I just found other Black girls and friends who were like me. I found this duality that, yeah, I can wear my hair in braids and twists and at the same time be very committed to wanting to do well in biology class. There is no choosing.

Being Black was just so nuanced for me. There are so many different levels in terms of the culture. I am very, very particular about liking Black artists and Black music, especially R&B music by women. I'm not going to apologize. I don't feel like I need to go out of my way to like the Red Hot Chili Peppers just so people think that I have some type of balance to my personality. If everything I like is Black, oh well.

I'm very unapologetic about saying, "No, I've never watched Star Wars. *I don't know who Bon Jovi is." That's not my life. I didn't grow up with that. My mama raised me from when she was a twenty-three-year-old Black girl growing up in her thirties. You think a thirty-year-old Black woman was listening to Bon Jovi? Not to say that there wasn't any, but that just wasn't my lifestyle. I grew up listening to Mary J. I grew up listening to things that she could relate to, and that's very implemented into me. I'm not apologetic about that being who I am.*

I do think there [are] a lot of similar shared experiences. I think technology brought that closer to us, TV and the media and things that we were exposed to help us. The internet helps you realize that all the time. Tags like #Blackparentsbedoing or #thingsBlackmamaswillsay. The idea that none of our mamas ever had McDonald's money, for all of us to know that that means, I think that is a shared cultural experience. It's also like "taking over for the '99 and the 2000," you know Juvenile's about to come on.

Our culture has always been rooted in communal and safe spaces. I think at the foundation most Black people just want the same equality and freedom. I think being in America for so long now for so many hundreds of years I think Black culture in America is very unique.

I think the girls in the hood are probably the leaders of the carefree Black girls. Girls that have been fighting every day, getting kicked out of school just because of the culture that we live in. I care about those girls the most because I understand they're the most vulnerable people in our society. Even though I love her to death, the Zoë Kravitzes of the world are the most privileged people. I think she's very beautiful and the most amazing, very talented, but she's necessarily not my, like, carefree Black girl icon. For me I'm looking at the Cardi Bs and people like her who literally are "regular schmegular" girls from the Bronx who just started making Instagram videos.

Think about Cardi B's story. She might not have everything right. She'll probably say something problematic. I think about how she was young, she was a stripper and she just decided, "You know, I'm going to make funny videos on Instagram. I think I'm funny. I think I'm cool. I think I have talent. I'm going to do this . . ." and gained millions of followers just based on her personality.

Now when I think of how she's like, "I want people to take me seriously as a music artist and a rapper and really be in my craft and still stick to who I am . . ." I value that too. I'm not like, "Damn, is Cardi B out here wearing Black Lives Matter T-shirts and wearing her hair in natural Afros and flower crowns?" That doesn't make her more authentic to me. If she's wearing her red burgundy weave, but she's still about that life and about people from the hood and making sure that we're doing well and trying to set a good example for other girls to do it, that's more authentic to me. You know what I'm saying? For me, in terms of Black culture, the spectrum is endless.

If you are a Black person that listens to Bon Jovi and you really, really like it, I'm not going to be like, "Nah son, you not real, you not authentic." That's just what you like, and if you love that, and that's a part of you and what you are, you're still part of the culture.

I do think social media has [enabled] a lot of people to tell their stories in ways that we traditionally haven't been able before. It's been able for us to relate and connect on certain things, even like quirkiness. Issa Rae, I think she's so dope and so cool. When Awkward Black Girl *came out that was very revolutionary for me and a lot of my Black girlfriends. I can't say that me and her are alike, just exactly the same, but there was nuances there in terms of awkward. I do think it was a normalization of things that me and all of my friends that deal with and do that you just don't get to see Black girls be that way. You get to see the Seinfelds and the Liz Lemons and Tina Fey get to be that way, and so I was like, "Yes. This is so neat. This is so cool. We're quirky."*

I think that's what the culture is now, or at least what I observe, is just more people trying to push through to fight to be more of their authentic selves. I feel like if you're Black, you're Black. I think the more I become authentically me, the more people see the differences within our culture and the differences in the type of people that we are. I think more people need to see all sides of us, not just the dope, cool parts of it, but, like, see me when I'm talking about some smart shit, listen to me.

I think so much of our culture has yet to be exposed. There's only the small pieces that people want to take from. I don't know what it's going to take for more of the boringness of us, if that's a cool thing to say, for people to get exposed to that, too.

I genuinely care about fun, cool stuff on the internet and people who are sharing that space. I care a lot about Black people being able to share in that space because just as much as it can be a harmful space for us and people can penetrate it and have things to say, whether it's trolls or people coming at us and being very verbally violent on the internet, it's become such a universal communal space.

People talk about Black Twitter all the time, but Black Twitter is Twitter. It is the biggest platform in terms of a shared communal space of people with similar interests all around the world vibing on like one big inside joke after another every day. A lot of times just me being in tune to that helps me get through my day. I've got to know what the TL is talking about. The FOMO is so real.

This is the internet, but it matters. It matters to a lot of people, even if people are too cool to say it matters—it matters. I think it is that community space. The majority of the world isn't a safe space for us. There are very few safe spaces for us outside of our homes or our churches or certain schools or places that we built and created on our own terms. The internet has allowed for us to create a space on our own terms.

chapter four

BLUE COLLARS

WHEN MY PROSPECTIVE BEAU WALKED INTO THE DORMITORY OF MY WHITE-ASS university wearing a factory onesie plastered with his name on the front, I nearly died. It was sometime in the early 2000s when bling bling and neo-soul both jockeyed for a place in my heart, and I was still searching for who I was, still trying to front for the White boys and girls who believed affirmative action was the only reason I got a seat next to them. More than anything, I was still trying to figure out how to get that so-called success I had been dreaming of for years. In my mind at the time, I knew it didn't look like the working class, and right there in front of me, standing in a navy uniform and construction boots, was a living, breathing representation of the working class—everything I was trying to escape.

I remember not only being embarrassed by the blue-collar chic he so casually flaunted around these White folks, but being *astounded* by his pride. Back then I naïvely thought my time in college was about breaking away from the blue-collar life that so many of my family was bound to. I thought I was leaving a reality where breaks and lunches were timed.

Where some manager/overseer clocks your every move as you numbly pass the hours and people tell you what to what to wear or how to dress. Back then I thought I was supposed to aspire to a Black professional life filled with chocolate bodies wrapped in perfectly tailored suits and ties, clamoring for mimosas at bottomless brunches where you talk equally about Barack and Beyoncé. Signs that you "made it."

I know now that my shame was stupid, having nothing to do with the American Dream. But my bougie blinders were so thick that day that I didn't even stop to think that he might have enjoyed working with his dad, who had gotten him the job. Plus, his dad was making a great salary—more than I've ever made and far more than my mom at the time, who labored away in the boonies of the Midwest to get a graduate degree and had to deal with being called things like a "Negress." I didn't stop to think that this dude was also learning about the world—albeit in a different way from the way I was. No, at that moment my disdain for my date was clear, despite my liberal rhetoric about working-class rights in the classroom. I had become one of those stuck-up women that Tyler Perry rails against in all his movies.

I hadn't thought about that day in years, though I remain good friends with him. I'd forgotten about it even as I watched Issa Rae's HBO show *Insecure* and sneered when her lawyer friend Molly dumped a "good" non-college-educated dude after she got accepted into an elite Ivy dating app. I shook my head with disgust, like *she* was tripping, though I failed to realize that I sometimes have had my own uppity ideas.

Thinking about that day made me realize how Black millennials, particularly those who are college educated, often disdain working-class life or at least see it as something that is different—unequal to our own professions, though many won't admit it. Perhaps it is because we are so often taught that if we're not professors or lawyers, then we haven't "made it." Perhaps it's because we don't have a culture that reveres and upholds the Black working class in the same way as the White working class. Or perhaps I was just acting "brand new," uppity, forgetting where my family roots came from.[1]

Instead of being a revered group, the Black working class is perceived as something else: an underclass. When and if the working class is acknowledged by the media, it's almost always through a lens of Whiteness, not Blackness.[2] During and after the 2016 elections, the trend was particularly egregious, as the op-ed writers and reporters tried to humanize and understand this group. Headlines like: "Is the White Working Class in the US Being Ignored?," "The Struggling, Rural, White Communities That Feel Like Nobody Cares," "Stop Demonizing the White Working Class," "Rural White Working Class Neglected," and "The Great White Nope: Poor, Working Class, and Left Behind in America,"[3] peppered newspapers and websites around the country and the world.

The few articles written about the Black working class often talk about the group as poor or pathologize it. "In general there is a tendency to not talk about Blacks as workers. This hurts the whole dialogue," William Spriggs, an economist with the AFL-CIO and professor at Howard University, told CNN in 2016. "They are an underclass, not a working class, lazy, not hardworking. The notion of the White working class implicitly embodies a view of White privilege. It implies that things are supposed to be different for them, that they aren't the same, that they aren't going to face the same pressures."[4]

Black workers, however, face many of the same pressures as White workers: they're worried about NAFTA; the decline of unions, which boosted their pay and benefits; mine closures; and high taxes. Their struggles may even be more intense, because they're often under more financial pressures than White workers in similar positions. For instance, a 2016 report in the *Washington Post* found that a White worker without a bachelor's degree still makes more money than any other race or ethnicity. The median salary for a White worker with a high school diploma makes $706 dollars a week, while their Black counterpart only was $578.[5]

There's less data specifically on working-class Black millennials, but we see similar patterns emerge and know that overall more Black millennials tend to be working class or low-wage workers. Research has found that 25 percent of White millennial workers would be counted as low-income earners, making three times the poverty line or less, but an astounding 43 percent of Black and 40 percent of Hispanic millennials would be considered low-income earners, showing a clear gap between race and class even within the millennial generation.[6]

Part of the misrepresentation of the Black working class might have something to do with the fact that the working class as a whole is misrepresented in our popular culture. In 2015, 43 percent of Americans without a bachelor's degree made up the labor force and would be considered "working class," but there's been much confusion about what the working class actually looks like. On the whole the working class, defined here as those without a four-year college degree, isn't comprised of those with industrial jobs and never has been. In 1940 about a third of working-class people had industrial jobs, though half worked in the service industry. Even in the 1960s, when industrialization was at its peak, factory workers only comprised 37 percent of the working-class population. Today those trends for the working class remain. A study released in 2017 by the Center for American Progress (CAP) found that over three quarters of the working class today are employed in service jobs like retail and health care.[7]

White folks overall are underrepresented here: they only make up 59 percent of the working class (versus 64 percent of the population), though according to the same report by CAP, three-quarters of a century ago, Whites made up a nearly proportional share of the working class. Today Black workers make up 14 percent of the working class (and are 13 percent of the population), and Latinx workers 21 percent. By 2032 people of color are set to make up the majority of the working class.[8]

The trend with Black millennials follows in that same pattern. Black millennials are more likely to work in sales, food, and personal service, and less likely than their White and Latinx millennial peers to work in (slightly) better paying blue-collar jobs, often because of last hired, first fired seniority policies that usually disadvantage Black workers. Add in the decline of unions and fewer regulatory policies under Trump, and one can only wonder what life will look like for working-class Black millennials in the future.[9]

ꕥ

ON AN EXCEPTIONALLY WARM FALL DAY IN KEYSTONE, WEST Virginia, in late 2015, two City Hall employees fought over a black and silver holiday wreath. The wreath in question had been a gift to the county, and Von, the sixty-something city manager, was ready to hang it up along with the more traditional red and green evergreen wreaths that were peppered throughout the office. Brandi, her twenty-nine-year-old assistant, argued that a black wreath made one think of death and not optimism. Von seemed to think about the request for a moment, holding onto the gift. "We're not depressed," said Brandi glaring at the wreath. "We're not in mourning," she said, reflecting the optimism that Black millennials and Black folk overall are notorious for, despite living in the poorest county in an already poor state. She went about putting up other Christmas decorations, breathing heavy sighs, until the boisterous Von relented and the uniquely colored wreath was put away for use during another year, or perhaps never again.

Holiday cheer is certainly not associated with Keystone or the county it lies in, McDowell. Poverty, death, and dying are usually connected with this part of West Virginia—coal country—though its residents bristle at the charge. The media often depicts coal country as a crumbling area, with derelict houses and a drugged-up population that has lost its way amid coal's decline. But today, in Keystone, despair seems like a foreign concept. Yes, there are falling-down houses. Yes, a man walked up to me begging for change as I drove up in my "nice" rental car, and yes, an old coal worker complained about not getting his black lung benefits. But as a long train carrying coal wound through the sleepy mountain town next to a group on ATVs, the county's latest venture into tourism, coal country didn't seem dead just yet. It was beautiful, and in fact it seemed to be alive—or at least trying to survive in a country, and with a media, that is determined to proclaim its end.

Keystone is not just any coal town, but a historically Black coal town, a coal town that used to be the so-called Harlem of the mines. It was a center of Black excellence, Black talent, Black labor, and, of course, that American Dream, the one you almost never hear about.

It seems that you can't talk about coal without talking about the beloved White working class, but stories of Black people and Black coal miners in coal country are rarely discussed. As I drove through McDowell County, I wasn't shocked particularly by the poverty or the few blighted houses that looked just like Detroit, Chicago, or any city I've been to. I was taken aback by Black people, young Black people, living in the mountains a few miles away from Confederate flags and coal mines. Up until then I didn't know that Black folk lived in Appalachia, or if I'd heard about them, I certainly didn't know about their experiences. Rocking long locs, cute braids, and Timbs, they looked like they could easily be on the streets of Harlem, Newark, or even Atlanta, but here they were, Black millennial mountaineers just trying to get through the day.

McDowell County was a part of coal country where many young Black men and women came to make their dreams of middle-class life happen. It played a big part in the development of the coal industry and helped build the area that was once known as "billion-dollar coalfields." In the 1950s, at its peak, over twenty thousand African Americans lived in McDowell County—24 percent of the county's population. In a state where Blacks were only 6 percent of the population, the contrast was stark. The number of Blacks in McDowell was so unique that the area was dubbed "The Free State of McDowell," a name it still retains. McDowell was an anomaly in that sense, but like elsewhere in the region, residents were ensconced in the world of coal. Records show that Blacks had been mining coal since at least the eighteenth century as slaves, but they really began to flock to the region as the railroad and coal mining industries expanded at the dawn of the twentieth century.[10]

In the 1930s, coal was booming, and work was plentiful. Across the United States the number of Black coal miners increased to over fifty-five thousand, and West Virginia was no different. According to *Blacks in Appalachia*, by William Turner, in 1930 Black coal miners made up about 21.8 percent of the population of Appalachia, making about $118 dollars a month. Nationwide the typical salary for a Black person at the time was only $537 dollars *a year*.[11] This wasn't to say that life was all good, but despite rampant segregation—in housing, schools, and even the kinds of coal jobs (Blacks and foreigners tended to have the lowest-paying, back-breaking, nonmechanized jobs)—Blacks in the area experienced many more liberties in West Virginia than they did in other parts of the country, especially in the Jim Crow South. They enjoyed things like voting rights, political leadership (including the first Black woman to become a part of a legislative body in the United States), and integrated unions.[12] Even the nation's first (and now only) memorial to African American soldiers in World War I is located in Kimball, which is in McDowell County.

With its high population of Black doctors, lawyers, and entrepreneurs, somewhat a result of segregation, McDowell, particularly its unofficial capital, Keystone, became a haven for those who wanted a better life. And it lived up to that promise for awhile. At a time when Jim Crow was making life harder for Blacks around the country, Keystone, with its plentiful commercial activities surrounding the coal industry, plush entertainment, more liberal homeownership laws, and a thriving red light district (Cinderbottom), became the hotspot for Black life in coal country.

"Everybody had money. The poverty levels were very low here because there were so many peripherals of the coal industry. Restaurants. Shopping. Cars. Hospitals. It was a thriving community," said Clif Moore, a state delegate for McDowell County. "It was sort of like little New York.

Like a little Manhattan. Everything was popping." But as the industry became more mechanized in the mid-twentieth century, Black workers, who often occupied less-skilled positions, were the first to lose their jobs. What had once seemed an all but certain gateway for African Americans to enter the middle class began to close. Many left the area. In 1950 12 percent of West Virginia's miners were Black; in 1960, the number shrank to 6.6; and by 1980, less than 3 percent of Blacks were coal miners in the state.[13] According to the most recent data from the Census in 2017, there are about 1,900 Blacks working as coal miners, out of 43,000 left nationwide.[14]

Coal has always had its booms and busts—you can see it in historical pictures of poverty in Appalachia and the current ones that focus on the dilapidated storefronts and homes—but this time, folks say, it feels different. Cecil E. Roberts Jr., the head of the United Mine Workers of America, noted the change in the industry. "In the past we always knew that the demand for coal would rebound and the jobs would come back," he said in a report by the *New York Times* in 2015. "This time, there is no such certainty. Fundamental changes are underway in America and across the world that will have a lasting impact on the coal industry and our jobs." But African American families who have lived here for generations say they're reluctant to abandon the region, even as coal's decades-long decline enters a death spiral. Coal production in Appalachia fell almost 45 percent between 2005 and 2015 (compared to around 21 percent nationwide), as tougher environmental regulations and cheaper natural gas choked off demand for the fossil fuel.[15]

Counties like McDowell, now the poorest in West Virginia, can feel it. Instead of talk of expansion and growth, conversations often center on mine closures, empty streets, closing businesses, and the high amount of drug use. But many Black residents here praise the benefits of living in the region, including its physical beauty, the close-knit family life, and the friendly Southern manners, which they say, distinguish the area from elsewhere in the state. "It's a different kind of Black folk here. If you put ten people in a room from McDowell with ten people from ten other cities in the state of West Virginia, you could pick out the people from McDowell. They dress differently; they talk differently. They carry themselves differently. They have a little arrogance about them," said Moore with a grin.

In President Obama's final State of the Union address, he promised to help the folks of coal country find a new way. "Now we've got to accelerate the transition away from old, dirtier energy sources. Rather than subsidize the past, we should invest in the future, especially in communities that rely on fossil fuels. We do them no favor when we don't show them where the trends are going. And that's why I'm going to push to change the way we manage our oil and coal resources so that they better reflect the costs they impose on taxpayers and our planet." But Brandi's great-uncle, Buck, like others here, harbors particular resentment for the Obama administration. "He hasn't done anything for us," said the eighty-eight-year old-man, leaning back on his couch now covered with photographs and memorabilia from his time underground. "If he were running again, I just couldn't vote for him. And I've been a Democrat my whole life." Donald Trump is promising to build the region back up again. But most people are just holding their breath.

When Buck first started working in the mines, Franklin D. Roosevelt was president. It was a dangerous gig, but he didn't worry much about safety, even after watching his brother almost die in a motor accident underground and his father lose an eye in a roof collapse. He said he didn't witness much discrimination, either, a fact I admit is hard for me to believe, though I heard it repeatedly. "I had some of the nicest White friends that you would ever want to meet," Buck told me. "If colored people and White people just got to know each other, they wouldn't have the feelings that they have. In the mines we were all in there together. All of us could have been covered up in there together." In 1959, as automation hit the industry, Buck was laid off. Two years later, he was rehired, but he later learned that some of his colleagues who'd served shorter tenures in the mines were brought back before him.

Angry at the nepotism, Buck got more involved in the union. He served as union trustee and president, then became an official with the United Mine Workers of America. He retired fifteen years later as a district director of the Welsh Office. Looking back, he said, the union is what helped him stay in the coal mines so long. It's also something that he worries is going away. "The company doesn't really want to give you something. The union makes a lot of big demands, but to be union you've got protection on your job." Buck believes that the younger generation would go into mining if they could, but without role models and the lack of available jobs he believes that coal miners will eventually fade into history. Buck, who was also mayor of Keystone, reflected with sadness on the thriving community, "People will come here to look at what it was one time. But it will never be like that again. There's just nobody to follow. These kids won't have any inspiration about wanting to go." He tried to get his only child, Johnny, into the mines, but he chose a different path and ended up working in the steel mills and then a hospital before his death almost a decade ago. However, his grand-niece, Brandi, and nephew, Galvester, still have hope for the future of coal.

~

BRANDI LIVES IN KEYSTONE WITH HER THREE KIDS. SHE SAID the town is a great place to raise a family. "When it snows, it's beautiful, and my kids can go out and play," she said. "They'll see a deer running through the woods, and they get so excited. You don't have all the crime. All the gunplay and weapons, you don't really see that." She said she's never experienced blatant racism, though there is a shop close by in Bramwell that carries Confederate flags she won't go in. She thinks the flag is racist but doesn't worry about the symbolism. "I've never had any personal experience with blatant racism. I think it has to do with the image that they portray with Appalachians. I have family in Ohio, and when I go out there, they automatically assume missing teeth and banjos and hillbillies. I think it's all stereotypical, really. I think what sets me apart, I'm country music, rap, and R&B. My brothers are like that too. My mother loved country music. It may be the environment, but I think it's more the person. If you're open to trying new things. That has more to do with it." More than any sort of race issue, or even drug use in Keystone (she admits more young Blacks may be dealing than using opioids), jobs, she said, are the problem.

She thought about working in the mines but ultimately decided she wasn't cut out for it. She went to college for a bit at what was then known as Concord College. A few weeks into the semester, her mom died, so she withdrew. The next year she started at another college, Bluefield State, then got pregnant with her daughter, and came back home. She landed a job at Walmart, which was the largest private employer in the state between 1998 and 2016 (it now ranks number two after WVU Medicine), where seven of her family members were also employed. She started at $8.50 an hour plus benefits and was then promoted to a pharmacy job, where she earned $11.75 an hour. "Most people try to get jobs at Walmart. Walmart and fast food restaurants. If you look at it, there aren't that many more opportunities for young people just starting out." Since May, she has worked as an assistant to the city manager.

Her thirty-seven-year-old brother, Galvester (also known as Junior), focused on getting a job in the mines, just like his grand-uncle Buck. After a stint at a mine as a security guard, and forty hours of coursework in mine training, he landed a job driving a 777d rock truck at a strip mine. He liked the job and the pay, but after exactly five months and two weeks, he was laid off. He needed to find a new job quickly, so he took a position as a school bus driver. "I do enjoy being a bus driver," said Junior, but he'd go back to the mines if he could.

It's understandable why. The median salary for a bus driver in the southern part of West Virginia is $30,837. The average coal miner there makes $84,959.

Soon after I left, I found out that Brandi and Junior's relatives at Walmart would soon be on the job market too. In January 2016 the retailer announced it was closing its McDowell County store by month's end.

~

IN THE NEXT COUNTY OVER, TWENTY-FIVE-YEAR-OLD JEREMY works at one of the few coal mines left. Jeremy never set out to work in a mine. Unlike others in the area, he didn't have family in the industry. His biological father was a police officer, and his stepdad owned his own roofing business. The only students at his high school who talked about the mines were those whose parents worked in the field. His teachers and guidance counselors didn't encourage people to work in the mines; they encouraged kids to go to college. Besides, if anything, he was afraid of the mines. He'd heard of how dangerous they were and, on top of that, believed it just wasn't something for Black folk. "I didn't know about it. [I thought] it's more of a White job, more White people doing it than Black people doing it. . . . You hear all the stories about how people get killed, how dangerous it is. I was afraid of it, didn't know nothing about it." So instead, he got a job as a mechanic.

However, when a friend's father who had worked in the mines for thirty-two years told him a few years ago that it was a career where he could make six figures, Jeremy jumped at the opportunity. He had a wife and three kids to take care of, and it seemed to be one of the most lucrative options available. In a state where the average Black household income is $50,000 a year,[16] it's easy to understand why Jeremy was so excited. His fears of getting crushed or developing black lung never abated, but the opportunity seemed too good to pass up. So he turned it all over to God and went to work. It helped that each shift prayed before they went underground. It made him feel safer and more secure. After five years, his wife, a cheerleading coach, was ready for him to give it up, but he knew there weren't many available jobs where he could make that salary, and he wanted to provide for his family. "If putting my life on the line is what I have to do to take care of the people around me, that's what I'll do." He decided to work on attaining his roofing license so he could potentially take over his stepfather's business one day, but he still thought that coal was the future.

Jeremy didn't mind the work; he was in a union and felt they were looking out for him as a worker. He received 100 percent health coverage, and his co-pay was only twelve dollars. His coverage was so good that he still marvels at the fact that after a motorcycle wreck that caused $32,000 worth of damage, it only cost him $24 to fix his bike. "You can't beat it," he said.

But it hasn't been all fun and games. Jeremy had a tough time when he started working in the predominately White mine. He said there was name-calling, teasing, or at worst, being ignored. "It was hard on me at first. I was called the N-word when I started working underground, people not talking to you, just walking by you like you're invisible. They put people in a category. If you're Black, there's nothing good about you—especially if you're Black and taking a White person's position, where another White person could be. They just don't like it." Jeremy was one of just a few thousand African American coal miners left in the country, and, according to him, one of 13 Black employees of 430 at his mine in West Virginia. "It's been days I wanted to snap, go crazy. They'll push your buttons and see how you're going to react or see if you're gonna go off. But now that I know all the guys, and they got over that I'm Black, it's been pretty good." While not excusing his fellow miners' behavior, he holds no grudges. In fact, he called the miners his second family and his "brothers." "I can't blame them. Their parents taught them that. That was passed down. You look on the news, and the media is making Black people look so bad nowadays that White people judge off that." Being in a union, he said, helps mitigate some of that. "Nonunion mines they can call you everything under the sky and get away with it. Union mines, you can't get away with it."

Jeremy would love to stay in coal, but as the industry continues to decline, he's not sure about his future. In October 2015, his employer announced it was laying off more than two hundred people—roughly half its staff. Jeremy kept his job, but his overtime hours were capped, costing him about $2,300 a month, he said. He was relieved, though, to still have a job.

He wondered if politicians are really committed to keeping coal alive and back in 2016 was thinking about voting for Donald Trump. He said that while there are "enough" Black people who liked Obama in the area, they probably don't work in the coal mines. "We don't like Obama 'cause he don't like us," he said. Instead, he was hoping that Trump would relieve some of his economic burdens. "He talk a good game," Jeremy said. "We'll see if he stick to it. I mean, who wouldn't want to pay less taxes?"

Two weeks after I spoke with Jeremy, on the day before New Year's Eve in 2016, he was laid off. But as he was making plans to start a job as a truck driver hauling cars and heavy equipment cross-country, he was called back to the mines. Since then he has been laid off from the mines again and now is working in roofing and other industries.

UNIONIZATION HAS BEEN THE KEY TO CREATING A SOLID BLACK middle class and could potentially be one of the biggest boons to Black millennial upward mobility. But the security that unions once brought has been in decline since the late seventies, making it harder for workers like Jeremy to achieve what Buck and others of his generation managed.[17] There are some positive signs for the union movement, especially among young people such as recently formed unions at media outlets like *Vice, Fusion,* and the *Los Angeles Times* and the gains made by striking school teachers in states form West Virginia ro Washington. But there have also been more ominous trends: the shuttering of website DNAinfo/Gothamist after its workforce voted to unionize, the failure to organize auto workers at a Nissan plant in Alabama, and, most importantly, the US Supreme Court ruling that it's unconstitutional for public sector unions to collect fees from nonmembers, in *Janus v. AFSCME*, a decision that upended nearly forty years of precedent.

In the past, unionization was often confined to manual laborers or government employees, but as manufacturing declines and blue-collar work shifts to the service industry, the face of unionization is trying to change with it. Now you're more likely to find Brown, Black, and queer low-wage service workers leading the change.

BLEU WAS COMING HOME FROM A LONG SHIFT AT CHIPOTLE AS I peppered him with questions about life in the fast food industry. It was a dark January night as the country was waiting for the inauguration of a new president. Bleu, full of Southern charm, was passionately recounting the fragile precariousness of his existence, his fight to just survive, as he drove through "the Neck," one of Tampa's notorious Black communities. He didn't drive through the area much, but his usual route was closed, and he was forced to take a detour. He didn't seem to mind. He was driving slowly anyway, because I was a thousand miles away on the phone and he wanted to make sure I understood each word he was saying about the state of Black millennial workers. Less than ten minutes into our conversation, Bleu went silent.

At first I thought I was unclear with my line of questions or had somehow offended him. The silence persisted. Baffled, I called out to him, but then I heard a man's voice in the background. "Please give me your license and registration," the voice boomed through the phone with the bass of an authoritarian who was not about to fuck around. Bleu was both calm and frantic as he told me he would have to call me back.

The irony was too real. I had just asked him what being a young, Black, low-wage worker meant. He had talked about the difficulty of getting jobs, about being stereotyped as being lazy or slow, and then he started to talk about the things that happen when he leaves work. "It's not like it stops, you know? Discrimination against Black and Brown people, it never stops. Some people think that just because we had a Black president, that racism has kind of disappeared, when really racism, it hasn't gone anywhere." Trump's win, he said, points out the racism in our society even more. "Not only do you have to worry," he said, "about not having food to eat, but as a Black person, you have the added burden of just trying to make it home alive."

And then our conversation came to a halt. Bleu had been pulled over by the police.

∾∾

BLACK WORKERS HAVE IT ROUGH. NOT ONLY DO THEY FACE THE burden of facing discrimination based on age, class, and employment status, but they also deal with the other usual burdens of being a Black person in America. The words they use to describe their treatment in the world is "low," "uncared about," "spoken down to," "disrespected," but surprisingly to me, a (barely) white-collar worker, they liked their jobs. They wanted to make customers happy and took pride in making things look nice and right or providing a warm meal. What they hated was not being valued and being undercompensated for their efforts. And they hated that race still seemed to play a role in this. Janelle Jones, a policy analyst at the Economic Policy Institute, said intersectionality was evident in the struggle of Black young adults. "Young Black workers are just getting hit in so, so, so many ways, so many overlapping issues of discrimination. You have race, which matters. For women, you have gender, which matters. You have being young, which also matters. Something that was helpful for Black workers three decades ago is that they could get out of high school and be able to find really good union jobs with health care and with a retirement plan. That's harder for anyone to find, but it's going to be particularly hard to find in an environment where racial discrimination in the labor market is still running rampant."

No one seems to understand this, as politicians, business leaders, universities—everyone really—continue to push expensive degrees, while Detroit dies and manufacturing's end seems more prominent with each passing day. No one seems to understand the plight of young millennial workers like Bleu, who is demanding more equitable pay from his employer. Bleu came to fast food work like many of his peers: because it was the only job available to him. As a resident of North Carolina, he knew his options were somewhat limited, even though he graduated from a public charter school with top grades hoping to be a forensic scientist. The reality was that he needed to help his family out, so when graduation day came, he found the best job available. It was at a fast food restaurant.

Bleu was following in the footsteps of his mom, who had been a window clerk at Taco Bell until he was born, and then got a job driving buses. He watched her leave their home every single day, weary, only to come back home and play a guessing game with the overdue bills about which would be paid that day. Most of the time they got by, but at other times they sat in a dark house with the lights turned off. They made it work, though, and Bleu was content. When their clan started to expand and his mom gave Bleu some siblings to play with, things got even harder. He didn't mind the extra company, but their meager resources were taxed even more. As he grew older, he decided that he would try to wrestle that fate away from his brothers, erase the past that was plagued by hardship. "When you're a kid, you really don't know the struggle. You just know you want things and you can't get them because your mom has to pay the bills. I always knew we were, like, behind and we were what we called in school 'poor.'" It wasn't as if he were an anomaly: other families in his area of North Carolina were also trying to make ends meet. Struggling was the norm, survival was the dream, and it seemed everyone was just trying to make their own way. No one understood that better than Bleu's mom, and she was determined that he have a better life. So she enrolled him in a good elementary school and made sure he stayed out of trouble. She didn't make it to every basketball game, or even to many, much to his chagrin, but he was happy for the strong bonds they had as a family.

Bleu knows his life could have ended up different, that he could have ended up on the streets hustling, but he knew that wasn't his path, and he chose to stay in school and work on his basketball game. As he reached the end of high school, he was confident that forensic science was the field for him, and he enrolled in college. Soon he realized that even though his mom had gotten a "good" job as a bus driver for the local school district, that slight bit of financial comfort, that sweet taste of safety, that feeling of relative stability was hard to come by as the family remained on the margins, despite the fact that she was working all the time. He knew he had to put his dreams on hold to help his mom out, so he turned to the restaurant industry, the sector where job growth is exploding,[18] especially for Black and Brown people, to become a cashier at a fast food chain.

At first Bleu tried to balance his job with his studies at his for-profit college, but after three months he got behind on his payments—around $75 a month—and had to drop out. "I had to quit going to school because I didn't have money to pay for the fee to go to school. I didn't have enough money for that and to be able to take care of myself, and take care of my family, so I had to choose and I took care of my family." It would be the beginning of nearly a decade-long career in the fast food industry, a career he likes but where his pay has remained close to or at minimum wage (as of 2018, the federal minimum wage is $7.25 an hour, and Florida's is $8.25).

When a setback happens for a young Black worker, it's often not a minor nuisance of inconvenience but can turn into a life-changing event—like that dark winter night when Bleu was chatting with me, and two officers, one Black and one White, pulled him over because they said he ran a stop sign. They let him go with a warning, but Bleu said it's the ultimate example of how precarious his life is. "Imagine if I got a ticket. Now think about how would I pay my bills and pay that ticket and pay whatever court cost that they would give me if I had to go to court?"

He continued in a huff: "Making $200 every two weeks doesn't leave much room for incidentals like this." In 2015, an investigation by local television WTSP found that African Americans are stopped in that area more than any other race, making up 54 percent of all arrests by the police department, though their population is just 26 percent. Police officials said that the arrest rate is part of a no-tolerance crime policy and has led to a drop in crime. "If you commit a crime [in Tampa], no matter what your color is, you're likely going to jail," the Tampa Police Department captain said.[19]

In the fast food industry, Bleu said, Black folks have to prove themselves—first by just getting into the industry, which he says can be hard, and then after being employed, you often have to deal with stereotypes like being lazy or slow, all on top of recognizing that your pay may not be equal to your White counterparts. But Bleu likes his job. He said he likes meeting new people and intends on staying in the industry, though he knows people look down on him for doing so. Fast food work is harder than people think and takes a lot of organization and communication skills, he said, exasperated, noting that most people wouldn't last one day in his shoes.

His day starts at seven a.m., when he wakes up and then catches a ride with his neighbor to his job at Chipotle. He gets there by eight, punches the clock, and begins getting everything prepped and ready for the day when the store opens. Bleu said it is hard work, but most workers put love and effort into making the store run. When they open, he cleans up some more and begins to deal with customers. That part can be satisfying or challenging. "Some customers may have a good day. Some customers may have a bad day, but it's up to you as an employee working at Chipotle to always have a good attitude and always come in there ready to work. Even if your lights are out or even if you get put out, evicted, right before you come to work, you're still expected to come with a nice attitude and have a nice smile and be friendly, and the customers are always right, you know." He said he doesn't get a chance to sit down and take a break, so he's basically on his feet running around the whole day—going from the back to the front of the store. He estimates that he probably runs a mile inside the restaurant every day.

Despite his hard work Bleu had a tough time making ends meet. He left North Carolina for Tampa in 2013 so that his mom would have one less mouth to feed and to find better opportunities. But things haven't always worked out as he hoped. He's been homeless, he's felt cheated by jobs, and he's been let go from a few places and quit others. His checkered work and home life was not unusual for low-wage workers in the fast food industry and for a while he just accepted things for what they were.

One day, when a worker came up to him at his job at Arby's and asked if he wanted to make $15 an hour, he was flabbergasted. "I was like 'Yo, you crazy? $15? That's too much.'" Later that night he read up on low-wage workers organizing and thought it over. He remembered his Grandma repeating the mantra that nothing in life was free. Looking at his stagnant wages, which remained at $7.25 an hour at the time, he decided right then that he wanted $15 an hour and joined the nationwide Fight for Fifteen campaign. Soon after that, Bleu was calling up Dennis Ross, his member of Congress, to lobby him to join their fight. Ross flat out told him no, he said, asking why he would want the government to control how many hours he could work and how much he would be paid.

According to Bleu, Ross then launched into a story about mowing lawns at twelve years old and running his own business. Bleu wondered just how much Ross's family really relied on their twelve-year-old's income. "What kind of job did he really have to get? It sounded to me like he really don't work. He just wanted to do something to pass the time or something like that. He didn't really have any responsibilities at the age of twelve."

Ross's response didn't deter Bleu. He just started to work harder, recruiting other workers to join the fight. Some people were skeptical. Some were confused. Others just didn't want any "trouble." He tried to sell the campaign by arguing that worker-led movements were what led to Martin Luther King's and Rosa Parks' successes, and that disruption was the key to success. "How would you be able to live your life the way you want to live your life without the people that came before you and paved the way for us? How would you be able to do those things?" A lot of people were afraid of going against the managers, but like the overseer on the plantation, he said the managers often didn't have money either. "We're going out to these big corporations that make millions upon billions of dollars every year, and the only thing they do is put it in their pockets, or, like McDonald's, they buy back their own shares."

Bleu ended up at McDonald's after being let go from Arby's because he says he let his girlfriend in after closing, something that was against the rules. He continued to be active in the workers' rights campaign and worked on an action around safety and health, a matter close to his heart, since he was a grill cook. After one action, his name and face were all over the media, and his manager the next day decided to give him a personal tour of all the ways McDonald's was on the up and up. He showed him the first aid kit, the gloves, all of the equipment that they were using to promote better safety. Then he put him to work at the front window, where Bleu could no longer see the health conditions at the restaurant. Retaliation, Bleu thought, for speaking out. Soon after he had another run-in with management. His brother was in jail, and he needed to take some emergency time off to deal with it. Management said it was okay, he said, but he also had scheduled time off to protest the McDonald's shareholders meeting. When he came back to Tampa, he was fired. He was told that, despite the fact management had approved his time off, he was let go because he was still on probation.

He got another job in 2015 at Checkers. He had problems with scheduling, didn't like management, had a beef with another coworker, and said the tension could always be felt in the air. Management, he said, even told the employees they would be fired if they took off work for a one-day strike. Three of them went on strike. Others wanted to go but were afraid they would lose their jobs. When Bleu came back to work, nothing happened. Later management fired him for another incident—speaking back to a boss—but he can't talk about that because of impending litigation.

A few months ago he applied for the job at Chipotle. He's been there for three months. He's continuing to fight for $15 an hour, fight for a union, and fight for the rights of other workers beyond those in the fast food industry. "It didn't start with us, so it's not going to stop with us, you know?" He thinks that the fight is going to take a while before they see results, but he's vowing not to go anywhere. He says his American Dream revolves around equity—not equality for all. As he explained it to me: "Basically, if someone has a million dollars, and I have $10, and you're being 'equal' by giving us both $10, so now he has a million and ten dollars and I have $20, we're still not equal though. He still has a whole lot more than I have. We need to figure out how to have equity across the board and get me to a million dollars, you know?"

Bleu is optimistic, though he reminds me that the American Dream has left behind young Black workers for so long that it's hard to believe there is a dream left. "A lot of people come to this country saying that they're chasing the American Dream, and they're still running. They're running after it. Forty acres and a mule is what my ancestors were promised, and I haven't seen forty acres yet. I haven't got my mule yet. My grandma, she's talked about that a lot, like 'I want my forty acres and a mule,' and I want my grandma to still have her forty acres and a mule. I want her to say, 'My grandchild has fought for me to get my forty acres and a mule that I was promised.'"

~~

Despite being nearly ignored entirely during the 2016 presidential election debates, Americans still care about organized labor, especially American millennials. A Gallup poll in 2017 found that 61 percent of Americans approved of labor unions—a shock to me. The historical approval has averaged around 62 percent, since the question was first asked of the public in 1936, though those numbers hit a low of 48 percent in 2009. And while Americans overall believe that the power of unions is waning, millennials generally view unions favorably. A Pew study from 2017 found that 75 percent of millennials ages eighteen to twenty-nine approve of organized labor—the highest of any group—though they're less likely to be in one.[20]

According to the Bureau of Labor Statistics, only 9.4 percent of folks ages twenty-five to thirty-four are in a union, about the same percentage as it was in the early eighties. There's good news for union advocates though: in 2018, a study found that 76 percent of new members in unions were thirty-four or younger.[21]

Recent stories about Fight for $15 victories, a group composed largely of people of color and women, have been inspiring organizers. Yet these victories seem to be the exception, not the norm, and organizing remains more challenging than ever, especially for Black and Brown workers. As millennials worry about increasing job fragility, unions worry about organizing in the Trump era and after the Janus decision. Critics say, for example, that SEIU already spent less on Fight for $15 in 2017, but the union claims it is just "shifting gears" and changing strategy.[22] A long hard fight for better wages and conditions may still be a challenge for young organizers looking for change. It's something Keisha learned all too well.

KEISHA JUST WANTED TO WALK AROUND VERSAILLES SOMEDAY like Marie Antoinette. If that didn't happen, she just wanted to see the ocean and take a stroll down a beach—a real beach, that is, with bright sky-blue water she could swim in and sand that could be felt between her toes, unlike the manmade Indiana Beach, the only beach she'd ever been to. She wasn't sure if any of that would ever happen. Keisha was a housekeeper in Indianapolis at one of the biggest hotel chains in America, and given her financial circumstances, she had to temper her fantasies and face a harsh reality. She was thirty-one and made less than $10 an hour. With a stack of bills to pay, she could barely make ends meet, even after sharing expenses with her husband. And though she was eligible for a hotel discount to help cover costs for her dream vacation, she soon realized a European getaway was out of her reach and probably would be for a long time. Her mother-in-law ended up using the discount instead.

THE MONDAY AFTER KEISHA AND HER HIGH SCHOOL SWEETheart got married they were fired from their factory jobs. They were late to work. The newlyweds had been employed at the company for six months as part of a temp assignment, and Keisha said she had never been tardy previously. She was frustrated, but it was 2002, and work seemed to be plentiful enough, so she shrugged it off and found a job at Ruby Tuesday's Restaurant. She didn't love the gig, so when her mom's friend told her about a job at a hotel in 2007 making more money—and more importantly, with more benefits, she jumped at the chance. She had been struggling to find decent health care, her husband was having trouble getting a job, and the opportunity to make things look neat appealed to her. Going in, she never really thought about the down side of hotel life. In fact, she thought hotel work was going to be a good fit for her lifestyle. She wanted a position where she would keep busy all day and not get "bored and drool on a desk." It was more stable than the restaurant job and temp positions she had had since the factory job, and after all she always liked making things "pretty." But within two months, Keisha lost twenty pounds, was sore from changing beds, had cuts on her arms, and was not getting proper sleep. Her thighs throbbed in pain, as if she had done "a thousand squats" in one day, and her shoulders hurt from carrying wet shower curtains filled with mold or mildew. Add in lifting heavy mattresses, hauling around vacuum cleaners that weighed over five pounds, and pushing carts with supplies and linens, and her body was exhausted.

Even more frustrating was the constant pressure to clean as many rooms as possible, often between fifteen and eighteen in an eight-hour shift, regardless of the condition of the room. Like her coworkers, she said, she soon found herself fighting exhaustion with what she calls "housekeeper's steroids" (5-Hour Energy Shots) and pain with ibuprofen, naproxen, Thermacure patches ("a godsend"), and a muscle rub. To top it off, the low wages ($7.50 an hour in the beginning) and lack of affordable health insurance benefits were stressing her out.

After a few paychecks Keisha realized she was not going to be able to pay for health benefits—an important need, since she had been trying to get pregnant for ten years—or be able to move out of her bug-infested apartment. She was disappointed. As the recession began to take hold, and her husband was trying to find steady work, the couple, just like so many others living on the margins, spent their nights figuring out which bill could go unpaid. She said it was obvious that management didn't care about the complaints of the workers, but rather than quit, she decided, at the urging of her family, to figure out how to make a difference from within. When she heard whispers of a group that was trying to organize workers, she seized the opportunity to make real change. A few weeks later, she was sitting in one of the first meetings of UNITE HERE! in Indianapolis, an American and Canadian service industry union that had just come to the city to help workers improve their employment conditions.

According to UNITE HERE!, Indianapolis is the largest US city without a single unionized hotel. The president of the local chapter said that he believes the average hotel housekeeper in Indianapolis in 2018 makes about $10 an hour, whereas the workers in a neighboring city like Chicago make $19.72 an hour, plus he said, they have "way, way, way better insurance and retirement benefits."[23]

In cities like Chicago, where hotels are unionized, organizers say health care is free for many workers. Back then, UNITE HERE! demanded that hotels increase wages, instill regulations on the number of rooms housekeepers are required to clean (they say they've heard of workers cleaning as many as forty rooms in a day, while a typical union hotel worker cleans about sixteen), end the overreliance on temporary contracted workers without benefits, and employ safer working conditions. They focused on three hotels to unionize in the city: the Westin, the Hyatt Regency, and the Sheraton Keystone Indianapolis.

Keisha, a self-described shy military brat with honey-blonde braids, wasn't exactly sure what taking on her employer meant. She didn't have any experience with politics, wasn't an activist, and on top of that, got butterflies at the thought of public speaking. More importantly, she was afraid of losing her job. She always had problems standing up for herself, but thinking about how badly she wanted to have a child, and seeing the working conditions of her coworkers deteriorate, she pressed on and decided to take on a fight with the $200 billion industry. "I got tired of struggling. [My husband and I] have a lot of financial problems and trouble paying our rent. Sometimes we are torn between putting groceries in our fridge or paying rent or the light bill, and we just didn't want to go through that anymore. The banquet workers and the housekeepers are pretty much like a drum line: we are the pulse of the hotel; we're the heart and soul," she told me.

~

STATISTICS SHOW THAT UNION PARTICIPATION INCREASES WAGES overall, particularly for African Americans, and likely for Black millennials as well. Unions are commonly credited with helping people of color enter and remain in the middle class. The Economic Policy Institute found that Blacks and Hispanics in particular have a far higher union premium than Whites—making about $2.60 and $3.44 more an hour, respectively, than nonunion counterparts. Yet unionization also has its detractors who aren't convinced that it's good for Black workers and think that in the long term employers will just reduce staff to deal with the added costs.

~

Over the last few years, it's been hard to watch television or pick up a newspaper without hearing about workers fighting with companies for things like higher pay and better benefits. Not all of the coverage is positive. Instead of people championing the "little man" fighting for their "rights," many, particularly those on the right, are angry at the workers and the unions that represent them, saying they are greedy, disruptive, and whining at a time where they should be happy just to be employed. One columnist even noted, "Unions have become selfish, extremely greedy, and even thuggish in their never-ending quest to take in as much as they can for themselves, at the expense of everyone else who crosses their path."[24] In 2012 an op-ed in the *Chicago Tribune* noted of striking teachers. "Plain and simple, it is about the union's drive to protect Chicago's incompetent teachers at the expense of students and good teachers. We must not be fooled by the rhetoric that teachers are striking in the interest of students. Baloney. This strike is about protecting political power."[25] Over the past few years unions have been accused of disrupting school schedules in Arizona, instigating nasty political fights in Wisconsin, causing a ton of bad calls during NFL games, leaving the public craving their favorite snacks like Twinkies, causing protests at Wal-Mart during Black Friday, and leaving New Yorkers "starved" during a walk-out at several fast food restaurants like McDonald's and Taco Bell.

Keisha is not sorry about her activism. She wanted to make the public understand just how important it is for employees to have ways to engage management with their problems and concerns. In a perfect universe, she thinks workers should be able to talk to their bosses without these sorts of organizations, but in a world where capital is king, she believes that collective action is sometimes the only way to make the powers that be understand you mean business.

Many people never think about all that happens to make a dream vacation possible when they check in to a hotel, but Keisha hoped to change that. She wanted the world to know about the struggles that housekeepers were having at Indianapolis hotels, as they scrubbed their days away on their hands and knees. She wanted folks to understand the physical burdens, the tubes of BenGay, the exhaustion, and the low wages that hotel workers have to endure—problems she says that can be fixed if they just had a stronger voice to advocate for them.

Keisha believes unions play an important role in helping workers secure better wages and benefits from megacorporations that often only look out for the bottom line. She has read up on the history of organizing, and begun to learn more about the connection to race, politics, and activism. "All throughout history you see Black women particularly saying, 'We want better wages and better working conditions,' but dignity is also a really big part of it. I feel housekeeping is a very respectable profession, but we do get disrespected a lot," she said. Keisha wanted to have a better future, so she dedicated herself to become a part of a labor movement that's increasingly being led by Black, Latinx, and Asian women and men around the country. In recent years, Black workers have had the highest union participation of any racial and ethnic group, though among the millennial generation, 9.8 percent of young Whites are in a union, compared to 7.8 percent of Black millennials.[26]

While we may hear about Black men organizing, like the Brotherhood of Sleeping Car Porters in the 1920s, Black women like Keisha, 11.7 percent (or 1.1 million) of whom are in unions, have played an important role in organized labor movements too, whether in the fields during the post-Reconstruction South or as domestics in the North. Black women have historically organized themselves for the same reasons as Keisha: they want better wages, improved working conditions, and, most importantly, respect, even in the face of racial and gender discrimination. (It should be noted that despite their high participation in unions, Black women are not strongly represented in leadership roles. A report by the Institute for Policy Studies found that less than 3 percent of Black women who reported union membership had elected positions.)

Keisha started off small, attending meetings about two to three times a week. Then she passed out fliers and began speaking to colleagues and their families about their experiences at the hotels. Horrified at the stories she heard, she signed a petition later that year that was sent to her management formally asking for a union. When it was ignored, she and other organizers ramped up their efforts. It wasn't glamorous work, but it was a small step in getting the union off the ground.

One of the toughest decisions she had to make was whether to go to a workers' rally after hearing that bosses from other hotels were encouraging their employees not to attend. She decided to go anyway and was handcuffed and arrested along with forty other people for civil disobedience by blocking a sidewalk. That first time she was arrested, she was scared, but she was released, and the offense was taken off her record after union lawyers intervened. She didn't get in trouble at work but was clearly shaken up. Still, it wasn't until she had to speak at a city council meeting about the poor conditions of hotel workers, with her bosses in attendance, that her new role as an "activist" became fully clear. "My general manager was there. I was sweating bullets; I was shaking like a leaf. I was thinking, 'I'm going to be called into [my manager's] office, and I'm going to be fired, or my boss is going to be like, "I need to talk with you,"' but I didn't get any of that, nothing negative came from it."

~

In the first year or two, Keisha thought the workers were making progress. They didn't get a union, but her employer started making changes. Employees got lockers to secure their personal items, better food was served in the cafeteria, and bad managers were given the boot; still when the tough issues came up, like deciding on the rules for organizing, the hotel managers refused to relent or ignored their requests all together. UNITE HERE! had made a push after the Super Bowl in 2012. They argued that since hotels in the city got a big boost from the game, charging as much as $2,000 a night for rooms that would regularly be $150, some of those earnings should be passed down to the workers. But even with the support of the NFL Players Association, nothing had materialized.

As the weeks grew to years, workers became weary. People at Keisha's job began slacking off, thinking that a union was just about to form that would protect them. Some got fired as a result. Others just disappeared. The numbers at meetings—once up to a hundred workers, according to Keisha—started to dwindle, and those who were left were frustrated that things weren't happening more quickly. Local and national politicians and even President Obama declared their solidarity with the hotel workers in Indianapolis. But when a beloved bellhop and friend lost his job of fourteen years and was told to reapply as a temporary employee, changing his salary from $8 an hour to a little over $3, Keisha wondered if their actions were actually making a difference. "Sometimes I think it is not going to happen. They're going to keep staying lawyered up, and we are not going to be able to get through their sea of lawyers and red tape."

Keisha believed in the power of organizing—well, she wanted to believe in it. She wanted to believe it could be a reality, that it could lead to a better life, but as the continued burden of being a poor low-wage worker overtook her life, her faith in the movement waned. Her coworkers increasingly feared for their lives, and her housing situation became more stressful. As she dealt with evictions, bad roommates, and hard-to-live-with family members, she had a rough time focusing on organizing. She was afraid to tell leadership what was going on—the shame of poverty rearing its head—and she stopped attending meetings. For that price, she said, union leaders went silent on her, stopped speaking to her altogether. "I couldn't continue my union [work] because I didn't believe I was making a difference, and I was having my life turned upside down because of debt. I was too embarrassed to say that I had to concentrate on setting things straight because our living situation got precarious and I couldn't get around the way I needed to." By 2014, her husband found a stable job, and Keisha had had enough. So she left the hotel after seven years. She never received a pay raise of more than a dollar an hour.

Today, Keisha's not sure if unions are a total solution to better treatment in the workplace, though she believes they may be helpful. "I think unions are a good start. We as people no matter what ethnicity need to stick together, especially now, when there are powerful entities in existence that are dividing people within their own ethnic group or nation. This melting pot we live in is bursting at the seams, and I feel a little frightened for our younger generation." She doesn't see a lot in the media about organizing the hotel workers in Indianapolis anymore, and sometimes she misses it. She thinks organizers may have taken their campaign underground until they can get their numbers up. (A representative for the local UNITE HERE! chapter said they simply haven't continued because of "lack of resources.") By the time she quit the hotel, she was the only one left fighting. Everyone else, she said, was too scared of losing their jobs to take the movement any further.[27]

For now she is driving around the country with her husband as part of his new truck-driving gig. For a while she would just sit with him as he made runs, and they lived from hotel to hotel room. She didn't have a permanent address, and it was hard to apply for jobs, but she was content on the open road. She is entering a new, more settled phase in her life with her husband. They have just gotten an RV and plugged it into a friend's house, so she is less worried about housing now. She's happy to have traveled to thirty-five states and is working on writing books—especially vampire novels and poems. She is hoping to go to beauty school (though she had to drop out earlier, and now it's hard to enroll somewhere else because of that debt) or find something where she can control her own hours and wages. She still hasn't made it to the South of France yet, but a year after she quit her housekeeping job she made it to the beach, in both California and Florida, an accomplishment she said was "cool," particularly collecting seashells, and perhaps proof that one can still achieve one's dreams without economic riches. Keisha, who is helping her husband raise his daughter from another relationship, has yet to see a doctor about having children, and she's still trying to find the right insurance that won't cost too much. Right now she is working on raising money to get a book published and for a new laptop, because Suki, as she affectionately called her old computer, "bit it."

Keisha's story reflects a group that seems to be working harder than ever—productivity is in fact up—but is still falling desperately behind.[28] In March 2017, she finally decided to take another job as a cleaner in downtown Indianapolis. Her friend was a supervisor there, and they needed workers. She works Monday through Friday, better than her hours at her previous job. She likes it so far and said there's less pressure to be perfect. However, nearly a decade later, Keisha is making less money than she did at her hotel job.

MILLENNIAL MOMENT: **FORTY ACRES**

DAVON, AGE 28, RAEFORD, NORTH CAROLINA

I grew up in Pittsburgh, Pennsylvania, so I'm a city kid. I've been gardening and playing in the dirt my whole entire life. My aunt and my grandma got me into gardening so I was always around plants. By the time I went to high school, I was wanting to go to school for botany. I was looking at wrestling at the University of North Carolina-Pembroke, and they had a botany program. I got accepted, came down, and that's where the story starts to turn.

My freshman year I decided to join the army. I was a first-generation college student. I grew up in a single-parent household, where my mom often worked two jobs just to get us through. She wanted me to pursue higher education, but she couldn't pay for it, so I took out a lot of money, close to $40,000 for my freshman year. At that time, 2007, we were ramping up in Iraq and Afghanistan, and the recruiters were recruiting heavy. They came with a nice offer for student loan forgiveness and offered a nice enlistment bonus.

I did not think they would call me up—I really didn't. Two months after I volunteered, I got the call, "It's time to go." I'm like, "What? I'm in Algebra class."

So I did that. We got to Iraq. Did that. Got pushed to Afghanistan. While in Afghanistan, I got to about month number 8 to 9ish, I got hit by a IED. That IED changed my whole entire life. I broke my L1 and L2 [two vertebrae in spinal column] in my lower back, and I suffered a traumatic brain injury. When I woke up in Germany, my life was different. I was different. I didn't know how I was different, but I knew I was different. I didn't want the same things anymore. I didn't want to be a botanist anymore. By the time I got back into college to finish my degree, I was feeling kind of lost. In transition. I developed narcolepsy. Trying to go to graduate school was gonna be out because it was very hard to stay awake under a microscope.

I graduated, and nobody would hire me because of the narcolepsy. I have a son—he was about two years old at the time—it was like, "How am I going to provide for my family?" They told me to go to college, I served my country, and it sucks because I was almost unhireable to a certain extent.

The county that I went to school in is the largest agricultural county in North Carolina. Looking around, I was like, "How is it that we're the largest agricultural county, but we have the hungriest people in the state? This don't make no sense." I started really diving deep into it, and I started going on farms and volunteering. Come the end of 2013, I met a doctor who had about 500 acres of land, and he was looking for a new farm manager. He was like, "Your resume looks pretty good. I think that you'll be a great fit, so here goes the farm. Good luck!"

That farm saved my life. At the time I was still kinda lost, turning back from suicide. I needed to be mission driven to continue my life, and so feeding my community became that mission. Farming became so therapeutic to me because these animals, they don't care about your past. They take you on face value. They don't care nothing about what you been through. I needed that. I needed somebody not to judge me.

Do I get the same reception as my younger White farmers get? Oh, no. I think the bright side to being a millennial farmer is, it's different, but it's the same at the same time. Racism and segregation in farming has not left. We tend to think that we're past that, but we're not in farming. I'm in a White-male-dominated field. It's incredible that when I go to meetings, I'm normally the only Black there.

I just don't get the same access to information, the same [access to] funding, the lending practices. I don't have the same access as my White counterparts. How are we ever gonna be on the same playing field? The FSA (the Farm Service Agency), they still need more cultural sensitivity training because when I go in the office, I feel like the reception is kinda like, "Are you lost? Are you sure that you have the right place?"

I was at the Farm Bureau conference last year, and there was probably, out of about four hundred plus White young farmers, about five or ten Black farmers. So I asked the president of Farm Bureau, "What are you doing for diversity?" He was like, "It just has to happen." Well, how is it gonna happen when your stance is not a reflection upon it? People of color, we're looked at as low, but we run this industry still. I think until we start to look at it as that, we're always gonna have problems when it comes to racism. I feel we look down on ourselves because we're working in these chicken factories, or we're picking these vegetables. And it's like no, you're the conductor of this industry. Not them. They may own it, but you're the reason why the industry is as profitable as it is in America. Because of you.

People say, "Well, do you ever get intimidated?" No, because I feel like I'm representing my people. We were brought to America for the sole purpose of a free economic state of slavery, so agriculture is built on the backs of Blacks. It's a privilege and a honor to me to be an African American farmer because for me to have the legacy of the last four hundred years, for me to still have this and trying to make a profit for [this] today, that means the world to me. There's no other career that I'll ever do.

When you think about the food that you are consuming, you need to know where it comes from! If it don't come from somebody who looks like you, that is a problem. Because when you don't control the system, you don't control the outcome of the whole equation. I do care about making money, it's very important to keep it going, but that's not what drives me to farm. What drives me to farm is making sure that my community has access to local organic produce, that it comes from somebody who looks like them. To me, that means more than any dollar to me because it brings it all full circle.

People laugh about the forty acres and a mule, but that was going to be very important for Black survival. You have the forty acres. You have the mule to cultivate the land. So you're almost self-sufficient. Well, that didn't happen, and throughout history, when you look back at Black farmers, we've always had the shit end of the stick. If it wasn't them trying to take our land, [it was] them not giving us the access to loans that White farmers had. It has always been something. People always ask, "Why should a Black man in the South, in today's kind of cultural values and economic views, why should you farm? Because you are not gonna make it." I hear that all the time. People look at this as like, almost still like slavery. We spend trillions of dollars in the food system, but as Blacks, we own none of it. That to me should be alarming to you. That should be a wake-up call!

I think the brightest spark that I get is when I have young Black kids come out there, and they look at me and they look at my background and the fact that I'm farming, it's like a positive to them. When they get to eat the food that comes from somebody that looks like them, that gives me pride. The fact that I can get my community access that they would not have if I wasn't there, that's worth a million dollars to me. Good food is a privilege in America. And to me, it's not a privilege. As an American, it is your God-given right to be able to eat the best food that we produce. African Americans, I tell them all the time, good food is preventative medicine. If you eat good food, and you do a little exercise, that goes a long way.

My grandma always say, "When you put your hands in the dirt, you know, you will never be the same again." After being injured the way I was, you know when I put my hands in the dirt, it's like everything just changed for me. Feeding my community became a mission that for me I cannot lose. In Afghanistan, we lost that mission, but if we lose this mission on trying to feed African Americans, we are going to be in a world of hurt.

chapter five

PAINTED WALLS AND TEMPLES

PATRICK STILL REMEMBERS WHAT IT FELT LIKE AS A CHILD TO PAINT THE WALLS OF his own house for the very first time. They were scribbles really, but it was one of the few chances when he'd have the freedom to do something so innocuous as painting, and the only time when he wouldn't face repercussions from parents worried that a landlord would find his youthful art less than, well, artistic. When you're a young kid, there is nothing more liberating than having your own room to decorate with your interpretations of the world. Your bold stroke of red there. A smattering of yellow there. In a world where walls are erected to cut people off, these decorated walls did the opposite. For Patrick, they opened the world up, gave him the freedom to celebrate his art and express himself. That year that he spent painting walls was the only time he lived in a house that his family owned. He now wants to buy a property of his own, a house or condo where the walls are his to paint, but he's not sure when that will happen.

As a young boy, Patrick lived at his grandmother's house on seventy-five acres of land outside of the city of Cleburne, Texas. He slept in the same room as his mother, father, and brother, until they finally moved into a rental of their own. After a few more years of saving, his parents were able to purchase a house in the city. It was his father's dream come true. Patrick loved the house, but his joy was short-lived. Barely a year into their move, his father, then a police officer, was laid off and unable to find work within any reasonable distance from their new home. The only job he found was as a parole officer in Beeville, Texas, five hours away. They needed the money, so they packed up their home and moved to the small community that was trying to turn itself into a new "prison hub."[1] His dad was heartbroken that he had to leave the home he worked so hard for and wasn't ready to relinquish his dream just yet, so he decided to keep the empty house as well as pay rent on their current place. It worked out for a while, and everyone eventually adjusted to the new living situation. They would go back to visit their old home in Cleburne, but the visits began to decrease as maintaining the house started to become a burden. One day Patrick, who was then a freshman in high school, walked in on an argument between his parents about money. They were having trouble keeping up with the mortgage payments on their home in the city, and it was now being foreclosed on. Eventually they lost the home. Looking back almost a decade later, Patrick realized that the year he lived in that house was the last time he lived anywhere for more than a year.

Losing it, and moving from place to place, he admitted, changed his views on homeownership. And slowly he began to think that renting was best, since you didn't have to be tied down to one place. Throughout high school and college, as his childhood memories of painting his walls faded into the past, he didn't want to live in any one place. "It definitely had a psychological effect on me because I no longer knew the importance of owning something. I just believed that renting was the best way."

~

Patrick's ideas around not wanting to own a home are reminiscent of that of many Black millennials, and sometimes millennials overall. Research shows that millennials aren't buying homes at the rate our parents did, and homeownership rates for those under thirty-five in 2016 hit an all-time low.[2] Millennials, studies found, are delaying the process, renting, and even living with their parents more than previous generations. The reasons for this change vary from student debt to lack of income growth. There has been no shortage of theories and think pieces as to why millennials aren't buying: One is that we like the freedom of being nomads. We are obsessed with sharing, and renting mollifies all these needs. Blake Morgan, writing in *Forbes*, blamed millennials' lack of interest in ownership on the experiences of people like Patrick, who saw what their parents went through during the Recession and didn't want to replicate that: "Being a 'NOwner' looks attractive to many millennials who don't want to suffer like their parents and grandparents did."

While this may be true, thirty-five-year-old Australian entrepreneur Tim Gurner implied that it's the entitlement that millennials are so notorious for that also may be impeding them from buying. "When I was trying to buy my first home, I wasn't buying smashed avocado for $19 and four coffees at $4 each," he told Australia's *60 Minutes* in 2017. "We're at a point now where the expectations of younger people are very, very high. They want to eat out every day; they want travel to Europe every year."[3] Many millennials weren't buying his argument. They said it wasn't just avocado toast holding them back, but a world where they have outrageous loans, out-of-control health care costs and other expenses previous generations did not. Recent studies seem to confirm that analysis. It's not, they have found, that millennials don't necessarily want to own homes; we just can't afford them.

However, as millennials get older, and a large number of us head into our mid- to late thirties, we still seem to be replicating the patterns of our parents, and the so-called millennial housing crisis no longer seems as dire. In February 2018, one headline at Bloomberg even read, "Millennials Are Out of the Basement and Into Buying Homes." The next month the *Chicago Tribune* noted that millennials were finally making "the leap to homeownership," citing a recent study by the National Association of Realtors that found that millennials are now the largest group of homebuyers. But as the real estate industry breathes a collective sigh of relief, and despite all the glee over the increase in homeownership rates by millennials, it remains clear that there is a big disparity when it comes to race.

Black millennials are not necessarily part of this new trend of homeownership. Even as millennials age and the economy allegedly strengthens, Black millennials have the lowest rate of homeownership and the highest rent rates. According to Census data from 2016, only 27 percent of Black millennial households own their own homes, compared to 51 percent of White millennial households, 40 percent of Asian households, and 37 percent of Latinx households. Yet what those statistics tell me is that the story is more complex: it's not just about the millennial generation eschewing homeownership, but about a clear gap between Black and White millennials.[4]

Derek Thompson writing in the *Atlantic* points to two groups, which he labels "the supermobile" and "the stuck." He shows that the emerging millennial housing crisis wasn't just because of the stereotypical overeducated White kids who were struggling, or the new gig economy, but because Black and Brown young adults were pulling those numbers down. "The primary reason that the U.S. now has a record-high number of 18-to-34 year olds living with their parents is not because some rich White twentysomethings are taking a year after graduation to save money. It is because Black and Hispanic Millennials who didn't go to college, or did not finish college, are more likely to live with their parents than any time since the late 1800s." He goes on to say, "The decline in Millennial homeownership today is a single simple statistic masking a complex distribution of motivations. Rich, urban, college-educated, and supermobile Millennials have elected to trade their 30s for their 20s

BLACK MILLENNIALS' HOUSING

RACE/ETHNICITY	OWNERSHIP RATE	RENTING RATE
White	56%	44%
Black	31%	69%
Hispanic	39%	61%
Asian/Pacific Islander	43%	57%
Other	42%	58%

SOURCE: US Census Bureau, 2016 American Community Survey data, from Steven Ruggles, Katie Genadek, Ronald Goeken, Josiah Grover, and Matthew Sobek, Integrated Public Use Microdata Series: Version 7.0 (dataset), University of Minnesota, 2017, doi.org/10.18128/D010.V7.0.

when it comes to buying a home. Meanwhile, poorer, less-educated, and stuck minorities have often traded homes and apartments for their childhood bedroom."[5]

His theory makes sense when you look deeper at the disparity between Blacks and Whites, and financial issues are surely at play. However, while a lack of wealth is tied into Black millennials' low rates of homeownership, there is a fair amount of anxiety related to owning a home among Black millennials—no surprise, since Black families were hit the hardest during the housing crisis. As Black millennials come of age, not only are they dealing with the residuals of the housing crisis, but they also face the sobering statistic that this is one area where Blacks have made no progress. Homeownership for Black Americans overall is about 40 percent, virtually the same as it was fifty years ago.

Patrick, who identifies as biracial, said that while some Black families like his girlfriend's have owned property for decades, the culture doesn't propel homeownership, partially he said because of the legacy of redlining. "We don't care about owning in the African American community because we grew up with parents who were essentially redlined. Who were told that 'you aren't going to get a loan for this house.' More millennials grew up with renting as their way of living than owning, and I think that really affected the millennial generation."

Patrick didn't even know what redlining was growing up, and as a senior in high school, watching Obama get elected as president, he admits he was one of those people who thought, "Oh, maybe racism is over." But after his college years at Howard University and a stint as a Marketing and Outreach Consultant for HomeFree-USA, a nonprofit housing advocacy group, Patrick said the inequality in housing is clear, despite the equal housing laws, which he said don't often protect Black home buyers. "You still will get denied a loan if you're Black and trying to move into a predominantly White neighborhood. They just . . . they won't say it's because we're redlining you—we're just denying you this loan. It can make people skittish on the home buying process." Aside from the discrimination factor, Patrick agreed that many of his Black peers actually love the idea of a home but are worried about the potential liabilities that come with it.

Though millennials get criticized for not wanting to be tied down to one place, he said that mobility is necessary not because of flighty, youthful indecisiveness but because of our economic reality. "We are redefining what the American Dream is," he told me. "Black millennials are always looking to improve from the situation they grew up in. They want to do better and be better than their parents. Being able to move from city to city, or from apartment to apartment matters to the Black millennial bouncing from job to job trying to find their career. Freedom has always been something Black people, not just millennials, have fought, bled, and died for. Today Black people, especially millennials, are dealing with rampant unemployment in their community. What else can they do other than pack up their life and move to a place where there are more opportunities available to them? Being able to freely move from location to location helps the Black millennial discover themselves, their career, and what role they play in society."

Even when they do consider home ownership, Patrick argued, things aren't always easy. "Black millennials struggle with homeownership because, unlike White millennials, homeownership has always been a struggle for us." He believes that since White households own homes at greater rates, many White millennials haven't worried as much about where they will lay their head at night, whereas many young Black millennials have been exposed to precarious housing situations since they were young. "Black millennials have been dealing with the struggles and complications of homeownership way before they ever thought about purchasing their first home, while the White millennial may not have to deal with these same issues." Still, his thinking has evolved, and it's not that he doesn't ever want to own a home. "I've come to the realization that renting is paying somebody else's mortgage. Renting is paying for somebody else to own the property that I live in now. I don't get freedom to paint the walls of my property. I don't have freedom to do whatever I want to do to my property. I have to rely on somebody else, and that person may or may not assist me."

He said that things are slowly changing for his generation and thinks there may be less attachment to homes as a stand-in for the "dream." Homeownership now, he thinks, is also about having an investment, and millennials might be quicker to rent out a house (something his parents didn't try) rather than let it go into foreclosure: "We want to use the home to make money for us, for ourselves, as a new source of income. I've been looking at owning a home more as a place to rent out more than I am as a place to own and stay in and plant roots."

~

A RECENT STUDY BY SOCIOLOGIST MEREDITH GREIF FOUND THAT homeownership means different things to Black and White Americans. The report posits that while White people had higher rates of homeownership and lived in better neighborhoods, people of color tended to value owning a home more. "For minorities, the highs of homeownership are higher while the lows are lower," she said, noting that "homeownership may be considered a double-edged sword."[6] "For Blacks, owning a home, particularly in a more advantaged community, may evoke a feeling of having 'conquered the odds' by achieving homeownership in the face of historical and current obstacles."[7]

Now that Patrick is convinced about the benefits of homeownership, he is worried about other things and knows the process will be different for him. He is concerned about discrimination, which remains rampant in the housing industry, and he is worried that if he wanted to buy a house, especially in a Black neighborhood, the mortgage company might charge him higher interest.

He isn't wrong to be concerned. America has a history of discriminating against Black homebuyers and those wanting their own land. In 1862 Blacks were practically excluded from the Homestead Act, which gave more than 270 million acres of land to over 1.6 million settlers for a nominal fee. One study at the beginning of the century found that 46 million descendants of homesteaders may still benefit from the policy.[8] A small number of Blacks did try to benefit from the act, traveling to places like Kansas. These folks were known as Exodusters; and though in the thousands, their numbers were far below those of Whites who were given access to land.[9] Communities were also allowed to create racial zoning laws, which restricted where Blacks could live, until the Supreme Court struck those laws down in 1917 in *Buchanan v. Warley*, but in its place racial covenants became a popular tool to essentially do the same thing. In 1934, when the Federal Housing Administration was created to help usher in a new generation of homeowners, once again Blacks were excluded. While practices like redlining and blockbusting were used to keep Blacks out of housing during this time, White homeownership soared from 46 percent in 1940 to 65 percent in 1960.

The Fair Housing Act of 1968 sought to end discrimination in home buying and renting, and for a while incremental progress was made. By 2004 Black homeownership was at its highest rates ever: 49.1 percent owned a home. Yet discrimination still lingered, and disparities in the industry, particularly around lending, continue. For example, a 2018 study by the investigative journalism group Reveal found that "modern-day" redlining was pervasive in a number of areas around the country. Their yearlong study showed that Blacks and Latinxs were denied conventional housing loans at "far higher" rates than White people in sixty-one metro areas in the United States. Housing policy, in fact, has been and remains so detrimental to Black Americans that today their homeownership rate is about the same as it was when discrimination was legal.[10]

Black Americans and lower-income populations are often the target of unsavory housing practices, which are so pervasive in large part because of a lack access to credit. One result of the Recession was that African Americans, who have more of their wealth portfolio tied up in their homes than others, and who also often live in neighborhoods with lower home values, were disproportionately affected. A 2014 Pew report noted that Black families lost 43 percent of their wealth between 2007 and 2013.[11] Beryl Satter, a professor at Rutgers University, told the *Washington Post* that Black people still have limited options for financing. "Choices that Black Americans have had for housing loans have been predatory loans, or no loans," she said, noting that there has been "a complete revival of redlining in a slightly different guise."[12]

ON JANUARY 12, 1865, AFTER THE FALL OF SAVANNAH, TWENTY Black religious leaders from the city's five historic Black churches met with Union general William Sherman and Secretary of War Edwin Stanton to talk about what Emancipation would look like. According to historian Andrew Billingsley, the well-dressed group was clear in what their vision of freedom looked like, and when asked directly about what they wanted, they didn't hold back: they wanted land. In an account recorded by a local newspaper, Garrison Frazier, a spokesman for the Black leaders, said, "The way we can best take care of ourselves is to have land, and turn it and till it by our own labor—that is, by the labor of the women and children and old men; and we can soon maintain ourselves and have something to spare. . . . We want to be placed on land until we are able to buy it and make it our own." Over a hundred years later, Billingsley applauded their foresight, noting that they understood what many "contemporary advocates of social progress" had not: "The secret to independence is land." For a brief period, it seemed the United States government shared the vision those twenty men presented that night in Savannah. On January 16, 1865, General William Sherman declared that four hundred thousand acres of confiscated Confederate land be redistributed to almost four million enslaved people. The order, known as Field Order Number 15, gave confiscated Union land on the Southern coast stretching from South Carolina to Florida, the Sea Islands in Georgia, and some main land areas to newly freed Blacks, in forty-acre plots. It also established that the land would be solely run by Black folk. They would later order that a mule could be loaned to the settler in addition to the forty acres. The African American population was ecstatic, and by June 1865, forty thousand Blacks had moved to what became known as "Sherman land."[13]

Their joy was short-lived. After Lincoln's assassination, Andrew Johnson ascended to the presidency, the order was overturned, and the land returned to the previously slave-owning rebels. As scholar Henry Louis Gates wrote, "Imagine how profoundly different the history of race relations in the United States would have been had this policy been implemented and enforced; had the former slaves actually had access to the ownership of land, of property; if they had had a chance to be self-sufficient economically, to build, accrue and pass on *wealth*. After all, one of the principal promises of America was the possibility of average people being able to own *land*, and all that such ownership entailed."[14]

Homeownership has long been a path to the middle class and a symbolic fulfillment of the American Dream for Americans. However, one cannot forget the intentionality in all of this. When the government began promoting homeownership and all the matters involved in the "home" in the early twentieth century, it took the onus off institutions to solve domestic problems and turned them into individual, moral concerns. In the Black community, this idea was particularly influential. Booker T. Washington was convinced that homeownership was a path to not only economic freedom but proving Blacks' "respectability" as American citizens. Even before that, in a manual on how freedmen should behave, White Union general Clinton B. Fisk wrote to African Americans, "You must learn to love home better than any other place on earth. . . . You should always be thinking how you will make it prettier and happier than it is." He further specifies what the home should look like, mentioning having a "nice fence about your dwelling . . . glass in your windows," as well as "a little paint, a little whitewash, a few yards of paper, some gravel walks and a few flowers."[15]

While Black folk were being told this, however, the reality in the early twentieth century was that it was hard for anybody—including Whites—to own a home, and the Depression only compounded the problem. Determined to help ensure this dream become a reality, the government created the Federal Housing Administration. The FHA insured bank loans that would cover 80 percent of the purchase price of the home; however, it did so by explicitly excluding Blacks and other people who lived in or near Black communities from these loans. In 1944 the GI Bill gave veterans subsidies for mortgages. Once again, Blacks were often denied these benefits. Their denial was devastating: between the FHA and the Veteran's Administration, which administered the GI loans, $120 billion worth of new housing was financed between 1934 and 1962. Less than 2 percent of those funds went to Black and other non-White families.[16]

Lorraine Hansberry's famous 1959 play, *A Raisin in the Sun*, based on her father's lawsuit against the city of Chicago concerning restrictive racial covenants, defined the value of homeownership for a new generation. As the character Mama talks about her dreams of a house, she says, "It's just a plain little old house but it's made good and solid and it will be ours. Walter Lee, it makes a difference in a man when he can walk on floors that belong to him." It's a sentiment that has remained prevalent in the Black community, so much so that nearly fifty years later, another play about Black housing, Bruce Norris's *Clybourne Park,* won the Pulitzer Prize in 2011. In the wake of the Great Recession, the effect of the housing crisis on Black families was measured not in terms of the loss of wealth, but in terms of access to the American Dream. "Homeownership has become an indispensable part of being a full participant in American society," National Urban League president and CEO Marc H. Morial said. "An erosion of homeownership rates among African Americans represents not only a devastating financial loss but a barrier to full participation in the American Dream."

I don't know if the problem is that as Black folk we place too much value on homeownership or that the undermining of ownership in the Black community has made Black millennials less willing to purchase homes, but these are the issues on hand as young Blacks weigh the decision to buy a home. Despite these factors, Wells Fargo has learned through a series of consumer surveys with Ipsos Public Affairs that African Americans view homeownership positively.[17] According to the 2016 survey, 90 percent of African Americans say homeownership is a "dream come true," 79 percent say it's essential for building families, and 51 percent are considering buying a home in the next two years.

I BOUGHT MY FIRST HOME IN AUGUST 2005, AS HURRICANE Katrina hit New Orleans. The confluence of historic depravity, government incapability, and racism had destroyed the city. To this day, communities there, and particularly Black communities, have never fully recovered; their homes are gone, and their legacies and histories in the city erased. But I wasn't thinking too much about that when I left my mom's house one August day. I was too nervous and scared about the day ahead. I had taken off of work from my job as a production assistant at Fox News to get ready for the big day, excited that I would now have a visual marker of success. It had been months in the making—years really. I was obsessed with homeownership, perhaps inspired by President Bush's "ownership society" agenda, which he had been advocating for years. "We can put light where there's darkness, and hope where there's despondency in this country. And part of it is working together as a nation to encourage folks to own their own home," he said.[18] The events of September 11 had corrupted my view of the world, yet I was still somehow feeling hopeful. Of course I was. I was twenty-five, just a few years out of college, and everything felt possible.

I had just broken up with my first true love, but I was ready to prove I was the mythical independent woman both my mom and Beyoncé had drilled into my head. A slew of friends had bought condos in Washington, DC, where I had gone to school. Almost everyone in my immediate family owned their own home: my grandparents, my great-aunt, and most importantly my single mother. She bought her home a few years after I was born and constantly talked about how tough that was to do in the 1980s—so tough that she had to get her boyfriend at the time to co-sign for the house. Even though he never made a single mortgage payment and was eventually taken off the agreement, a statement she boldly and intentionally touts every chance she gets, she was always clear about the importance of owning your own things. It meant having control over your life; it meant freedom.

At the time, I was making crap money—$28,000 a year, nothing much when you live ten minutes away from Manhattan—but credit was free-flowing, and I qualified for a $250,000 loan. It wasn't a lot, but with a little bit of savings and some money that my mom and great-aunt promised to give me, a privilege a lot of Black people don't have, I knew I'd have enough for a sizeable 20 percent down payment. My mom and I looked everywhere for a place to buy: Harlem, which I was priced out of, but also halfway convinced by my mom that the market there was too expensive (mistake #1). Jersey City, where the quality apartments were a little out of my reach and the neighborhoods I could afford weren't ideal (mistake #2). I was frustrated but determined. My mom convinced me to get over my ideas of living in the city, because, she said, by the time I was thirty, I wouldn't care how close I was to the bars or clubs and buy a place in my suburban hometown that I could afford. I sort of felt at peace. It was the wrong decision (mistake #3), because I still love the city. I relented because I wanted to feel stable. I wanted to own something, even though I hadn't really thought about why, or what it would mean long-term. Mainly I relented because I saw the look on my mom's face when I put in a bid for my apartment on the East Hill.

The East Hill neighborhood in Englewood, New Jersey, was on the other side of the tracks from where I grew up—a railroad literally divided our town. Englewood had been a mixed community for decades, something the town has touted for ages, though that integration comes with a caveat. There were designated places where Blacks, Browns, and Whites could live, even if just informally, and my family was from the "Black" side of town, the Fourth Ward. The East Hill was the premier posh neighborhood in the First Ward. It was the neighborhood my mom got pulled over in one Halloween night in the 1960s for DWB—driving while Black. It was prim and proper, and very few of "us" lived there. Some years ago, when we found out that the comedian Eddie Murphy had moved there into a house with thirty-two rooms, we were proud. But he had fences built up, and I could never see the inside. We'd drive by, but his dream, too, felt distant from the community I knew. It still felt like a million dreams away.

Not that we felt constrained or restricted. It was just where we were comfortable and where our community was. My family, for the most part, was unapologetically uninterested in integrating neighborhoods. If White folk didn't want us there, we didn't have to be there. Instead, they built up their own communities. In 1954, fresh from Harlem, my grandfather and grandmother bought two plots of land. They planted a garden filled with an array of vegetables, and my grandfather planted a beautiful, thorn-covered rose garden, with rows and rows of beautiful pink and red flowers that I was expressly forbidden to touch. They worked hard at maintaining their house and worked harder to keep it beautiful and "respectable." When I, like Patrick, attempted to paint their walls with Crayola creations as a child, I got a whooping that I still remember, because they didn't want their walls dirtied.

They loved being homeowners, and soon their other friends starting moving in from the city too. They even convinced my Aunt Dee to move from the Bronx after her divorce and bring along my great-grandmother. They seemed even more excited when my mom finally bought her own house six blocks away in 1986. To say it was a fixer-upper would be an extreme understatement, but it was hers, and they were proud. They came over and helped her till the land, put flower beds down, build a new kitchen, and everything in between. There were good times in all those houses, shared with people and a community my mom also had known for decades. I remember barbeques and birthdays, happiness and joy, Kwanzaa parties and lemonade. There were some painful memories, too. I remember watching my grandmother be carried out on a stretcher from her house and her dying soon after. The mouse that terrorized the kitchen for a month created a fear I have yet to get over. I remember, too, the solemnity that hung in the community after a young Black man was shot down by a cop down the street from my aunt's home, and the concern when my childhood friend found a gun in the park near my house. But whatever house I was in, it felt like home. And we owned them all.

My wonderful experiences growing up in a home aside, I, much like Patrick, saw homeownership as a wealth-building tool. I didn't envision grand parties; I didn't see my children settling in my condo or a lifetime of memories there. I just thought it made sense not to pay rent and to be able to do what I wanted to do with a place. After meeting another realtor at an open house who referred me to a mortgage lender (mistake #4), I was happy. I was especially psyched because I was dealing with all Black realtors and brokers, I loved that they were the ones who were helping people acquire wealth, helping them own the land. It felt as if it wasn't just me winning: *we* were winning. Despite the fact that I'd gotten an adjustable no-doc loan from National City (a bank that no longer exists) meaning they didn't verify my income but just my employment, and that my mortgage would "adjust" in a few years, I was confident that this was a good decision. Unlike other mortgage representatives my mortgage lender told me I needed to get out of this loan in two years and get a conventional mortgage. She sort of warned me this was a shitty deal, but also took a "by any means necessary" approach to Black folks owning property. I understood. Plus, I was confident that I'd be making more money in a few years at my job and assumed I could take the risk. My mom said she'd back me up, if anything went leftways.

Having that all figured out, or as much as a twenty-five-year-old thought they could, I marched up to my new, small, one-bedroom apartment on the Hill, satisfied. I started thinking about a redesign. My mom tried to figure out how many Black people lived in the building. Even my Aunt Dee was excited about the purchase and said it would be perfect place for her to retire to in old age, when her house would be too much work. It felt as if I'd broken barriers.

At the same time, I worried that I'd betrayed my race somehow. I didn't buy in the "hood," in my old community. I wanted to buy someplace that I thought would be a better investment, set in the East Hill, a Whiter neighborhood, the property value would probably hold better. I should have realized that owning a home didn't really change how the government, or White people, saw me. But back then I was too high off that idea of the Dream to realize otherwise. A few days later on TV, I watched Black homes wash away as the president flew over, looking at them from above. Their homes, their property, their blood and tears meant nothing to so many in the nation, who saw people who looked like me as savages looting the streets.

In the years after, I saw the joy in the faces of some old church ladies when I told them I'd bought an apartment on the East Hill. Instead of rolling my eyes at the dated, sometimes irritating "you go girl" affirmations, I saw the pain in their eyes when they told me their stories of segregation on the wrong side of the tracks. I remembered the history of redlining and the GI bill policies that were meant to exclude people like my grandpa, who fought in World War II and still managed to buy a home. And I felt privileged that I had my own home to go back to when I visited Mississippi years later and sat on only the steps that remained from so many of those houses that floated by in Katrina's wake.

My apartment didn't require too much renovation, and in two years I got a nearly $45,000 raise and refinanced my apartment with a conventional lender for a thirty-year, fixed-rate mortgage that kept my loan at a decent level. The downside was that this was 2007, and the housing market was about to bust. I found out my apartment was a little underwater. I figured I could hold out, but then I decided to get a PhD. The apartment became a burden on my graduate student stipend, yet I didn't move out. Much like Patrick's family, I wanted to hold onto my "piece" of America. I took out a small loan to pay for the condo fee. Ran up two credit cards and even used a $14,000 bond that my grandfather had given to me (mistake #5 zillion). I should have rented the place out or found someplace cheaper to live, but I was still proud that I was (barely) holding my home together. When I got a notice in the mail a few years after the financial bust, I felt weak. Dizzy. The letter said that my mortgage company had been charged with giving subprime loans to Black and Brown people around the country and asked if I wanted to join a class action suit. I stood there and read it again and again. I had been the target of predatory lending. Sure, I knew that my income made me a target. I'd heard the words of the broker. But because of my race? It hadn't ever crossed my mind. I was devastated.

I know the history of this country, know the history of redlining, know how my grandparents were locked out of neighborhoods because of their skin color. But for some reason I was still surprised. I hadn't lived any fucking dream. I hadn't broken any fucking barriers. The little piece of America that I had to scrimp and save for was just as racist as ever. I would say I was mad, but more than that, I was hurt that I had been lulled into some kind of false bourgeois comfort that made me think that my life was different from my predecessors' lives. Sure, I had made it up that Hill, but at what cost?

I left the letter open on my dining room table for months. Ignored the others that followed. I was never able to send back the form to join the class action suit. I couldn't admit that I had been duped. I wanted to have something that felt like mine. I wanted to play "American" for a bit. To feel that this was my society too. It was in that moment that I realized my error. This country wasn't mine. It still isn't. So I let the letter sit. Watched as my pride died a little every time I glanced at it, until the date had passed and it was too late. Years later, I got another notice. The mortgage company had decided to settle the discrimination case with the Black and Brown homeowners. To make up for their malfeasance, the mortgage lender would pay $200 to each of those who had signed on to the class action suit. Sometimes I'm still mad about that money I lost.

Ten years later, I'm out of the apartment but still in New Jersey. I've become a landlord, and I'm living in my great-aunt's house. She was too old to live alone, so she moved into mother's house until her death a few years ago. The apartment isn't underwater, but it's not exactly making me money either. In fact, while the rent my tenant pays covers the mortgage, it doesn't pay my condo fee. I keep going back and forth as to whether I should sell. I probably should. After having to replace a floor and losing income for nearly a year, the appeal of being an owner has worn off. And the reality that I still can't sell it for what I paid for it makes me bitter every time I step through the door. Yet there is something special about owning one's home, and it keeps me hanging on (along with the mortgage interest deduction on my tax return). I know I'm not alone.

~

PRINCE GEORGE'S COUNTY IN MARYLAND, ON THE BORDER OF Washington, DC, has the highest family income in a majority-Black county in the country. It's known as a beacon for Black homeownership. But it also felt the brunt of the recession and has not recovered in the way the adjacent White counties have.[19] I wanted to know how Black millennial homeowners in this wealthy community were managing. I stopped by Home-Free USA, a nonprofit organization that helps people, particularly African Americans, buy homes. They work with many of the banks, like Wells Fargo, that people claim are responsible for the recession, but they also help people who have historically been underserved by the industry get into the housing market. It was there that I met Christina. She was attending one of their home-buying seminars. At the end of the vibrant session led by Marcia Griffin, one of the founders of the organization, Christina, who is twenty-eight, waited around to ask about whether she should buy a home. She was assertive but also a little shy. She had money saved, she said, but not a high-paying job, and only makes $38,000 a year. Yet she knew it might be time to finally leave her parents' home. I was surprised when Milan, Marcia's daughter and vice president of marketing and outreach, told Christina that she might want to wait. Christina looked disappointed but also seemed to understand the economic reality.

Milan is part of a team that wants to see young Black people buy homes, but she also wants to see them keep them, and is determined to not sell a false dream. She recently gave her cousin in Houston the same advice she offered Christina. Her cousin called her wondering whether or not to buy an investment property at a foreclosure auction. She was willing to pay $11,000 up front, but it was an "as is" property that she had never laid eyes on. Milan was nervous at the thought of it and advised her cousin to pass on the offer. She told her that buying a property you have never seen is risky for your first home purchase, and she didn't want to see her sink money into something that might require a deeper investment. It's not that Milan doesn't believe in homeownership for young Black millennials. She just knows what they have to contend with in order to buy—and keep—their homes.

Milan grew up in Washington, DC, to a family of entrepreneurs and homeowners. She was privileged, she said, went to good public schools, but also grew up, like most middle-class and upper-class Black people, close to the hood. "It was an interesting 'boughetto' dynamic of being uptown and not really being hood, and then really meshing with, at a deep level, the real hood," she said. Her dad owned the largest mortgage servicing company in the nation, and her mother owned a store in the posh Willard hotel in DC. When her father lost a big HUD contract, followed by the revelation of a plot to rob her mother's store, they both decided to start a new business together. Her dad had noticed that a lot of the borrowers at his mortgage-servicing business were African American, so together they started a new business aimed at helping Black people get loans.

Home and land ownership had always been in her family's blood. Both sets of Milan's grandparents owned land. Even her great-grandfather, who was born into slavery, owned property in the nineteenth century. As a mixed-race man who identified as Black, he didn't qualify for a mortgage. So he got the White daughter of the slave master to sign a mortgage for him so he could buy land. "Because she signed her name on the dotted line so my great-grandfather could own property, you have now started a whole lineage of property owners," Milan said. She believes the studies that find that people who grow up in a home owned by their family are more likely to own a home themselves. One recent report in 2016 noted that children whose parents owned their own home were nearly three times as likely to also be homeowners.[20] The legacy of homeownership in her family certainly influenced her attitude toward it.

Still, her experiences represent that of a minority of Black millennials. In 1994, the year that the Census began tracking ownership by race and ethnicity, 42 percent of Blacks owned their own homes. That number was much higher for White families: 70 percent were owners. That disparity is the same today. According to Census data from the first quarter of 2018, 72 percent of White families own their own home, compared to 42 percent of Black families.[21] Add on the fact that White millennials marry and partner at younger ages, and more crucially, that they have more resources and more access to wealth (especially inheritance), and it's understandable why Black millennials are not becoming homeowners at the same rates.

The disadvantage is more than just financial. Milan describes it as "psychological trauma" that came with the foreclosure crisis, which she believes affected not just low-income young Black people but professional ones with graduate degrees. Many millennials she works with still see homeownership as out of reach, or they don't think about it until they're almost forty—a mistake, she said, as they lose vital years of wealth building. In an age when her peers have 401ks and not pensions, a home can offer another avenue for stability. "I love being a homeowner because it gives me a lot of options," she said. "I can make money without having to spend a lot of time. With work, you have to be physically present. I don't have to be physically present with real estate. Once I get that bad boy off the ground, and I really screen my renters right, the amount of time in comparison to what I make is very slim."

When I ask about all the potential pitfalls of homeownership, Milan is frank about the risks and knows that while she purchased homes at the right time, she may also suffer during economic downturns. She admits that things like student loan debt, poor credit, and lack of access to down payments prevents many young Black people from entering the housing market, but she also blames the government for failing to help people understand the benefits of home ownership and mortgage companies for their decreasing interest in the Black homebuyer. She admits there are some "halfhearted" attempts to promote homeownership to Black people, but none with the full gusto that will especially attract young Black millennials at the national level, to help them see owning a home as not just owning a place to live but creating an "entrepreneurial venture."

While Milan does gush about how much she loves the financial leverage real estate provides, I suspect that it's about more than that for her. When Milan finished up college, she decided to move back in with her parents in DC, though it wasn't long before she bought her own house. "It gives me really a true pride with an ownership because it gives me a different connection to where I am. If these kids walk past my house, they cussing, all this other kind of thing, throwing trash everywhere, I'm also going to check you because now we are part of a whole community. If I was renting, I'm basically borrowing a place from you, so I wouldn't have the same connection. So I have a deeper love for those I'm around because I own my place. And you learn how to be neighborly in a different way. People look out for me, I look out for them, so it's a level of love." Now she owns two properties, one in the District and one in Florida, and couldn't be happier.

~~

Milan is particularly sanguine about Black homeownership as a pathway to upward mobility, but she may be an exception. Many Black millennials are still dealing with just having a place to lay their heads at night, particularly those in the LGBTQ community. In New York City alone, the total number of homeless people ages eighteen to twenty-four, was about 1,706, according to the *New York Times*, though the number is thought to be "significantly" higher. Like Christina and over one-third of Black millennials, Maya still lives at home. She is debating the benefits of ownership while trying to figure out her own situation. Right now she barely has enough for rent on her own. She lives in a neighborhood that's rapidly gentrifying and with each year becoming more unfriendly to artists like her. She's no stranger to housing issues, having had to shuffle around when she was a teenager, but she's also not sold on the idea that ownership is as liberating as Milan makes it sound.

~~

It's a cloudy, unseasonably warm winter afternoon in Brooklyn's Bedford-Stuyvesant neighborhood, and Maya and I are standing in front of the recently closed Ms. Dahlia's Café. It had been a staple of the neighborhood for ten years, and Maya is shocked about its shuttered doors. As she peers in, a passerby tells us the owner died recently, and the family decided to close the café. Maya had sent needy youth there for jobs, and now she's now thinking about what will happen to them. She's wondering in general what is happening to her beloved neighborhood, as gentrification in Brooklyn continues. She hopes, in the least, the location can stay Black-owned, she mutters, as we head for a Haitian spot a few blocks away. We sit outside Kafe Louverture, talking about the changes the community has seen as Biggie's "Juicy" plays on a car radio.

Twenty-one-year-old Maya, an artist, activist, filmmaker, and teacher, has lived in Brooklyn nearly all of her life, and after a short stint staying with an aunt in Manhattan, she's living with her parents again. She is trying to make it work, but she has set a deadline to leave if she can't. "Have you ever lived with Black parents?" she asked. I laughed. "You can live in a Black household, and you can pay rent, but still not have the same freedoms that you would if you were paying rent in your own household," she said. "Or you can not pay rent at all but contribute to the house in different ways, which is fine, but still you're twelve. You kind of just want to throw up your hands and be like, 'All right. All right.' And then with Caribbean parents? Oh God. It's a whole other level." She's partially joking. She said her parents are her biggest fans, and while they get on her nerves, and she gets on theirs, they manage okay. "It's all copacetic as frequently as possible, but I still have aspirations of my own, so I need to get out. In order to feel good about myself, to feel fulfilled within myself and then also for my parents to feel like their swan has also done well in the world." As soon as I open my mouth to form an "awwww," she adds that they are still pressuring her to leave. "It's like, 'You about to be twenty-two. You need to be thinking about other options.'" She doesn't disagree.

Maya saw her parents struggle with housing when the recession hit in 2008. As it was for Patrick and many other millennials, it had a profound impact on her. Maya grew up in a three-bedroom prewar building in Prospect Lefferts Gardens, right across from the Botanical Gardens. It was a railroad apartment and under Section 8, the program that provides housing assistance to low- and moderate-income families, but it was nice, Maya said. Her grandmother, aunt, and mother lived there for forty years. It was their home. It was all they knew. And Maya loved it. It was everything to her. Sundays in the springtime were her favorite, "frolicking" in the grass filled with sunflowers on the property. It was her happy place. But in 2005, when her grandmother died, the landlord seized the apartment. He said that her mother wasn't on the lease and took the family to court. They fought for six or seven years, she said, until her mother finally grew weary of the battle and decided it was time to move on. Maya was thirteen. They moved in with her dad's parents for a few months. She shared one bedroom with her father, mother, and sister, but she had fun. Soon her parents decided that they were going to enter the public housing system, and they moved into a shelter. It sucked, she said, but at least it wasn't too far away from her old neighborhood.

Her parents are both in the arts. Her father is a musician, but he has a day job to support the family. Her mom is an art teacher. They worked hard, but during the recession they lost a ton of money in their 401ks, which held much of their cash. It was hard, she said, because they had been saving money. Her mom especially had been investing, but it just "evaporated," Maya said, with a sadness that's quiet and frustrated. Times were tough, Maya was grieving for the loss of her grandmother and for the loss of her childhood home, and then suddenly she was tossed into the shelter system. Instead of acting out, she saw it as a moment to mature. "It was like, 'Okay, you can't lash out the same way; you can't have your lapses of insanity. You kind of just have to be as supportive to the family unit as possible.' I'm the eldest, so I tried to be as responsible as possible, as far as my hormones allowed me to." On top of all of that, her mom had a new baby to take care of. It was rocky.

To this day she's still bothered by people who think people end up homeless because they've done something wrong. The experience changed her idea of what a home means. "When you think of home, you think of a space that you created that's internal and external. You hold space for it inside of you because you directly put energy into creating it for who you've grown to be. And then it's the external space of 'Okay, this is sanctuary. This is my temple. This is where I come to lay my head at night.'" She realized that an actual home is much deeper than that. "Home is where you make it. You could have a cardboard box, and it could be home. It may not be the ideal home, or it is the ideal home for you because you have the ability to be a nomad. Some people truly like living that way."

Eventually, the family pulled through, and within two months they left the shelter for a Victorian house in Prospect Heights, where they lived for two years until the owner sold the house to a poacher. The owner's children had taken out loans against all the equity in the house, and the woman couldn't keep it up or pay back the loans. Maya's family was given a month to move, and after the renovation the house was rented to two White families. Still, her family landed on their feet. They found a three-bedroom apartment in Brownsville, and that's where she has been living for the last four years, with the exception of that quick move to Harlem. She loves the area and said it still has that Brooklyn charm. "It's a mixture of 'don't fuck with me, but you fuck with me, right?' I like it. It's historical. There's still farmers over there. There's a man over there who harvests bees and honey, and he has a chicken coop," she said, laughing. "There's still chicken coops out in Brownsville!"

She wants to own something one day but doesn't feel that it's a particularly American thing. "I feel like everybody, anybody who comes from anywhere, their dream is being able to be like, 'I own my land, I own my property, I have my farm, and I can sustain myself.' Yes, that's a part of what my aspirations are: to be able to own the deed, own the land, and own the building." As Black folk, she said we must push for more when it comes to ownership, more than the traditional 40 acres of land we were always told we were entitled to. "I've always had a problem with the 40 acres and a mule type thing because it was a section of land that was allocated to you. It wasn't the land that you were entitled to, because you were definitely entitled to more. You were working on 140, but yet you get 40 acres of that, and a mule to work it? You raped and pillaged the whole entire continent, and I get 40 acres of this space? Get out of here!"

Maya isn't sure what's going to happen next. As a creative, with parents who can't financially support her, she's not sure how she is going to make it in New York City. She's thought about moving to Canada but decided it's too cold. She started looking at the prices of houses in the Caribbean, and Costa Rica especially appeals to her. But she feels stuck. She said while New York still has things that people romanticize about it, it's increasingly feeling like a city for the 1 percent. "You can't move to the West Coast, Silicon Valley, it's the same thing. Can't move to Middle America, because the way that Trump has affected the racial divide is just like suicide going over there. So you move down South. Or you leave the country. A lot of us are okay with facing the possibility of living in Costa Rica. It's cheaper. Ecuador, cheaper. Blacker. The food is better. Like fuck it, I will take the whole new experience and be a part of a whole new culture." She pauses, and thinks of her next words some more, "I mean you can pick up and go, but . . . You can pick up, but where are you going? The thing that motivates you to pick up and go is knowing that you have an alternative space to go to. It's like you *hope* that you stumble across a place to be." The risk, though, is something she knows too well: "landing back to the homelessness thing."

IN THE LAST FEW YEARS ALONE THERE HAVE BEEN A RANGE OF lawsuits alleging discrimination in the housing industry by big and small companies. In 2012, Wells Fargo, the nation's largest home mortgage lender until 2018, was sued by the Department of Justice for discriminatory lending practices. The case charged that Black and Latinx borrowers were steered toward costlier loans than White borrowers in similar circumstances. The bank never agreed to wrongdoing but agreed to pay $175 million in order to avoid further litigation. In 2015 and 2016, journalists at Reveal showed that TD bank proportionately denied more Black and Latinx mortgage applicants than any other US bank in 2015 and 2016: it turned away 54 percent of Blacks and 45 percent of Latinxs, three times the industry average.[22]

In 2016 BancorpSouth agreed to a $10.6 million settlement in a case that accused the company of telling its loan officers to "turn down" mortgage applications from non-Whites more quickly and stop giving "borderline" applicants of color credit assistance that Whites would be eligible for. The case also cited an audio recording of a loan officer commenting on their policies on race, saying, "'They need to get their credit up,' and 'stop paying their damn bills late.'" In 2017, a group of realtors in Mississippi settled with the National Fair Housing alliance for steering White homeowners away from Black or mixed-race communities and never even responding to queries from Black would-be homeowners. That same year JP Morgan Chase settled a $55 million case that accused the bank of affiliating itself with brokers that charged Black and Latinx buyers $1,000 more than their White counterparts. During that same time, the City of Philadelphia filed another discrimination case against Wells Fargo, also noting that Blacks and Latinxs were charged higher amounts for fees and mortgages than their counterparts. The lawsuit charged that Wells Fargo had a "history of redlining" in Philadelphia that dated back to the 1930s. The bank said it was prepared to defend its "record as a fair and responsible lender."[23] (Previously, Wells Fargo committed to helping increase Black homeownership, saying that it would lend at least $60 billion to Black borrowers over the next ten years. To assist with this initiative, it is working with Black organizations around the country.)

These are just a few examples, suggesting that discrimination is not some anomaly or unique. In fact, these practices are so egregious and pervasive that in 2018, a week after the anniversary of the Fair Housing Act, the *New York Times* editorial board published an article titled, "Blacks Still Face a Red Line on Housing." The piece said that fifty years after the act was first passed, the continual discriminatory practices against Black and Brown people in the housing industry remain rampant and urged the government to be more responsive to these practices: "In a sensible world, the federal government would be suppressing predatory lending while beefing up programs that provide affordable home mortgages and refinancing arrangements. Instead, the Trump administration and Congress are gearing up to gut federal fair lending protections and make it easier to hide emerging patterns of predatory financing."[24]

Perhaps it's because of the president's history with racism in the industry as a budding developer himself. Trump came to prominence in the early 1970s after he and his father were sued by the Department of Justice over discriminatory housing practices against Black people. They ended up signing a consent decree, which did not include an admission of guilt but stipulated the ways Trump and his company would desegregate their properties. He considered it a victory.[25]

In early 2018, the Trump administration took away enforcement power from the Office of Fair Lending and Equal Opportunity, a unit in the Consumer Financial Protection Bureau that deals with discrimination cases in lending, including home mortgages. The administration believes the group is too aggressive in its mission and is trying to change that. Instead of oversight of companies day to day, the group will now focus on advocacy and education. Previously the bureau helped to get payouts from lenders that it found had systematically charged people of color higher interest rates and other fees than they had for Whites.[26]

~

ASIDE FROM CONCERNS ABOUT THE $90,000 IN DEBT HE WILL have after finishing graduate school, it is the "Black tax" that Patrick is most troubled by when it comes to homeownership. It's understandable why, with the staggering number of these cases and report after report online stating things like, "Redlining is alive, well and dangerous," "Remember Redlining? It's Alive and Evolving," and "Barriers to homeownership still exist for people of color," which to him and any young Black person is reason to pause at the idea of ownership.[27]

As he begins to seriously think about buying a home, Patrick, who is now driving full-time for Lyft while he works on starting a nonprofit, has become a lot more interested in Black-owned banks, something he and his friends previously knew little about. He is hoping to learn more about them and other aspects of homeownership. Now that he understands the history of redlining, he doesn't think much will stop Black millennials from buying homes—not Trump's presidency, big banks, or Blacks' lack of wealth. "Black people don't give up. Black millennials are coming into their own right now, and we're in that same mindset. We're not going to give up. We're also hip to the fact that we are going to be discriminated against no matter what happens. Whether it's buying a home, getting a job, we're going to be discriminated against because of the color of our skin because that's the way America is."

MILLENNIAL MOMENT: **THAT CRAVING**

African immigrants are more likely to have a bachelor's degree or higher than Americans overall. They are also less likely to live in poverty and more likely to be married and have higher household incomes than US-born Blacks. Breaking it down by ethnicity, research shows that Nigerians are the most likely to have degrees—almost two-thirds do so—and often the pressure to excel is high.[28] Black millennial immigrants seem to replicate these patterns. They too have higher educational attainment and incomes than US-born Black millennials. This group and their children can sometimes get the label of "model minority," but first- and second-generation Black millennials say it's more complicated than that.[29]

BJ, AGE 33, BROOKLYN

My father is a government employee for my country, so I was a diplomat's kid in Switzerland. I came here when I was still documented, I was kind of like in a "privileged" situation status. My parents were still living in Geneva when I came here, and then subsequently they were reposted. My dad had to go back to Nigeria. When you're overseas, in terms of Nigerian politics, they pay you in dollars. Once you get back home, they pay you in Nigerian currency. Therefore, you lose a whole lot of value in the exchange rate. I came here on a scholarship, washing dishes, occasionally parking cars.

It was a cultural shock. I'm from Nigeria. It's a big, populous country, diverse. Then I go to Switzerland, and it's a smaller country, neutral country, but still, developed country. Progressive country. Then I come to America. The perception of America is like this big land of opportunity. You think you're going to go to the beach, and you're going to see something like Pamela Anderson, you know? Unrealistic expectations, really. I landed in Pennsylvania. Amish country and going to a Mennonite school, where a lot of the Amish don't believe in electricity. My first host family did not have a TV. They say Africa's third world, but we had a TV, you know? I lived in Switzerland, TV. Then I come to America, and it's supposed to be a better place, but here I am with no TV.

[People would ask] "Do you have an elephant? Do you ride a donkey to school?" or whatever. Those are all part of the high school experience. The American high school.

I graduate. I go down to West Virginia. They do believe in electricity, but maybe they can't afford it. You're getting different exposure to poverty, which is more akin to, like, an African experience. Appalachia actually reminded me of a lot of Nigerians, good people, good-hearted people. Maybe different in terms of not too diverse, but their concerns are the same. They want to live; they want to eat; they want clean water. You're stuck with opportunities that you have.

You're always aware of the racial dynamics. Rednecks, big Confederate flags, those sort of things. I'm African, and yeah, that's acknowledged. That sentiment just kind of went away to some degree. It disappeared more so into the everyday struggle. They don't really care too much because you're not eating so much more than they are; they're not really noticing you because their focus is on them trying to eat.

I've worked for $5 an hour. I've worked for $7 an hour. I've worked at a corner store. Delivered pizza. I've worked at car washes, a Christian kind of camp. I've climbed ladders and painted; I've dug holes, sheetrock. I've delivered flyers. I was selling marijuana. I was still going to school. It was profitable; otherwise I wouldn't have done it. It's not real profitable. It's a get-you-by thing. Most people don't go into it with a business plan. Most people just spend it on a day to day—you get food, and then you go to a club, or you know, you like some chick or . . . You can pay your bills. It wasn't like

I was going to get rich. I wasn't doing it on that kind of level. The space I was in wasn't really conducive to that kind of movement, but you can get by, so I got by.

My last semester, actually, that's where the issue kind of starts. I didn't have the requisites, credits, to graduate. I had to take on partial credits, and as an international student, partial credits do not qualify you to retain an international student's pass. Therefore, I became undocumented. I completed my requisite credit requirements and graduated, but I graduated into an undocumented status. There's really no remedy for that unless you get sponsored by an employer. This is also at the time where there's a lot of talk in Congress *or the legislature about potentially changing immigration. There was always a hope that there would be a normalization. Day to day, you still have to live, so you work under the table, work for cash.*

It's challenging. A lot of times you're like, "What is it for? Why did I go to school? Why did I go to college?" I have a college degree, and I expected, or I thought and I wished, that I would be following a professional footstep. It just turned out that along the way, the rules are changing. I've chosen to keep fighting. Maybe I'll give up next year, but I hope not.

Before taking this job that I'm in, I interviewed for two jobs. There was a construction job and this job, paralegal. I was offered both. Both paying comparable wages. I brought it up to my mother and my brother. They both said, "No. Fuck back-breaking shit or whatever. You sit down in an office." I actually enjoy construction. There's sometimes nothing more beautiful than watching paint dry. It's almost like an instant gratification kind of thing, in a sense. What you build, you see. If it's good, it stands. Sitting behind a computer, it's like, not seeing what you're creating or what you're making. That was something I took pride in, in construction, personally.

I'm still not where I want to be regardless of which job I'm doing. My big goal is to become an attorney. Graduate law school and then the big goal after that is . . . maybe make something better for somebody else, you know, legislation or something that affects a larger population.

There are people that think African Americans are lazy and want to do whatever, but Africans, or immigrants, are hungry and therefore will put up with whatever bullshit. I definitely experience it on interviews. I worked with an employer that just basically hired Africans. This was a packing place.

Then also, my current job, I feel like . . . I don't know if I got it because I'm African. I think I got it more so because I have a bachelor's degree, but I feel, right or wrong, I feel like because I'm African and I brought up that I'm still going through the immigration process. . . . I went to the interview for what was to be the office manager. The job that I got offered and I got accepted was a paralegal. When they called me for the interview, the pay is different. Supposed to be 15 to 20 [dollars an hour]. I was offered something that pays 15. There's no 100 percent way of knowing this, but it's like yeah, you could have this person do this job or something similar to the job for a lower title, smaller pay. Occasionally I'm asked to do things that I believe do not pertain to my job. I kind of feel like it's due to the fact that yeah, I'm Black, and yeah, I'm immigrant, and my immigration status is not so good. . . . I can't be as vocal [as] say somebody that was White and be like, "No, I'm not going to do that. I'm going to tell HR."

Most of my coworkers are Americans or African American. I guess occasionally, when I talk, my accent might come out, or maybe my mannerisms are different. There's a little bit of tension with that. Nigerian jokes. Or not maybe jokes, but Nigerian queries or questions kind of resurface again. Kind of those things like, "Oh yeah, what do you guys believe in? Are you Christians?" Those kind of annoying questions that are maybe not bigoted in their intent, just like ignorance. I find it kind of ironic, big city population, diverse, but there's still a misunderstanding or a mistrust.

I would say, generally speaking, immigrants are more hungry, have more of a gut, but then you know, a caveat would be it's all based on the individual. Generally speaking, the immigrant has a little bit more of . . . that craving. Maybe not the fight, but the craving in them. That is what being an immigrant is. They are seeking something better. They're extra hungry.

The American Dream is not "getting by." At least it wasn't supposed to be. There's a dream that's changed, and maybe it's changing. It hasn't changed enough to define a new destination. I still believe that the new American Dream is still sort of what it's been or portrayed to be. You're supposed to have a comfortable life, not a "getting by" life. They used to depict it with the house, two kids, the car in the garage, the picket fence. That's still the American Dream. It's comfortability; it's not a hand-to-mouth existence.

I do not have it.

I'm still working on it. I'm still pursuing, Still chasing the dream, whatever. Shout out to Martin Luther [King].

KUNLE, AGE 32, NEW YORK

Kunle is the executive director of Everybody Dance Now! an organization that uses dance to provide a positive platform and outlet for underprivileged youth. He has been dancing since he was sixteen, but he ended up at Harvard training to be a doctor, a dream for many in this country. Soon Kunle realized that medical school wasn't his dream. He wanted to be a professional dancer.

I grew up in Memphis, Tennessee. This was confusing a bit because my parents were still definitely holding onto their African culture and tradition but trying to slowly adapt to understanding American values. I feel like I never really fit because I was, in terms of the African American and Black kids that were generationally from America, I didn't fit in with them because my parents were all about the education and studying. Growing up, people were saying, "Oh, why are you acting White? Why are you caring about your grades?" I never really fit in that culture.

We had a schedule of when we could watch TV, and I didn't know anybody else living like that. I definitely pushed to kind of fit more into "American" culture as quickly as I could, but I never really lost values, from my parents, of sacrifice. I started to adapt, like eating more American foods and doing things like sleeping over at friend's house, which my parents did not understand at all. They were like, "You have a house. You have a bed to sleep in. Why do you want to sleep in someone else's house?" They didn't know that was a thing because it was nothing that they were used to or grew up with, so it was slowly understanding and finding myself amidst the voices of my parents and the voices of my friends, really trying to identify who I was.

Success was going to a good school, of course excelling. College wasn't enough—you had to do something else, whether that be law school, whether that be medical school, whether that be some PhD or something. My dad's a PhD in physical therapy. My parents grew up with nothing. Education saved my family. My dad was supposed to be a farmer, but he made it. He made the decision that he was going to go to school, and that kind of changed the trajectory of our lives, so education for him was security. The more education you had, the more secure your future was, the less you were going to have to worry and never end up in the poverty that they had to experience.

I applied to a bunch of schools, got in them. My parents were like, "You're going to Harvard." I was leaning towards Columbia at the time because I ran track and field, and I just kind of clicked more with their coach, but, yeah, ended up going to Harvard. I went there with the intention of going to medical school afterwards, so I was a biology undergrad on top of premedical courses, and my thing was "I am going to be a doctor. That's how I pay back my parents' sacrifice." That was my initial plan after the four years.

I wanted to hate [Harvard] just so I could hold it over their heads like, "I'm here and I hate this place," but I couldn't. I think my year to that point had been the highest percentage of African Americans that were accepted. I think it was 10 point something percent of our class and I just started to meet people like me. The people I met were amazing. I started to see there's so many Nigerians and Africans that made up the population. We shared common stories of growing up and how strict our parents were and all these kind of things, but it was also sad because it was like, "Oh, there's some values here that aren't being replicated in the Black American experience," so these numbers are really skewed. If you took that 10 percent [of Blacks] that made it in, I'd say 80 percent were second-generation immigrants or international students. Students are coming from Senegal and Ghana and stuff like that directly, and the rest were, "Oh, my parents were African." It's crazy.

I think it made me realize how much slavery impacted not just the individuals but the mindsets of the communities that were later formed. I think the [Black American] kids I work with today, there is just generationally a culture of "do the best you can, but don't really expect much." That was the opposite of what I heard growing up. Growing up it was like, "You can take over the world if you want to, but you got to put some hard work in." Even just the value of family, just seeing how many kids I work with, they come from broken families. My parents were never affectionate at all, but I knew they would never, ever separate because they value family that much. No matter what argument, the kids matter. It's something I never had to worry about and same thing with the friends I met at Harvard. Their families are all together. They had that support from them. They had that encouragement, and they had that expectation. I think that might've been the thing. The expectation was excellence.

I don't really see that in the communities we're working in today. I don't see that because, again, if families are broken, then sometimes they don't have either parent, and they're just doing their best to get by, so it's hard to tell a kid like that, "Okay, the standard is excellence." I understand why they're not being pushed as much. I think there's something in that experience. I'm not sure the cause of it, but it's just American-born individuals went through that process of slavery that I think had an effect, a ripple effect of just the mindset. I think, coming here, my parents were not about that. My parents were like, "You can do whatever you want to do."

It's funny. My parents are racist. A lot of immigrants are when they see Black violence like, "Oh man, why are people doing this?" I think they spoke more negatively about the Black communities growing up than my White counterparts. I know I didn't share their sentiments. I think they [thought] that yes, this [racism] exists, but that doesn't mean you give up. That means you work harder. It doesn't mean you blame someone. That means you do what you have to do.

My parents are like, "We didn't come to America for you to chill, for you to be comfortable. We came to America for you to make it and change the face of what [our] household name is in the world." I had no excuse because they came from nothing in Africa. My dad, the first clothes he had was his school uniform. I have no excuse whatsoever. Whatever racism that might exist was worse when he was in the South in the '80s than it is now. So it was just also seeing what he had done and achieved kind of set an example. My mom came to the states in her thirties and went to nursing school and was probably the oldest person in her class, but she did it. I think having those models of achievement is something that is really important because then as much as people can tell you it, if you see it, then it's more tangible.

I think great things are formed out of pressure but I think pressure also keeps you from taking a step back. I felt like I was on someone else's path for four years of college. It's hard to take a step back when there's so much pressure on you to exceed and keep on moving and things like that.

I was on my parents' dream, you know, until I realized, I can't define my existence off of their happiness. The first decision was, "No, I'm not going to apply straight out of undergrad," like a lot of my friends did. I worked in the clinics two years, realized that I couldn't see myself going back and studying another four years, training another four years after that, just to end up doing this thing I wasn't really passionate about. So I kept up dancing, I worked in the day, and I'd just go take classes, teach class on the weeknights, then on weekends. I realized I got to keep this in my life. I was okay saying, "You know what, I'm in my twenties, and it's okay to try and figure things out. I was definitely worried [about my parents]. But I was more worried about what would happen if I just lived this life that wasn't mine.

My parents will get over it at some point.

Hopefully.

chapter six

LUCK

WE COULD HAVE BEEN AT ANY COOL BAR IN SANTA MONICA. TELEVISION SCREENS were blasting the Final Four game as a group of people watched excitedly, yelling at the screen. Another group clinked their glasses together for a toast. The bar was crowded, considering it was late afternoon on a weekday, and no one seemed in a rush to move. There was a relaxing vibe, aside from the tension from the game, so much so that it took me a second to remember we were not at any random bar but in the headquarters of a billion-dollar beverage company in Santa Monica. Jaleesa, a twenty-five-year-old who worked in marketing for the company, greeted me with a hug and then led me into their cafeteria-like common area. I noticed, as we settled into some chairs in the common area, that there weren't any Black or Brown folks having any fun at that bar. I noticed, in fact, that with the exception of a cafeteria worker, we were the only two Black people on the entire floor.

As we began our conversation on what it means to be a Black professional in America, I wondered briefly if we should move somewhere else, worried that Jaleesa might get in trouble for her thoughts. Then I realized that Jaleesa didn't care one bit about what anyone thought, so I decided to dive straight into my first question about how it felt to be a young, successful Black person in America. Immediately she (rightfully) put my question in check. "What really bothers me is that whole concept of 'you made it because you're a Black professional.' I think a lot of the time Black people, because of the state of Black people in America, you never really make it. As much as I climb the ladder and be successful, I still have family members getting pulled off the street. I have grandmothers and aunts who don't have enough for their retirement and [their] social security check isn't enough," she said with a sigh. "I think with other races you kind of have the luxury of, you come from a wonderful background and people make it and you have access to resources, so you only have to worry about yourself. With the Black professionals, we have our families, and we have the burden of that. It's hard to feel successful when you have a lot of your people suffering and especially people very close to you." Even before that, she said, most people don't get how hard it is for many young Black people, especially those lacking resources, to get to the professional level. She said it's not for lack of intelligence or determination, but more about a system that wasn't really made for Black and Brown folks. Jaleesa didn't believe she was where she was because of hard work alone. Instead, she believed, she was able to expand her horizons because of chance connections with other professionals and thanks to some programs that were geared toward helping kids from the South Bronx. She acknowledged that she had a good work ethic, but mainly, she said, it was just pure luck.

THE BLACK MIDDLE CLASS IS THE ULTIMATE REPRESENTATION OF whatever "success" is supposed to mean in America. They are also the representation of everything that's failed in America. Perhaps more so today, this group represents the ultimate contradiction, the many paradoxes in our culture. These are the folks who "make it." Who often find economic and political "success" in the White world, get so-called approval from larger society, but also suffer from unequal economic, social, and housing conditions. They are found in newsrooms, classrooms, and boardrooms, even the White House, yet they remain as misunderstood as ever.

The labeling of who is middle-class and even who is a professional is sometimes tricky, especially in the Black community, where class position is sometimes determined by status rather than income and wealth. Some scholars use white-collar job status to determine middle-class status, others use income, and others include blue-collar workers, as well as clerical and sales employees. Some studies on the middle class omit fire fighters and police officers, while others consider them essential to the group. Disagreement over definition aside, the group has grown substantially by most metrics since the mid-twentieth century. An article in the *New York Times* noted that 21 percent of Blacks now make $75,000 or more, a number that has doubled since 1970, and 13 percent make $100,000.[1] According to a report by the Pew Foundation, Black adults have seen large income increases between 1971 and 2015, more Blacks are educated, and more are in professional positions. While those numbers obscure a precarious class position, and being Black and middle-class is still different from being White middle-class (more of the Black middle class is comprised of clerical and sales positions; the White middle class is located in professional and managerial positions), today 40 percent of Blacks consider themselves part of this middle-class group.[2]

We like to talk about the Black middle class as, to quote sociologist Bart Landry, author of *The New Black Middle Class in the Twenty-First Century*, the "bellwether of Black progress." It gives us hope that the American Dream is still achievable, and that if Black professionals can build stable, middle-class lives, so too can any Black person in America. In Black America, though, there's no such thing as a stable middle class. As Landry and other scholars have found, Blacks have a harder time maintaining a middle-class life, even if their income might qualify them. In 2016, the *New York Times* put it succinctly: "Nationally, Black and White families of similar incomes still live in separate worlds."[3]

There's always been a Black middle class. During Reconstruction, a modest middle class emerged compromised of landowners, mulattoes, and government workers called for by the new laws. When Reconstruction ended and the Freedmen's Bureaus were shut down, most of the upward mobility Blacks had made was lost. It wasn't until Jim Crow raged in the early twentieth century that another Black middle class emerged, this time comprised of those offering services to the Black community that Whites refused to provide. These professionals, primarily educated at HBCUs, lived in Black communities and worked as doctors, lawyers, and funeral home owners.

It was this group that Black sociologist E. Franklin Frazier observed was in despair during the mid-twentieth century and found they had "developed a deep-seated inferiority complex" because they were unable to relate to many parts of society. "In order to compensate for this feeling of inferiority, the black bourgeoisie has created in its isolation what might be described as a world of make-believe in which it attempts to escape the disdain of whites and fulfill its wish for status in American life."[4]

For those who were part of the Black middle class, the frustrations were mounting as neighborhoods remained segregated, incomes stayed unequal, and White folk were still in charge of many facets of society. But soon progress seemed to be on the horizon. The Black middle class grew exponentially after President Lyndon B. Johnson signed the Civil Rights Act into law in 1964. Johnson stated that the act, which eliminated discrimination in the federal government and in public places, would make it so that "the only limit to a man's hope for happiness, and for the future of his children, shall be his own ability." Just like during Reconstruction, the federal government seemed to be finally helping Black Americans claim their stake in the American Dream. As civil rights laws were enforced, affirmative action programs implemented, and desegregation measures taken up, Black people finally began to see their status change. They finally had access to more schools, White-collar positions, and managerial jobs. The number of Blacks in white collar jobs increased from 11.3 percent in 1969 to 17.4 percent in 1978.[5]

In 1974, *Time* magazine praised the government for bringing social and economic justice to the Black community: "With little fanfare, without the rest of the society quite realizing it, more and more Blacks are achieving the American Dream of lifting themselves into the middle class. They have become as well heeled, well housed, and well educated as their White counterparts. . . . They have shown that, reports of its demise to the contrary, upward mobility still operates in America. To be Black in the U.S. is no longer to be subordinate." However, beyond the lede, a truer racial reality was revealed, and the progress of the Civil Rights Act was exposed for being frustrating and socially stifling, and many were more frustrated than ever. In 1978 William Julius Wilson published his book *The Declining Significance of Race*, which many interpreted as saying that class was more important than race (there's much disagreement about this assessment). It seemed to give license to elites to focus on the Black poor, rather than the Black middle class.

For a while there seemed to be progress—Blacks were going to college, getting into more professional positions, and moving to suburbs—but it was never the same middle-class as the White one. Scholar Benjamin Bowser noted, that unlike the White middle class, which came largely from immigrant upward mobility, two of the three periods when the country saw a Black middle class emerge came as a result of federal actions to remove racial barriers. Once again, cracks started to emerge, and much of that so-called progress was seen as superficial. In 1993, the "rage" of this group was revealed in a book, *Rage of a Privileged Class*, by journalist Ellis Cose. Stories about the consistent racism and frustration about being middle class, about Black men not getting cabs, and about racism against Black elites came to light. And people were shocked at the lack of mobility they thought had mirrored the Huxtables.

It's not that there hasn't been any progress. But according to a study by the Urban Institute, it's harder for young Black people to hold onto even the precarious middle-class status of their parents. The study found that Black kids raised in the 1970s and '80s lost their middle-class status in adulthood, with over 35 percent falling to the bottom of the income distribution as adults—far more than their White counterparts. Even worse, the report noted that 25 percent of Black kids will make less than 80 percent—80!—of what their parents earned.[6] Theories as to why this decline is occurring range from structural to cultural, with scholars blaming failing schools, lack of enforcement of laws prohibiting discriminatory practices, the rise of single-parent homes, social isolation, neighborhood segregation, and the number of Black employees in the federal government.

Focusing on middle-class occupations, Bart Landry wrote about this group in his book *The New Black Middle Class in the Twenty-First Century*. In 1960, 10 percent of Blacks had middle-class jobs. That number jumped to 13 percent in 1970, and by 2010, 52 percent of Black people were working in middle-class positions as professionals, executives, sales, clerical, and technical laborers. Landry noted that when talking of the middle class, most people think about the upper middle class—professionals and executives—and choses to center his research there.[7] I follow in his path, by largely looking at this one segment of the Black middle class, Black professionals.

Eighteen percent of Black millennials are in highly skilled professions in STEM fields, health care, technology, and what the Census calls "managerial and professional" jobs, a number that has been stable but not growing for at least the last eight years (using another more ambiguous term, "white-collar" positions, we find the share of Black millennials also has been stable).[8] While there is grave concern about the high rates of downward mobility among this group, that's only part of their narrative; matters of race, colorism, dating, and workplace politics also remain an important part of the discussion young Black professionals are having.

~

By the time Jaleesa was growing up at the turn of the twenty-first century, the South Bronx had been burned down and was on the precipice of a revitalization. Its progress wasn't as fast as Brooklyn's, but it was on the come-up—at least in mainstream culture. J-Lo had made the 6 train infamous; and Fat Joe and Big Pun continued to solidify the streets of the Bronx as hip-hop's birthplace, where KRS-One and Grandmaster Flash first started out. It wasn't all gravy. The buildings may have stopped burning, but the ashes still clouded the skies. The murder rate in the Bronx was the highest in the city, drugs like Tango were the new talk of the town, and HBO was filming its *Hookers at the Point* documentary, about sex workers in the area. But for Jaleesa, the South Bronx was simply home.

On the surface Jaleesa's life is the kind of story that White liberals love to salivate over—that of a child who "overcame" and "made it out." You know what I'm talking about: a daughter of a teenager without a degree, a high school life filled with seeing dead bodies, friends with gunshot wounds. But that's really not Jaleesa's story. Jaleesa grew up in a tough neighborhood. She grew up with a Black single mom, who gave birth to Jaleesa at the age of eighteen, and a Puerto Rican father. But her parents remained close friends, and she had a good relationship with her dad. She was surrounded by her family, and it extended beyond blood. Her community was her family, and back then she wasn't trying to leave. She had no desire to even move across the bridge to Manhattan because she was loved and protected on her streets. Sure, she said, it was "traumatic." She witnessed drug use and was surrounded by violence. But there was humanity that the media never discusses when they talk about the gangsters and drug dealers around her way. They were supportive. The "best" fathers she knew of. They talked to her about how she should carry herself as a woman. She was cared for, "when people didn't care about the kids in the South Bronx." Protected when the cops didn't. And most of all, listened to about her future, and supported about her dreams. There were no accusations of "acting White," and the drug dealers encouraged her to go to college, to make something out of herself, so that she wouldn't follow their same path.

She was clearly upset that some of these same guys and her younger brother were recently picked up for having heroin and fentanyl worth $22 million—crimes, she believed, that many of them didn't even commit.

She tied it to the growth of private prisons, which is now a five billion dollar industry that has largely been built on the backs of Black men.

"It was rough growing up, but it was beautiful," she continued. "It gave me a toughness, and it gave me an edge. It helped me become a Black professional and not mask who I am as a Black woman because I'm very connected to the reality of Black people." She acknowledged that there was a lot of pain and anger in that environment, and she had to learn to deal with it.

She was eventually able to push past all that while attending high school in Harlem. It was a positive experience for her, though she noted that a Black counselor discouraged her from going to her dream school, Spelman College, an all-women historically Black university in Atlanta. "They're not going to pick no girl from Harlem, from here in this city," she was told. Jaleesa had first learned about Spelman from another guidance counselor when she was in middle school, and soon after she was obsessed. She wanted to get away. Do something different. She wanted to go there because she had met a number of Spelman women who were doing big things in the world, and she wanted to be just like them. When she was a senior, she ignored the words of that counselor and applied anyway. She got in.

Her parents were supportive, though neither had much experience with a four-year college. Her dad, whose profession she didn't want to mention, went to Bronx Community College and got his associate's degree. Her mom had worked at the post office since she was eighteen and never had the chance to go to college. They didn't have a lot, but they were both smart, and her parents encouraged her to make her dreams happen. It was hard, but with the help of the United Negro College Fund and a couple of loans, she was able to attend Spelman. She loved it, though she recognized how privileged she was to even go. She watched people sharing books, wanting to go on semester abroad but not able to afford it, trying to do the best with the little they had, and it was rough. There were people who got sidetracked, who had "too much going on," who got out of control, but that was not the majority of her peers.

Facing life after college was even harder. With very little guidance, she had to try to secure her footing as a young Black professional. Jaleesa got opportunities, she said, because of other Black people who helped her get in the door. She believes that she continues to be judged on job applications because of her ethnic-sounding name and attributes her first gig at a PR agency, and many subsequent ones, to Black people. The company she works for now has a lot of Black people, but she said that is because there were a lot of Black people who worked there to begin with. "You hire within your network. If your company is saturated with White men, it's going to continue that way because they don't even hang out with Black people. So how are they going to hire someone? How are they going to know where to get these people from?" That train of thought has been backed up recently by a book by Rutgers Business School professor Nancy DiTomaso, author of *The American Non-Dilemma: Racial Inequality Without Racism*. Writing about this phenomenon for the *New York Times*, she said, "Favoritism is almost universal in today's job market. In interviews with hundreds of people on this topic, I found that all but a handful used the help of family and friends to find 70 percent of the jobs they held over their lifetimes; they all used personal networks and insider information if it was available to them." She said if anything, people wanted to avoid competition and that they looked for "unequal" opportunity. "They want to find ways to cut in line and get ahead."[9] Yet it is often these same people, she noted, that get upset over affirmative action programs.

Jaleesa made it clear that if you're a Black professional in the workforce, it's not just a fluke. "You didn't just apply for a job. You got lucky. You got someone, and they looked past who you were and looked at your skills. But once you get in the company, that doesn't mean that things change." She cautioned that while companies have started to realize the importance of having Black hires and also the purely economic value in the Black consumer dollar, that doesn't translate into progress. "They care about our money, not our experiences." She believes this means that while companies often say they want diversity, it doesn't mean they really care about Black folk. It's just helpful to have them in the room, for the sake of diversity. She echoes a lot of the sentiments of the Black professionals in Cose's seminal work about the struggles of Black professionals that came out when Jaleesa was still in diapers. In *The Rage of a Privileged Class*, Cose wrote, "Many well-educated, affluent Blacks have already found their way out of inner-city ghettos, yet they have not escaped America's myriad racial demons. Consequently, they remain either estranged or in a state of emotional turmoil."[10]

As I listened to Jaleesa, I thought it didn't seem that much has changed. While more of us may be getting into the room, getting a place at the table, we still have challenges. We struggle with moving up, we struggle with our own professional insecurities, and then we struggle with that "Black tax." It's understandable why Black people often languish in lower-level positions and middle-management roles, and many have a tough time with the balancing act required to achieve true success in these worlds. "You don't want to be seen with an attitude, you can't be too aggressive, you can't be too hard working, you have to be mindful because a lot of things can be associated with negative terms with Black people, right, so you kind of have to be mindful of that," Jaleesa said. "Or you want to mask your Blackness because you don't want to just be seen as a Black person, so then everything that you do goes unnoticed. Or you're putting in work and doing things and giving great ideas, but then someone else gets the credit for it because you work for them."

It's still tough, even in an era when more people are claiming they are "woke." While millennials superficially may seem to want to be better on issues of race—a study by MTV and David Binder Research in 2014 found that they believe that our generation is more equal than the past—wanting to be better and being better are two different things. According to the study, 84 percent of millennials said their family taught them that everyone should be equal no matter their race, and 89 percent actually believed that people should be treated equally. But only 37 percent of millennials said their family even talked about race (30 percent for Whites, 46 percent for millennials of color).[11] It shouldn't be surprising, then, that an analysis from the *Washington Post* using the General Social Survey in 2010, 2012, and 2014, found that the attitudes of White millennials, gen Xers, and baby boomers aren't that different about Blacks and their work ethic and laziness.[12] Even among the so-called hip, cool millennial generation, racist attitudes linger. And sometimes those racist attitudes translate into racist behavior. A study by the National Bureau on Economic Research in October 2015 found that because Blacks experience longer times of unemployment, managers are more skeptical once they are hired. This leads employers to monitor Black employees more intensely, and because they are highly scrutinized, more mistakes are found, and they are more likely to be fired for their errors, creating a cycle that's hard to break.[13]

Jaleesa said that as a Black professional, it's a constant battle to prove your worth while facing daily microaggressions and sometimes flat-out racism. She told me of a conversation that happened when she moved from one area of her office to a nicer part, with a view. She was boxing her things up when a White woman made a comment to her and a coworker: "Oh ya'll came from the hood, y'all in the penthouse suite now." Another White coworker she was with replied, "Man, y'all in the hood, we just gentrified this area. We just made it better." Sigh. Like others I spoke to, she told me about getting called other Black people's names, even to the point where she sat down for a meeting with two people, and then they realized she wasn't the Black person they were supposed to meet with. I laughed. Heartily. But I realized it wasn't funny. I've been there.

Jaleesa reiterated how Black folk have to constantly prove themselves on the job, while White men walk into a room and command an audience, or get away with having a shitty attitude. She believes Black folks can't expect managers to say, "Oh, they're just having a bad day"—instead Black employees more often than not have to suck it up and smile, or they'll be labeled as being "difficult." She relayed another story about a professional exchange with a colleague over email that she said sounded a little "harsh." She asked the colleague to be a bit more mindful of his tone the next time, and he cc'd multiple coworkers about her response. Jaleesa's manager eventually came up to her and said next time she should just "take a walk" and not be so "emotional."

With all these labels, she said, it's challenging. It can also be confusing when White folks try to connect with you by talking about Nicki Minaj or something "really" Black, instead of treating you like a person. It makes you uncomfortable. Insecure. And it's hard to figure out where to draw the line and how to challenge people when they say or do questionable things.

This is something we watched Barack Obama, in some ways the ultimate Black professional, struggle with during his presidency. In her book *Changing Times for Black Professionals,* Washington University professor Adia Harvey Wingfield describes the problem Obama had when talking about race during his presidency. He learned early on, it seemed, just how detrimental conversations around race could be after saying that police acted "stupidly" after arresting Harvard professor Henry Louis Gates as he was trying to enter his own home, citing statistics about how Blacks and Latinxs are arrested at higher rates. His approval ratings plummeted, and the next day Obama backtracked on his statement. Wingfield said that if Obama can't even fully address race as the president of the United States, then it's understandable that Black people still have a "dilemma" in the workplace. She notes that the Obama case, if anything, shows that for Blacks it may mean that having a better job experience is contingent on "minimizing or ignoring the way race shapes their lives or other Blacks."[14]

In a sequel to his book about Black professionals, journalist Ellis Cose's 2011 book, *The End of Anger: A New Generation's Take on Race and Rage,* surmises that young Black people are more optimistic about their future than ever and don't feel as limited by their race as before. While he doesn't focus on the Black middle class, much of his intergenerational research survey is with Black alumni of Harvard's business school. While the survey found the group was less "angry" and more positive about their future than previous generations, when asked about how to thrive at work, they still saw assimilation as a key to success. In listing ten rules for "success," rule 10 was to "never talk about race (or gender) if you can avoid it, other than to declare that race (or gender) does not matter." Cose, who used data from over five hundred surveys and two hundred interviews with a range of Black people said that so many made the same point over and over again: any kind of discussion about race ensures marginalization. "The larger point, unsettling and unpleasant as it may be, is that honesty about one's innermost thoughts is not generally a good strategy for advancement. For to share certain views honestly—and perceptions about race seem to top the list—is to risk being seen as a divisive presence *who* probably doesn't belong on the team." I couldn't help but wonder if this was progress.

Even allegedly safe spaces like diversity trainings, Wingfield found, stressed Black professionals out. They said, more often than not, they thought it was a place where Whites were allowed to alleviate their feelings of racial anxiety and animosity, without repercussion, but where their true feelings were expected to be mollified. Much of this, she said, ties to the image that people have of Black professionals. She refers to Patricia Hill Collins's understandings of how Black professional men and women are read—as the "Modern Mammy," the "Black Lady," and the "Educated Bitch," while men are seen as sidekicks and unmasculine, compared to working-class or blue-collar men, who are seen as criminal or athletic. These images in popular culture, Wingfield notes, ensure that Black professionals stay in a subservient role: they learn that they must conform to have professional success. More problematic, she writes, is that these stereotypes "serve to justify unequal treatment afforded to Black Americans."[15]

Some of these things aren't new. Some of them were present when Cose wrote about Black middle-class professionals in 1993, citing their rage and frustration and the apparent shock of White professionals, who were waking up to the fact that their Black counterparts might not be satisfied. Yet things have changed slightly. Much of the racism today, especially in the workplace, is less blatant, the type of racism that doesn't leave a trail. There are no segregated bathrooms or blatant disdain for people of color, but instead it's more undercover, more subversive—displayed in microagressions, indirect or subtle acts of discrimination, so that it is often harder to prove a behavior or action is biased.

It's a problem Jaleesa often runs into. People want to understand her plight, see where prejudice is happening, but they want to see the receipts, and it's just not always that easy to do in this era. Often it happens in person, not over email. It can be something as subtle as a White manager not giving her direction on an assignment. And the action can rest inside that ambiguous gray area. Moreover, she sees a certain care White folk sometime give to their "own kind." It's different from the way Black folk get mentored. "There's a certain mentorship they give to their own people. There's a certain luxury they give their own people when they're new to a work environment. They treat them with care. They say, 'Oh they're making mistakes. We need to mentor them; we need to take care of them.' Us, they say, 'They're making mistakes. They need to go on probation; they need to leave.'" She thinks that this is in part because success for Black folks is impersonal to Whites. "There's just no connection because you don't look like them, because you don't share the same experience. So there's just not a concern."

She has found more guidance and mentorship from other Black folks, but that doesn't mean that all Black people share her view of solidarity. She told me a story about an office Halloween party at which, unsurprisingly, a White coworker dressed up as Harambe, the gorilla that was killed at the Cincinnati Zoo after a young Black boy accidentally slipped into his cage. Jaleesa noticed this coworker was carrying a Black baby doll as a prop that he kept throwing in the air. She was upset and offended, but when she told some other Black folks how she felt, they brushed it off. One woman told her just to leave it alone. "Some Black professionals have been so trained and taught to ignore stuff like that, they've normalized it."

∽∽

Jaleesa still has a tough time with people like that, though it seems she realizes this may become the norm as she goes deeper into the professional middle-class world, but she's certainly not used to it. In fact, when I ask her what it's like being a middle-class professional, she hesitates for a minute. "I mean it's so funny because you saying 'middle class,' and I'm realizing that I'm middle-class because being from the hood, I've always felt connected to that. But technically I am middle-class. There is a disconnect, and I think that's more the middle-class fault. When you start to become middle-class, when you start to have access . . . financial stability and just things that people you grew up with didn't [have] . . . because White people have so many resources, you aspire to that . . . which means you aspire to live in a neighborhood that doesn't include Black boys in hoodies walking around," she said. "It's crazy, you grow up feeling connected to those people, but then as you start to see and become more embedded into the reality of what American society is, you want to be removed from that. So you go from sitting on a train next to a young Black boy to holding your pocketbook because you felt threatened by that. You don't want to go to the hood spot because you no longer dress in hood clothes, so they're going to see you, and you think, 'Oh they're going to want to rob me,' or 'They're going to want to do things.'" She said she refuses to live that type of middle-class existence, but she worries how her life as a professional will influence her future, how it will affect her as a parent, and where she and her boyfriend will live.

She's already decided that she doesn't want her daughter, if she has one, to take ballet classes because Black women were told for so long that they couldn't. She'd rather her do something that "she's already accepted in," something that is authentic to her history. She also doesn't want her future kids to go to a traditional Christian church, since that too was used to oppress Black people. "I didn't go to school with one White person, like they're going to go to school with White people. And they're going to have White friends. Is my son going to want to date a White girl? Stuff I think about. How is that going to impact their Blackness? How is that going to impact their perception of Black oppression? Are they going to all of a sudden think that they're not oppressed because we live in a nice house in Los Angeles and we go to film premieres?" She is clearly stressed about these questions. "It's a huge fear for me because I know my kids are not going to experience their Blackness the way I did. I don't want that to cause them to have a false perception and false reality of the Black experience, because the reality is we're all in the same boat, and I think people need to understand that."

In the meantime she's doing on-air work in her downtime as a red carpet host and aspires to have a bigger voice as she climbs the corporate later. She hasn't forgotten about the South Bronx either. She plans to start a program there for underprivileged youth. In the office, she's focused on making the best of her professional situation. "As Black professionals, Black millennials do not have stability and security in the workplace. What differentiates us from every other race is we always feel like we could lose our jobs, and that's important because what that does to someone psychologically and how that impacts them. I won't know for another ten, twenty years, but it has to do something. It has to limit you in some way from feeling like you deserve a promotion, from feeling like you deserve a salary raise."

It was a White woman who told Jaleesa that she needed to make more money. It wasn't about her being some sort of White savior, but the fact that this woman had more confidence than Jaleesa did showed her how she had been undervaluing her worth. "I really want people to understand and sympathize that just because you're a Black professional, it doesn't mean you don't come in and question every day. Every day. When I have a doctor's appointment, I have to be late to the office. I'm worried. 'Oh my God, am I late too much?' 'Am I taking too many sick days?' 'Oh, I'm going on vacation for a week, and I'm doing too much?' 'I want to work from home. Everyone works from home, but if I do it . . . ?' You feel the need to always let people know where you are.

It's just—we never feel safe. We never feel comfortable. We never truly feel comfortable."

As I left Santa Monica, I realized I never asked Jaleesa a follow-up question about the recent arrest of her younger brother for drug possession. I'd heard about the federal bust, which had happened a few blocks away from where my boyfriend lives in the rapidly gentrifying South Bronx. I didn't really think much about it; Black and Brown men getting arrested by the NYPD is nothing out of the ordinary. Jaleesa was clearly upset by the arrest, but she didn't dwell on it. I didn't either. These types of stories are so much a part of the experience of the young Black professional in America that I hadn't even flinched. It felt normal, just a part of life. I shook my head, realizing how different the experience of young Black professionals is from our White millennial counterparts. We often walk a tightrope between the hood and the elite. We are always somewhere in between, code switching, pussyfooting around. It's a tough task having to operate with this duality. In order to deal with it, like many I spoke with, I recognized that you have to become numb to some things. Too many things.

AFTER MEETING WITH JALEESA, I KEPT THINKING ABOUT A brownstone party I went to a few years ago. It was the type of event I should have been excited to go to, but all I wanted to do was run away. Usually at these parties I feel either invisible or like some kind of token, the representation of the "few" of us who have made it. That night was no different, though it seemed invisibility was winning out. I scoured the room for familiar faces when I walked in. I found a few and happily made small talk for a few minutes after a few awkward minutes lingering around some food. I glanced around the room. There weren't many people of color in the room. Relieved, I saw a young Black man I knew from his social media presence. I tried, in vain, to give him "the stare." But he didn't even look my way. In fairness, I didn't try to speak to him either. Maybe he was shy, I thought. I gave him another look, a sort of knowing glance that said, "Word, you don't have my back?" He was more accomplished than I was. More successful. More at home, it seemed, in this crowd. He kept chatting with some White folks. I turned away. Maybe I didn't have his back either.

Losing interest in him, I saw a White woman I had written an email to asking about a program she ran. As soon as I approached, she disappeared. I noticed this happening all night. As I was in my feelings about this woman ignoring me, I ran into a man I'd sat on a panel with. He looked right through me. Maybe, I thought, it was because I changed my hair. Two other people I'd met before also seemed to have forgotten me and soon, I was just tired.

Invisibility is an unoriginal concept in Black thought, but an apt one to describe our existence, particularly as Black professionals. In some ways we are hyper-visible, when it comes to culture or as tokens of diversity, but who we are is often so obscured from the public and popular culture, and our humanity invisible. I sat thinking about these things, that night, which didn't turn out all that bad. I spent time with a bunch of lovely Black and Brown women I'd met, who recognized me immediately and greeted me warmly and had a few wonderful conversations. I also chatted with a few White colleagues with ease. But the other 50 percent of the time, I felt unimportant, unremarkable. Maybe it's that insecurity creeping in. In my professional life, I've always struggled with insecurity. I've always wondered, as Jaleesa did, "Am I good enough?" It started in third grade, when I switched from my public school with Black and Brown kids to all-White elite Catholic schools. I was still smart, still in accelerated classes, but I was never in the top honors program again. I will always remember how they looked at me. It was even more pronounced as I got older. I'll never forget one teacher's steely glare during my freshman world history class. She always called out my name with contempt, and my words, my presence, never seemed to matter to her. At some point,

I think, I gave in. I stopped raising my hand, I stopped studying as hard for tests. I convinced myself I was incapable. Perhaps my invisibility was cathartic to her. She gave me a decent grade, but the way my newly invisible presence pleased her stayed with me through my life. It was hard to reassert myself again.

Even in college, on graduation day, I remember one of my beloved professors telling me how my insecurity drove me, fueled my ambition. I think she was right, and still is, but I also remember her telling me that day in 2003 to get over it. I still haven't. When I was just learning about field producing in television, a job I'd long dreamed of doing, I started having panic attacks. I'm not sure if my bosses ever knew it or not, but my faint sweats and nausea weren't a result of sickness. It was panic. A trip to a shrink and a bottle of Xanax helped somewhat, but I couldn't help wonder if this is what "making it" meant. Moving on up? So nervous I needed drugs to help me get through? And that constant feeling of not being smart enough? It's probably no surprise that I ended up in a doctoral program, just to prove otherwise.

I was thinking about these things as I left that brownstone party, that party that I guess was supposed to be a sign that I'd "made it." It wasn't an anomaly. I'd been to several like it. I was kicking myself for spending an hour driving to the city, when I noticed I had a missed call and text from my high school friend about my old neighbor. He'd just been arrested. My neighbor, the one who always spoke to me no matter how many years had passed. My neighbor, who I sort of left behind when I went to the college prep Catholic school. My neighbor, who'd been arrested for drugs, who joined a gang, who had his house shot up. That neighbor, who asked my mom about me every time he saw her, had been arrested in another big bust for drugs and guns. I sighed. I wondered what the fuck I was doing out there with people who saw me as invisible when this one dude who saw me every time was suffering. Had this become my reality? Was this success? Talking about a book on upward mobility to people who had already showed me I was forgettable? Talking to folks who seemed to tell me that I only mattered if I accomplished something they could understand? Was that my Black professional success?

JALEESA GAVE ME GOOD INSIGHT INTO THE BLACK PROFESSIONAL workplace, but I had more questions, especially how the role of gender intersected with class. A recent study in the *New York Times* found that Black boys, even those who grow up middle-class and are from affluent homes and communities, earn less than their White counterparts with the same background. Succinctly put, rich White boys stay rich, while rich Black boys become poorer. The study wasn't exactly surprising, but it seemed an apt reminder of how race often supersedes class, particularly for Black men, even those who have the exterior monikers of success. So I reached out to Simon, chief technology officer for a small startup who lives in San Francisco.

Simon quickly glosses over what seems like a rock-star childhood that led him to MIT. He grew up in the suburbs in Southwest Florida. I could tell he was smart, but he said he just winged the whole college experience. I didn't really believe him at first, but after a few rounds of questioning, his story stayed the same. He wrote essays and applied to a few colleges; MIT was his top choice, but he wasn't sure if he would get in. His parents, who didn't go to college, didn't help him with applications. He proofread everything himself and hoped for the best. He was lucky, he said, that after he took the PSATs, colleges started swarming around him based on his scores, and colleges made sure he was interested in their programs. Maybe Simon is a genius, I really don't know, but he got into his first choice of college. He was happy, but in the end much of his decision around MIT also circled around funding. His parents didn't have any money to give him for college—his mom was a nursing assistant, and his dad worked construction. Aside from the University of Florida, MIT was the only place that gave him a good financial package. Plus, it *was* MIT, he said casually. He finished college only $20,000 in debt, an amount he thinks is pretty good in this day and age.

Looking back, he wishes he had more mentors during high school. He said there was only one teacher who seemed interested in helping him with planning his future, but he never really felt he had guidance about his career process. "I'm like, is it because I'm a young Black man and no one sees himself in me and, like, [wants to take] me under their wing? Or am I just an ordinary person that no one likes? It's one of those things where it's like, you are always sort of, is it because I'm Black? Is it something else? I don't know. I can't tell."

But while he lacked adult mentorship in high school, when he got to MIT, he immediately had support from MIT's community of color. He said they were welcoming and warm, and he made friends he has to this day. It was part of his survival, even in this supposed postracial country, because there were still so few students of color at MIT. They had to stick together; it was a necessity. He said MIT is a hard school for people of any color: it's a cold place, sink or swim, and depending on your background, you can get lost. But Simon said of his circle that it was nice not having to explain yourself, or not having to feel that you were representative of a whole race all the time. "There is a certain luxury of being one of many," he said. Fortunately for him and because of this extended network, Simon did well. After college he thought about consulting and working in banks, but he said they never really felt right—it was like fraternity brothers or "macho bros"—and eventually he landed at IBM. He said it just seemed to be a good match. The company appeared to be concerned about inclusion and tried to recruit students of color. It was a good job out of college. He was happy, too, that he got to stay on the East Coast.

Simon says he was lucky and acknowledged that the job interview and hiring process in the tech world are stressful. Though many years have passed since he had his start, his own insecurity creeps back up sometimes. "Even now, I've worked many jobs, and if I go to an interview, I'd still be sort of like, 'Is this person going to dislike me or think

I'm not as good as them, because of their impression of what I look like?'" In the tech world, he said, it's supposed to be a meritocracy more than other fields. Yet the tech industry is notoriously nondiverse. It's something a number of tech firms have expressed a desire to address. Google just started an incubator program for students from Howard University, for example. But overall the numbers are woeful: just 5 percent of workers in the tech industry are Black and Latinx (including 3 percent at Facebook and Twitter and 2 percent at Google).[16]

Simon says it's not an accident. "People are just hiring their friends, and typically your friends are probably not the best person for the job. There are so many people who I have encountered in my career who fit the profile for a tech person, White, male, maybe, seemingly smart, but then they get hired because they flip by with this profile, and they will talk a good game, but when it comes down to actually doing stuff, you just got hired because you fit the stereotype. It's kind of annoying," he said. "I have to just feel like so on point and so good. Be twice as good, sort of thing." Simon thinks this means he also has to dress better than his counterparts. Even in the super-casual world that feels *so* millennial, where hoodies and jeans are the unofficial uniform, Simon said he still has to be superior.

He tries not to dwell on it. "Obviously it's not fair. It's problematic. What am I going to do about that? I have a job, and I got bills to pay and that sort of thing. I can't obsess about the unfairness too much, because I would just get nothing done." So instead he finds his own ways to cope. "I feel like these are the things I almost got to block out because thinking about them makes me annoyed and angry."

But despite his attempts to block thoughts out, he still seemed frustrated, particularly when he talked about supervising people. He said that in his various positions he has had to manage people, but in one instance, he was getting more pushback and resistance from a young person, someone much more junior than him. He had an "inkling" that the person had an issue with him because he is Black, but he wasn't sure. Like Jaleesa, he pointed out that these days, there's usually so much deniability that you're often never really sure what is happening. "Everything is just so gray that you can't actually do anything because for an action to be taken, you need definitive proof. You need a series of emails from HR and other people backing you up and that sort of thing." It's hard, he noted, because people are particularly sensitive about being called racist. Today, no one thinks of themselves as racist; it's socially unacceptable. But racism is still everywhere. He used the tech world as an example: "Many of them [White people], especially in the tech world, are like, 'Well, White and Asian people are just smarter, that's why there is disparity.' We use beliefs that are sort of dressed up as scientific and such, but like under any sort of scrutiny falls apart. They will not call themselves racists, but they are just like . . . That's just how it is. This group of people is just better at this than this other group of people, whether they'll be women, could be color." Often times, he said, they won't say it's racism. They'll never say, "I'm not hiring someone because they are a person of color." "They'll be like, 'Oh, they're just not good enough.'" He said there is also this perpetual idea that when hiring, managers are looking for a good "fit." There can be a totally qualified candidate, but if the hiring managers don't see them as a good fit, which he said can mean seeing themselves having beer or hanging on the weekend with someone, then they get "bounced." "That is such a recipe for just hiring people you are comfortable with, and they look like you or reflect demographics you are comfortable with." Still, he's optimistic. He said the same tech world has democratized the tools to get ahead. It's opened up a whole new world and has given more voices the opportunity to get past the gatekeepers. He said that while "it's still sort of bad," and that the "giant" institutions have not still really invested in nurturing and grooming Black and Brown talent (we talked before the Google announcement), he thinks things are getting better, and he's generally happy.

It's not just his work life that can give Simon a headache. In his personal life, Simon, like other Black professionals I spoke to, is pulled in different directions. When he goes out, he goes to places where other upwardly mobile people hang out; he doesn't really go to places where there's a strong blue-collar presence. When he lived in Harlem seven years ago, there were certain fancy bars that seemed to cater solely to Black professionals. Now he thinks a lot of those places have closed, because Black professionals no longer need those segregated spaces (and, I suspect, because Harlem has been gentrified).

I asked him the dreaded question about relationships. I felt I had to ask: countless Black women, particularly professionals, have brought it up to me. Usually they're frustrated that Black professional men, they say, don't want to date them. I know a number of Black professional couples, but I understand these women's plight, especially in cities like Los Angeles and New York, where the competition over dating is fierce. As Simon explains it, "Being sort of like upwardly mobile, successful or wherever, puts you into environments, certain situations, et cetera, where it is you just run into more women of various backgrounds, and so it makes it easier to date them. This is how the world works. I've dated Black women; I dated a Black woman last night. I don't think, at least for me, success in any way implies not dating a Black woman." Instead, he said, it's actually the other way around. "I do know some people who were like, you should exclusively date Black women. I've been told this by Black friends I know. They are like, 'You are a "good one," and it is a shame if you are not dating a Black woman.'" In this post–Barack and Michelle era, he said, there's pressure for Black professional millennials to emulate that, to have this "idealized" Black love. "I remember a particular situation once where I was dating this Black woman, and we were in the train together, and an older woman was like, 'It's so good to see Black young people dating each other.'" It's those kind of societal "endorsements" that seem to annoy him. But he doesn't put too much stock in all that.

He gives back to MIT to help low-income students. He's working on outreach projects and trying to keep focusing on the future. When someone chastised him because he never had a job doing manual labor, he reveled in the idea. "Recently someone was like, "Simon, have you ever worked manual labor in your life for a job?" I was like, no. They were like,

"You just don't understand," and then I was like, I'm not going to feel bad about that because my parents busted their asses so I could answer no to this question." Still, Simon says he wouldn't exactly say that he has "made it." "To call myself successful would mean that I'm at an endpoint or something. I still feel like I have so much more to do."

His parents are both over sixty-five, they own a house, and while he considers himself upper-middle-class, he won't get any inheritance. He's secure, but he's also still helping his family out. When his mom wasn't working for a while and didn't have insurance, he had to make sure there was cash on hand in case something happened. He's relieved now that she is on Medicare, but it was a reminder just how different the lives of young, Black, upper-middle-class people can be from their White counterparts. His choices, he seemed to say, weren't exactly free. He was not exactly trapped but not able to fully just *be*. "One of the things I was thinking, 'Maybe I should have tried to be a photographer.' In reality, I didn't have parents to subsidize me while pursuing that sort of thing. Maybe that's something my kids could do, who knows?"

~

BEING A YOUNG BLACK PROFESSIONAL TO A NUMBER OF PEOPLE means keeping a low profile, not always speaking your opinion while pretending some postracial bliss exists. Even those who have vowed to be an advocate for Black folk have sometimes tempered their voices. Jaleesa never went to Human Resources to report that Black baby doll she saw being tossed in the air, and Simon still doesn't exactly understand the real reason why one of his supervisees was giving him pushback. And most professionals Cose interviewed knew never to talk about race if they wanted to get ahead in predominantly White spaces. That doesn't feel like the postracial, even-playing-field, color-blind America that many think we're living in. We are being killed in the street, gunned down by cops, and many of us are mad. Following the shooting of Michael Brown in Ferguson in 2014, there have been myriad protests, and Black Lives

Matter gained momentum. I spoke to a number of young Black professionals about how they were dealing with being Black during this Black Lives Matter era. They told me that they fear professional retaliation, rejection, or being perceived as a stereotypical "angry" Black person. It's tough enough to work in a system that privileges White professionals, they said—and taking on the role of activist makes it even harder. They have to confront issues surrounding free speech, employment, and respectability that, they believe, their White counterparts simply do not. But it hasn't stopped many of them from finding ways to continue to speak out against what they see is unequal and unfair treatment.

ON A SUNNY THURSDAY AFTERNOON IN EARLY 2016 TANISHA anxiously watched Facebook to check on a new clothing line she'd just launched. The limited collection featured sweatshirts and T-shirts with slogans like #GetSomePurpose and BAE—Become An Entrepreneur. Tanisha explained that she was trying to encourage more Black people to follow their dreams, just as she did four years ago, when she decided to become her own boss after a slew of corporate gigs. She founded a global marketing company based in Harlem, and she loves her work. But as friends, family, and clients streamed through her office space, the gregarious twenty-seven-year-old explained frankly how hard it is for a Black person to build a profitable business in today's politically and racially charged climate.

In the wake of the police shootings that summer in Minnesota and Louisiana, Tanisha, who also knows Jaleesa from college, was glad that young Black men and women were taking to the streets, their campuses, and social media to let America know that they were tired, frustrated, and angry. It was an exciting time for activism, said the New York native whose father used to call her "little Angela Davis." But it was both a blessing and a curse for someone like her—that is, someone who wanted to empower Black and Brown communities while simultaneously working in the very White world of marketing. Tanisha also makes a point of avoiding conversations about race and racism with her clients. Occasionally she'll tweet something about inequality or discrimination, but she believes that, overall, Black people who work in professional environments have to temper their activism more than their White peers. "I do think your reputation is everything," she said. "That's why I am kind of very selective about what I put on social media. When it comes to business, you got to take the emotion out of it."

By the following fall, Tanisha thought the climate had changed a bit. She said that after the violence that took place over the summer of 2016—first the shootings of two Black men, Alton Sterling and Philando Castile, by law enforcement officials, followed by deadly attacks on police officers in Dallas and Baton Rouge—she and her Black professional peers became determined to let their frustrations be heard publicly. "I'm still not a protester, but I have been a lot more vocal on my stance, because it's kind of insensitive to not say anything if you're Black with all that's happening. This is no longer a poor man's war or an urban war," she told me. "It's really looking at the justice system and how we're living as human beings on this Earth."

Twenty-seven-year-old Rebekah, a medical student in California, is part of White Coats for Black Lives. She understands the hesitation among Black professionals to speak their minds because of fears of offending or stepping on the toes of people who might hire or do admissions for a later job. She believed that she was facing even more scrutiny in the classroom by some of her teachers because of her activism. "I have felt more backlash as a result of being involved, but it is motivating me to become more involved and make sure changes continue to occur," she said. "As more publicity is being brought to this issue, more medical students will feel compelled to join because more people will be able to draw upon their personal experiences and feel a need to be involved." She said it's very easy to believe in a postracial society when your environment reflects that, but she said that the rise of Donald Trump and his racist rhetoric was blatant proof that we're not living in such a society now.

Traditional civil rights groups, like the Urban League and the National Association for the Advancement of Colored People, have always been bastions of the Black professional class. In some ways, newer groups, like Black Lives Matter and the broader coalition group, the Movement for Black Lives, which is more decentralized and often labels itself as a working-class organization, represent a shift away from this tradition and back to that of more militant groups in the vein of the Black Power movement or the Student Non-Violent Coordinating Committee. Still, the more radical message of Black Lives Matter seemed to resonate with many Black professionals, though in private conversations, they admitted that they still felt obligated to police their rage. Tanisha, who was a secretary for the Urban League in New York, believed there was more at play than just fear of retaliation. There was also a divergence of priorities between Black professionals and their lower-wage peers. "There are the educated, who focus more on politics and lobbying and understanding the law, and then there are people who jump on police cars and burn them up," she said. "People who are young professionals in those spaces and moving up—I think they are more focused on fighting inside than going out and marching. Their fight is just different."

This kind of divide is not new. During the Civil Rights Movement, groups fought over tactics and optics, often along class lines. This divide, and the tensions it provokes, is something that many young Black activists are concerned about. Kei, a twenty-six-year-old activist and former manager of a community workspace in Harlem and an organizer for Black Lives Matter, said there is a difference in the kinds of actions Black professionals participate in. Kei said these professionals often showed their support at a silent vigil, on Twitter, or at an academic conference, but were missing at more public or confrontational protests, where clashes with the police might be likely. This was particularly true of those working in more corporate environments, as opposed to creative professionals, teachers, and nonprofit workers. "I definitely see corporate folks as focused on assimilating up through the system," Kei said. "For some reason, they believe having a seat at the table is where you get your power from. Where, more so for me, it's great to have a seat at the table, but if what I'm saying isn't being heard, then why does the table even matter? Why should I care about getting in the room?"

The conversations around respectability seemed to crest for Black professionals particularly when Marissa Johnson and Mara Willaford disrupted a Bernie Sanders rally in Seattle in August 2015. "When the Black Lives Matter leaders ran up on Bernie Sanders and were screaming in his face asking him questions, my first reaction was 'That's not the way to do it,'" Tanisha said. "You are just perpetuating the stereotypes that they already have, and unfortunately our whole lives are about tearing down the stereotypes." Marissa challenged the idea that Black protesters have to act with a certain middle-class respectability in mind. "There's always this impetus put on Black folk to show yourself as morally above, pristine, or worthy of humanity that isn't placed on other people. It produces the desire to always be the perfect martyr," she said.

It seems difficult for young Black professionals to figure out exactly where to draw the line. "It's hard because you don't want to say, 'I have to conform to American standards,' when the standards never had me in mind in the first place," said Tanisha. "We have to unfortunately get past that first barrier of not being a threat." "It is a such a rarity to be a Black professional," Rebekah added. "We have to be conscious that unfortunately we are speaking for a race, even if I don't think I should be speaking for a race."

This isn't to say Black professionals and elites haven't been active in a myriad of ways. There have been Black professionals taking to the streets, donating money, getting arrested, and participating in die-ins. And organizers have said Black professionals in particular have been useful in trying to change the institutions they work in, whether it's creating new curriculum, organizing academic conferences and reading lists around social justice, and posting messages about police brutality. Even before NFL player Colin Kaepernick began his protest, Beyoncé and Jay-Z were quietly said to have donated money to help activists make bail after the unrest in Baltimore following the death of Freddie Grey, and the late singer Prince performed a "Rally 4 Peace" benefit concert in the area. Anthony,[17] a thirty-four-year-old organizer from New Jersey who works in public policy, said Black professionals were entering the movement in their own way. He used Will Smith and Jada Pinkett Smith's Oscar boycott a few years ago as an example. "That's their Black Lives Matter," he said. "Not to say that they're not concerned with guns being pulled out and cops, but they're saying, 'Hey, I'm worth $100 million, but I know because of the systemic injustices that happen in Hollywood I should be worth a billion dollars.'"

Tanisha also saw the movement broadening out. One of her friends started a political action committee to support Black politicians, and others were figuring out how they could advance this idea of Black power. "So it's no longer just Black Lives Matter, which is great, right? Because it also shows diversity in our communities and the power that we have overall. Our power isn't just by marching in the street and screaming, 'Black Lives Matter.'" Tanisha said activists were showing that their dollars and votes matter as well. "Point blank period: I think people are just tired. Tired of having to wake up every single day and see another hashtag or see someone else violated. It's out of control." Kei believes that as the movement goes on, young Black professionals will show more public support for the cause. "Young Black professionals have come to understand that, one, the system isn't made for them, and, two, what they bet on—what they put their money into, going to college, getting into student debt, all these things—is not really for them," Kei said. "They've just been sold a dream."

MILLENNIAL MOMENT: **5-0**

RON,[18] AGE 33, THE BOOGIE DOWN (SOUTH BRONX)

One of my friends was getting a ticket in my building. He was with my little brother, and I went over there because he was on the Row—he had just came out. He did something he wasn't too proud of. I went over there being a friend. You know, people change. He was getting stopped for a beer. So I went over there like, "Oh excuse me, that was my beer." For me it's a ticket; for him, he's doing ninety days. [The cop] still gave him a ticket. I went over there for nothing. So he's like, "Thanks, man. You tried." He had to call his parole officer.

I can feel the pain, you know. I hate that shit. So I went to get him a cigarette. The same cops was there. I'm going down on my bike, and I was like, "Now they gonna mess with me." They was just waiting to see if we picked the beer back up or whatever. I got off the bike. I sat down; they came over to me: "Let me get your ID." Right there alone I was like, This is personal. This is not procedure. If I was speeding, the procedure would be give you my ID; you run it; if I have a warrant, then I step out. Then you search. That's the procedure. Even if I have a bike. Just because I'm on a bike does not mean we going to war. I'm not dangerous; you see I live here. I wasn't doing any crime. He threw me on the wall. He called the 85 on me, and I know what that means. It's like "officer being assaulted"; that means that everybody come kick ass.

He's like, "You gonna resist arrest?" I said, "What arrest, what did I do?"

I had no record. Not even a warrant at that time, not even a ticket. So if you'd ran my name, I didn't have nothing. He changed my whole life because he was mad because of what happened and the way I spoke to him. I upset him some way, enraged him some way, and he showed power.

I went to the Boat. It's on Hunts Point. They call it the Love Boat, compared to Riker's Island. It scared me. The longest I been in jail is eight days, because of them, because of the false charge. Eight days. It's very, very scary. I seen people fighting over stuff—coffee, tissue, a orange. It's cold. They take everything from you. Jail is full of rapists, murderers, thieves.

I didn't have bail. It was like $1,500. [Bronx Defenders] bailed me out. If they didn't bail me out, I would've spent [Thanksgiving] in there.

It fucked up my whole, everything. I worked selling tickets. Eight days I was gone. I ain't worked since. I had one [interview] with the Mets that same year, and they looked [at my record]. And it showed resisting arrest and assault. No conviction. Pending. It screwed me over.

My résumé is good. I don't have no felonies; I don't even got no cases on me. And they seen that open case. I told my lawyer about it; I brought it to her attention. I was like, "Can y'all either hurry up with this case because I can't even get a job." I had to do a lot of weird things to sustain myself. It's been two years.

Luckily I had some kind of a support system. You got to eat everyday, and you need this, my kid needs stuff. She asking me for book bags, and even right now, like, I had to do a little babysitting for my brother's nephew.

It's like you're already been locked up. We ain't even do nothing, and it's still affecting you after because it's on your record. I had sixteen court dates. You can imagine. Every time I went to court, it was like, "Oh, we're not ready."

People go through worse. But like we in the hole. In the hole, like a six-feet grave, trying to dig out that motherfucker, right? And here come more dirt, kickin' more dirt on you.

Everything got cleared. If they hadn't bailed me out, I'd have been traded. I'm hungry, starving, and they waving steak in front of my face, and that steak is a cop-out. Take this community service. Take this time served. Take this disorderly conduct. You just want to get back to your life, your family. I'm telling you, I wouldn't even have fought for my freedom. I'd have been, like, "Yeah. You know what? I've been here for so long, maybe I did hit him." You start to contradict yourself. "Maybe I did?"

I just got my records sealed from that case.

It's racial. Everybody once stole something. White people take more stuff, but they not the ones that are focused on. I was just watching last night, like, with the Enron people. They stole so much money, took people life savings. How evil is that? You talkin' about a person who stole a pair of jeans? Compared to this Enron person? You can't compare that to million[s], you know? But that's the difference. We the only ones gettin' aimed at—like, that's it. Everybody doin' wrong, but they only want to lock up us. You think their kids are not smokin' weed? They not joy-riding in cars? They not doin' the shit we do? Partying and doing drugs they shouldn't do? But they the ones that's not getting in trouble. They comin' and trouble us. It's the Black people.

I think the only way, as a people, that we are gonna come together, is if we have an alien invasion. Did you hear this? An alien invasion. We all need help for that. I mean, a White president or Black president, we need somethin' that threatens the whole world. Like aliens come down, right? Now we together.

What does it feel like to be a young Black man in America? I used to say you were born with a felony. It's like a curse. It's a gift and a curse. It's more of a gift. Everybody want to be Black, but nobody want to be Black. You want to rock the hair styles, the dreads, the braids. Everybody want our culture, but they don't want to be us. Forget the curse, it's bittersweet. You already born with the odds against you. You make it out, God must know your name.

chapter seven

FAME

LOS ANGELES IS KNOWN AS THE CITY OF DREAMS. IT'S THE PLACE WHERE WE'RE supposed to fulfill our wildest dreams, satisfy all our hopes, realize our gluttonous desires for money, power, fame, and beauty. La La Land. Where anyone with a smattering of talent, guts, and grit trying to make their fantastical, over-the-top dreams come true. Los Angeles has always held this promise, if you somehow look beyond the pillaging of land, love of the almighty dollar, obsession with the superficial, and a litany of other sins. Starting with the Gold Rush in the mid-nineteenth century, when people ravished the city, to the Golden Age of cinema, Los Angeles, a city that was founded by twenty-six people with African ancestry,[1] represents the American Dream in ways that few other places do. Unlike New York, where Wall Street and the "Greed is good" mantra rule, LA promises something else: fame and celebrity.

For Black millennials, Hollywood may not be sold like the NBA or the rap game, but with the Gram, Snapchat, reality TV, and YouTube making damn near everyone a star (at least in their minds), the silver screen in some ways seems more accessible than ever. In the last few years,

Black industry professionals have picked up awards for acting, writing, screenwriting, and directing, not only from BET and the NAACP, which often are the only ones to acknowledge Black talent, but from the Academy of Motion Picture Arts and Sciences, too. These professionals have produced some of the most intriguing content about Black life, Black women, sexuality, and pain, and are finally getting the props that they have been robbed of in the past. It feels like progress. Almost.

There are still constant reminders that seem to tell us just how little our work and efforts are valued. We don't have to walk in back entrances the way Hattie McDaniel did back in the day, but we're still typecast and relegated to supporting roles. The sidekick. The friend. The list of grievances is too long. You've heard many of them before: lack of representation on camera, less power behind the scenes, less opportunity to break in, and so forth. And you will hear them again. Despite this moment in Hollywood, when *Black Panther* broke a billion dollars in sales and #oscarssowhite forced the Academy to pay lip service to the lack of diversity, little has changed.

Only four Black men and one woman have ever won a best acting Oscar in the award's ninety-year-plus history. In 2017, Blacks represented just 13.6 percent of characters in big film projects, according to a study by the University of California, compared to 70.8 percent of White characters. Black directors that year also represented just 5.6 percent of people who spearheaded films.

In 1932, an era when Black actors were overwhelmingly playing servants, predators, and slaves, a casting call looking for Black actors to be extras in the jungle film *Nagana* went out. It specifically emphasized the need for respondents to "resemble savages." Four hundred "savage-looking" Black actors responded. In 2014, a casting call for Black actors for the film *Straight Outta Compton* was posted on Facebook. It called for women of all ethnicities to apply, ranking them from "A girls to D girls." The A girls—"the hottest of the hottest," according to the advertisement—could be of any ethnicity but needed to have real hair. The next "level" were light-skinned, Beyoncé-like girls. The "C girls" were specifically African American, "medium to light skinned with a weave." And the lowest ranked? African American girls again. "Poor, not in good shape. Medium to dark skin tone." It was a throwback to the past.[2]

Sure, I'll concede that in some ways, particularly with the addition of streaming services like Netflix, Hulu, and Amazon, there is more programming with young Black millennials than ever before. Over the last few years, *Insecure, Atlanta, The Chi,* and *Dear White People* were released to critical acclaim. Yet I still hear stories of invisibility. And often it begins with lowered expectations, a protective shield that acknowledges the reality of what is valued in Hollywood, and what is often valued, they know, is not them. Black millennial actress Aja Naomi King never dreamed she could get anything more than the "friend" role. She never thought she could be a star. "When I first started in this industry, my goal was to be some best friend. The sidekick. I thought that would be an accomplishment," she told *Marie Claire* in early 2017. That this was the goal for this young woman, who not only is beautiful and talented but had proved her credibility in one of the most prestigious acting institutions in the country, the Yale Drama School, saddened me. Fortunately Aja pushed ahead, thanks to inspiration from other Black actors who were achieving more: Lupita Nyong'o and Viola Davis. Aja now has a lead role on Davis's Emmy-winning show, *How to Get Away with Murder.* But it's still too early to tell if she's the rule or the exception, or whether this moment of success for Black Hollywood will translate into permanent change.

IN 2017, I, LIKE SO MANY OTHERS, WATCHED AS *MOONLIGHT* LOST the Academy Award for Best Picture to *La La Land,* a movie I admittedly did not hate but that featured a nearly all-White cast reveling in the sounds of jazz in Los Angeles, working on making their dreams happen. I was in shock. Mad. Angry. And for a few minutes, I watched another story about unrelinquished dreams or at least dreams deferred, this time in real life, unfurl in front of me. In those few minutes, it was solidified and confirmed: this was the America we live in. An America that continues to award White mediocrity, where race still matters, and justice never seems to prevail. I texted my friends my rage. I sighed loudly to my mom as we ate a plate of nachos. This was Trump's America. This was the new system. The New World Order. I sulked into the couch, watching the confident White men proudly accept their award. The confident White men who looked about my age. The ones I know so well. The ones who dominate everything, work meetings, Tinder conversations, the chit-chat in the grocery store line. The ones who have the arrogance that their shit is the best, whether it is or it's not. The ones that stay fronting, keep getting funded, and collect all the awards. I was disgusted and annoyed. I hate those men, but I also simultaneously adore them. I wish I could be them at times, have that confidence that borderlines on arrogance and entitlement, that feeling that they deserve to be at the table no matter what. I watched as they spoke.

And then, in what many called some act of grace, the confident White men admitted an error was made. They had lost. Their confidence wasn't broken, and they seemed pleased with their benevolent selves as they handed the award to *Moonlight*, the real Best Picture winner. I was happy but heartbroken at the execution. It seems as if White folks always have to give us something, and when those confident and perfectly nice White boys handed *Moonlight* the award that night, in some ways, I wished Barry Jenkins had executed a Kanye-like move (RIP old 'Ye) and snatched that Oscar away from them. The moment stung. It still stings today. After all these years of fighting for a seat at the table, fighting to get on screen and off the Chitlin Circuit, after enduring a whole night the previous year of smug Academy members acting as if their shit didn't stink because Brown people were winning some awards, acting as if they had fixed the whole Oscars-so-White controversy in one award season, I sunk into my couch even lower. Confident White boys were still giving us things that already belonged to us, showing us that even in our moments of glory, America makes it about something more than us.

That was the place I was in, when I decided to leave behind the cold and stormy weather of the east and head west for a while to better understand the experience of young Black millennials who were trying to make it in Hollywood. Hollywood is a place where everyone wants their dreams to come true, but it's also a place that Black folks have struggled not just for visibility but for the power to create and tell their stories to the world. It's a place where despite all the odes to diversity, the experiences of Blacks (and seemingly all people of color) remain anything but equal. It's an industry that has taken decades to recognize powerful Black talent (hello, Viola Davis), while it ignores others (I'm looking at you, Regina King). It's an industry where Lena Dunham was able to write a one-and-a-half-page pitch that didn't feature characters or plot, one that she said was, "the worst pitch you've ever read," and get a TV show at the age of twenty-three,[3] yet no Black woman was even deemed worthy of an Emmy Award as a lead in a comedy series since 1986 (the phenomenally talented Tracee Ellis Ross broke that streak in 2017). It's an industry that has historically been so hard on Black people with a dream, where they make less, have their looks scrutinized and dreams constantly shut down, but one young people still turn to in hopes of defying those odds. And I wanted to figure out why that was. Lately, we'd been having some wins in Hollywood; we were more visible than ever, especially when it came to millennials. It feels in some ways like a moment, but I knew these folks and these films in many ways were the exception, and this moment could be perhaps fleeting. So I decided to talk to those who were still trying to make it, still trying to figure out their Hollywood story, to understand just what it meant to try to make it as a young person in Hollywood.

~

It was a cold and cloudy day. The flakes of snow had turned into mush after a spring snowstorm proved to not be the disaster it threatened to be. Yet for some reason the world still felt dark. The winter of the inauguration was still exceptionally frigid, and a chill lingered that seemed beyond thermostats and temperatures. The nation felt cold. I felt cold, and all I could think of was warm weather and palm trees, of something better than this dark gray city with piss-covered snow.

By the time I got to the airport, I was covered with nasty city soot from too much salt or maybe too much dirt. I tugged at the Black hoodie I was wearing that was supposed to tell the world not to fuck with me. To leave me the hell alone. I was annoyed and freezing but also feeling a bit optimistic. I had just spent my snowbound day before looking at reels of young Black people searching for some dream, and I couldn't believe how talented they were, how hopeful they were.

It seems nothing represents the American Dream more than Hollywood—well, the capitalistic version of the American Dream. It's a place of unattainable wealth, unattainable beauty, and often-unattainable dreams. But people have lived for it. They put their hearts and souls into being screen icons and gods even in an industry that all too often shuns them. I understood what working to attain your dream was; I understood wanting to have a voice, wanting to be remembered; but I didn't really understand Hollywood. I preferred to stew under the cold, sarcastic silver skies in New York until frustration caused me to run away. But that day in my thirty-fifth year, as I was trying to figure out my own American Dream, I headed west, with a bag full of Nutrisystem, tape recorders, and notepads. I needed to grasp what drove young people to one of the most written about, hardest, and unachievable dreams in the world: to make it in Hollywood. As I sat with my laptop open, listening to some new Radiohead song, I imagined this beautiful flight attendant, who did nothing but ask me if I wanted something to drink, had dreams that were beyond sky high and before I even landed I could tell my California dream had already begun in that silver bullet above the clouds. "Dreamers they never learn," the song went. "Beyond the point of no return."

~~

After a few days in Los Angeles, I walk into a crowded restaurant in Culver City. It was a Friday night, my third interview of the day, and I was tired. I had been listening to people tell stories about chasing their Hollywood dream all day, but I, with my nerdy political science background, still had a hard time connecting to the idea of it all. Then I met twenty-four-year old Kendra.

When Kendra was eight years old, she decided she was going to go to Juilliard to become an actress. To make that dream come true, she started praying. Over and over she would say, "Lord, I want to be famous. I want to make movies." She was serious and passionate and never relented in her request, though she's not exactly sure what drew her into the business. One of the first movies she ever watched was *Jurassic Park*. It came out the year she was born, and her interest in the industry was piqued. She fell in love with Kate Winslet after being "blown away" by her performance in *Titanic*, but what really solidified her love for the movies was watching a young star from Georgia by the name of Julia Roberts win a Best Actress Oscar for her role in *Erin Brockovich*. After seeing Roberts, she knew acting was what she wanted to do with her life. And she wanted to do what they did. She now realizes they were all White women, but at the time, she said, that didn't really bother her. She wanted to be like the people she saw in Hollywood movies, so she became, in her own words, "an "acting machine." She watched film after film, studying the acting craft. She took every theater class that was available in her small town in the Pacific Northwest. Awards season for her was better than the fancy high school dances, better than the Super Bowl, better, she said, than "anything in my life at the time." She had a ritual. Every year, for the Golden Globes and Oscars, she would put on her prom dress and pretend she was there. She had to be alone. She couldn't tolerate the presence of others. Later, she admitted that her friends and family would more likely be annoyed at her screaming at the television screen. She didn't care though—she was in heaven.

By the time high school rolled around, Kendra was auditioning for play after play. Yet it seemed her prayers were not being answered. She never was awarded any of the "good" roles in *My Fair Lady* or *The Sound of Music*, especially not the leads; and color-blind casting à la *Hamilton* wasn't yet en vogue. The one time her school produced a play that featured a Black lead—*Thoroughly Modern Millie*—Kendra was finally up for a major part, but, she said, the "only other Black girl" in her class got the role. It's a loss she said still "stings" today. Kendra was frustrated and questioned herself and her acting ability, but still never gave up. Looking back, she thinks racism may have played a role. The lead roles always went to White actresses, some who she said weren't as talented, but back then, she didn't understand all that. Back then, she said, she didn't even know she was Black.

Kendra grew up in Vancouver, Washington, a suburb of Portland, Oregon, on the banks of the Columbia River. She was the child of two working-class immigrant parents from Nigeria and Cameroon. She mostly has good things to say about the community, but it was clear from the way she talked about it that her dreams were too big for her hometown. "I came from a small town where there was one type of person. It was White, flannel shirts, goes hunting, that type of thing." She didn't mind that too much; it was more that a constant sense of inertia threatened to engulf her. "I was sheltered growing up but not by my parents, more by my environment. Washington is a beautiful state; there's a lot of trees and grass and plants and hiking and mountains. If you like that, that's fine. But if you were like me, where you want to see movies, you want to meet people, you want to do interesting things, it's not the coolest place to grow up. There wasn't a lot to do." Still she worked hard to fit in. She had some friends, but what she didn't have was a boyfriend, and that too was a part of a larger problem. "When I was in high school, I wore blue contacts 'cause I wanted my eyes to be blue, and I wore wigs because all the girls who had boyfriends had long hair and blue eyes. Maybe if I just got long hair and blue eyes, I would get a boyfriend too." She struggled with her identity for a while, but mainly she was focused on getting out and going to Hollywood. She applied to eight schools to study film, but only got into one, Syracuse. She attributes it to divine intervention pointing her down the right path.

She was excited about her move to the East Coast and arrived on campus ambitious and determined, telling her career advisor from the jump that she wanted to work for Paramount or Dreamworks. She didn't get to work for either of those studios, but she did manage to take a writing workshop with a prominent screenwriter and score an internship at the Cannes film festival in the South of France. Cannes was like a dream come true for her. She met tons of people on the red carpet and saw famous people from around the world. "It was amazing. This was all new to me because this is me, little girl from Vancouver who had these dreams, and I'm literally here living it. It was so exciting." But while she was setting herself up well professionally, when she came back to campus after Cannes, she realized how miserable her personal life had become.

During her freshman year, she had joined an all-White sorority. It was true to who she was at the time, and she loved it at first ("I would've felt uncomfortable if I joined a Black sorority," she noted). She was named best new member out of nine hundred new pledges because she was so involved, and she was even invited to move into the sorority house her sophomore year, which was a big deal. But soon things began to devolve. "I saw White privilege first hand. That is a game changer, let me tell you." All of a sudden she could see the walls go up; she could see the divide between her and "them." One was over money. Because she screwed up filling out her FAFSA loans during high school, she didn't get any money for college, so she had to take out a loan. It stung even more when she heard one girl complaining about her dad buying her a BMW when she really wanted a Mercedes. To top it all off, people often weren't nice to her in the sorority community at large, not just in her house.

Then there was the matter of the College ACB. College ACB was a rant website where you could post anonymous messages about people at your school. Kendra said there were many threads dedicated to her.

One person, she said, wrote, "Who's that fat, black monster in Alpha Phi?" As the only Black person in the sorority, she knew it was aimed at her. It was horrible, and she once again felt like an outsider. Her feelings were wounded even more when she went to frat parties. Just like in high school, all the girls would be dancing with a partner, except for her. She made friends, and people would talk to her and say hello, "but no one crossed that line." She thinks it's because they had never experienced someone like her. "I feel like the times that they saw a Black person, they were their maids, or they were housekeepers, or whatever." She decided to leave the house, and moved in with some forestry students. They were great. Humble. Grounded.

In an effort to move on, she enrolled in a study-abroad program in Prague, since it's a beloved city of filmmakers. Unfortunately, she continued to experience racism there, though it had changed from subtle to overt. No longer was it just the microaggressions—a person telling her she was "articulate," getting her hair touched, or saying she was pretty "for a Black girl." No longer was she dealing with comments hidden behind the wall of the internet. Now the racism was aggressive and blatant. In Prague she wasn't just the articulate one. She was a nigger. People on the street would stop and stare. They called her "Black devil." She was told she was a gypsy, that even the "bones in my body were Black." Soon she didn't want to go outside anymore. During the last few months of the program she stopped going to classes. She stayed inside and watched the sitcom *Modern Family* over and over again. She was disappointed but not yet ready to return to the cold Northeast, so she decided she would try a semester a little bit closer to home. This time she went to Hollywood.

It changed her life.

She interned, took classes, did everything "her heart desired." After she left work each day, she would stand in lines for movies and talks sponsored by the Writers and Directors Guild's of America. She didn't care if she had to wait two hours. Here she finally felt at home. She rattled off the names of the people she met: Geoffrey Rush, Marlon Wayans, Cuba Gooding Jr. It was a dream come true.

As an intern she learned what it was like in the industry. She did scheduling. Worked auditions. And it was there she realized something profound: she didn't want to be an actress. Knowing herself, she said she didn't think she could handle the rejection that was inherent in working as an actor. So she switched to producing and directing. She was still living her dream. When a television producer came to her class, Kendra was blown away. She took note of the fact that the producer liked handwritten letters, and when she begrudgingly had to go back to school, she made sure to stay in touch with the people she met, including sending a handwritten letter to that producer she adored. Six days after graduation and three days after her twenty-second birthday, she packed up the '98 Honda Accord she'd had since she was fourteen and headed to Hollywood with her mom.

Kendra was thrilled to have the support of her parents, which she said is an anomaly. In their African cultures, she said, many want their kids to go into medicine or the law and have so-called stable, well-paying careers, but her parents were different. They just wanted their kids to be happy. Her dad was an owner of a small janitorial company, and her mom worked as a teacher, so they couldn't help her financially, but they urged her to follow her dreams all the time.

The drive took two days, and she was anxious to get back to Los Angeles. She had already been reaching out to people to schedule meetings, but she was nervous about what the future held. She arrived at her new place on May 17 at three p.m. By three thirty she was emailing everyone she knew. She got six meetings, but she worried, like so many young women, especially young Black women, that she wasn't good enough and that no one would hire her. But when she went in for an informational meeting with the producer she'd met a few months earlier, she arrived in the middle of an office crisis. The receptionist had just quit unexpectedly, and they needed help. She happily offered her services and started a paid job the next day. Kendra's Hollywood story had begun.

Three months later their executive assistant decided she wanted to be the receptionist because the hours were better, and Kendra was promoted to assist two CEOS and the president of the company. She also started to work on her own side projects.

Around that time her brother, who is nine years older, left his career in civil engineering and decided he wanted to make music. They did a few projects together. She worked on a lot of short films, did a few festivals. A year in, she was getting fidgety at her job, but she was told that she needed more agency experience to advance further. So she left the production company to work at a talent and literary agency. She worked for the head of the motion picture production department. But it wasn't easy for her. The agent yelled at her constantly, called her an idiot, and treated her, she said, "like a dog." She became depressed and was scared to go to a job where she was getting screamed at for twelve hours a day. She gained weight. Her hair fell out, and eventually she had to shave her head.

After six months of that, she realized that she needed to make some changes. She started going to church and felt things were getting better. No longer was she filling her Sundays worrying about work the next day, but she was connecting with something she had lost since going to college. She managed to stay another six months and began looking for a new job. She had a couple of rounds of interviews at HBO, but her boss gave her a bad review, so she didn't get the job. Then a friend of hers told her about a position as a programming assistant at the cable network Starz. The Starz people immediately liked her, and when they offered her the job, she didn't hesitate to take it. Now she works on a range of shows like *Outlander, White Princess,* and *Howards End* doing development. It's the first job she's had, she said, where she really feels her input matters.

She's working her ass off and loving every minute, but said as a young Black woman in the industry the threshold for excellence is high. Even while working for the mean boss, she always would have to perform her job perfectly. She never thought of telling him off à la *The Devil Wears Prada*. She couldn't. She was the first Black assistant he had ever had. In her eyes that meant she needed to be a good example of the race. Being Black in the industry, she said, means having to teach producers and directors, who are often White, about the Black experience. You have to be the example you want to see them put on the screen. "When they write a script where the main character who is Black is either a drug dealer or a prostitute or a gangbanger or some kind, they possibly rethink that because they see you and they see this whole other different life." That means being "educated, cordial, pleasant," even as you're educating them on your culture and "lifestyle."

Then she said the thing that I've heard so often from so many people that I'm sick of hearing it and I'm sick of writing it: you have to work twice as hard. She said this applies to being Black and also being female. It's a habit she learned early on. If the other assistants are staying till seven thirty, she has to be there until nine thirty. If the others give a page worth of notes on scripts, she has to give two pages. She hates this reality, but she also wants to get ahead. It's a fact, she said, that even young White millennials who are her peers just don't understand. They don't understand that while they may have it hard, and while it's a universally tough industry, far fewer Black kids can call the head of a studio or a vice president and ask for an interview. She had a different experience. She had $100 dollars on her the day she arrived in Los Angeles and knew only a few people.

But it's not just monetary advantages; it's another type of privilege that people don't understand. They don't understand having to walk into a room and "prove yourself" because of skin color, though she thinks things are changing. She notes, for example, that BAFTA is no longer going to consider films that lack diversity in certain categories. While we talked before the #MeToo movement took off, she wondered if it's going to take the baby boomers dying off for things to really change. She's hopes not, and she's determined to make changes herself wherever she can. She keeps hearing that voice in her head that tells her she's not good enough, but she's ignoring it as best as she can, focusing instead on creating content for Starz.

As we took another sip of our drinks, Kendra excitedly told me it's a great time to be young and Black in Hollywood. People are just beginning to recognize Black talent, and they are beginning to understand the importance of diversity and telling a range of stories. She pointed to *Moonlight*'s Best Picture win. "We are taking steps to recognize, hey in the past it has been White, White, White, White, White, White, White, and now we want to bring in some color, 'cause what is a world without color?"

When she looks at her full body, natural hair, dark skin, and big lips and sees people like her on screen, it's promising. She also wants people—Black people too—to look at the community as a spectrum. To appreciate Issa Rae's natural hair and, at the same time, love Beyoncé's weave. To not require Black women be all one thing or another, to acknowledge the beautiful gray areas that lie between the Black and White. She uses Lena Dunham as an example. "I don't think Lena Dunham is my voice at all. Lena Dunham does not speak for me whatsoever. There is no one on her show that looks like me, that says the things that I do, that thinks the thoughts that I do. She is not a voice for millennials because millennials—I think the thing that defines us is how diverse we are." But, she said, and there is a big *but*, "She is a bigger girl who constantly is naked on her show. She's a strong writer and she has a voice that reached people at a time that those people aren't being reached. That's millennial women."

It's this kind of power, she said, that all too often Black people don't realize they have. "I feel like the roles that they get put up for too are still roles that are limited. Do not limit us. I cannot tell you the power that Black people have. Do not limit us. You look at our skin, and you confine us into a box based on our skin color. 'You can be a prostitute; you can be a drug dealer; you can be a crack addict.' No. I can be a fucking angel. I can be a queen; I can rule this fucking empire. I can do anything that I want to because I am a Black woman and because my struggles have been so real and I have lived my whole life sacrificing everything I want to do for everyone else. Do you know what kind of person that turns you into? To literally put aside your happiness for everyone else. That turns you into a person that this world just isn't ready for."

In 1924 a commentary by an unnamed actor was published in the *Chicago Defender*. He wrote, "I appeared in several motion pictures. . . . I acted the part of a coloured butler and in the other I appeared as a slave. I received less money for my work because I was coloured, and I am . . . disgusted, as every profession is open to the whites and few open to us. I am thinking what an advantage I would have if I were white instead of coloured."[4] His words stuck with me, not because they were particularly profound, but because of how closely they resembled what Kendra said decades later. I can't say I've only seen maids and butlers or slaves on screens, and given our circumstances, there has been progress, but Hollywood studio executives, 94 percent of whom are White, still seem to have a limited understanding of what they think "Blackness" is or should be. Black millennials are now able to reach audiences directly through new technology and social media, which means they can, to some extent, avoid the stereotypical roles if they want. But with so many at the top still not reflecting the diversity of America, it means we still aren't the ones in control of our narrative or representation in film or television (96 percent of CEOs in TV, by the way, are White too).[5]

We're in a weird position as millennials. Many of us, especially on the older side of the generation, grew up watching Black characters on television and big screen in the 1980s and '90s. On television, Black sitcoms ruled. We had Steve Urkel, Will Smith, Kenan and Kel, Martin Lawrence, Denise Huxtable, and the Mowry twins entertaining us. And at the theaters, urban tales like *Boyz N the Hood* and buppie fantasies like *Love Jones* ruled. Black stories were everywhere for awhile, with one writer in the *New York Times* noting, "black film properties may be to the 90s what the carphone was to the 80s; every studio executive has to have one." Black drama, until recently, has always struggled, but in 1997 there were fifteen primetime comedy shows on television. By 1999 the situation changed. None of the new primetime shows on network television featured a person of color in a leading role, and the NAACP threatened a boycott over representation. Six years later, there were only three shows. In 2008, as Barack Obama was about to take office, a new report showed once again no real progress, finding that the only lead on a new show for 2008 was a Black cartoon character and even he was voiced by a White person.[6]

Today, while networks like BET and TV One cater to Black audiences, and reality television has featured many Black characters, especially women, I still remain disappointed with our representation in the media. It became clear to me, after watching the rise and fall of Black television shows in the nineties and early aughts, that it was the bottom line—not Black folk—that networks and film studios cared about. After that heyday ended, I've never looked at Hollywood the same again. It was clear we were the outlier, a pawn used for profit at the will and whim of White folks—the people who truly held the power. I didn't give up on the industry, but there was no doubt I felt like a jilted lover.

Even in this moment, when it seems there are more opportunities available, it's still so far from being enough. Instead of expanding complex depictions of Black life and the Black experience, adding more Black managers and executives to their teams, and really trying to restructure the system so that it gives a fair chance to Black people, women, and all people of color, Hollywood is all too often satisfied with the same tired ways of dealing with race and still continues to fall into the same stereotypical thinking, with colorism and tokenism, and the belief that generally Black film and television can't be "mainstream." While I hope that the blockbuster successes and television hits have changed some of this thinking, Hollywood has a long way to go.

One actor, who wants to be called AB, has been dealing with some of this flawed thinking his entire career. When I first met him, I admit I was surprised. He's a light-skinned man, which in my mind is the prototype of a Black person that Hollywood loves. Someone who reads as Black but not, you know, *too* Black. Instead, his identity is both a blessing and a curse, depending, he said, on what is in vogue. As a biracial person of Filipino and African American descent who did not grow up in the United States, he's had to try to reconcile his own identity and race with a racism that he never really understood, in an industry that he says never quite saw him as "Black enough."

As he was growing up in Japan on a military base, Hollywood was a very distant place. All he knew of California was what he saw on television and in film. To him, it looked "amazing." He thought it was the "place to be" with beautiful people—a Disneyland of sorts. Watching television shows like *Baywatch, The Fresh Prince of Bel-Air, Boy Meets World,* and even movies like *Ace Ventura: Pet Detective,* made him fall in love with acting. He related to the characters and believed Hollywood was made up of a bunch of eclectic types, just as he was. "I felt like Hollywood would accept me for being awkward, or different, or weird, or biracial because everyone on TV had these type of TV problems that I feel like I connected to." And after moving to the West Coast, for a while it seemed he could fit in.

Right out of high school, he got his first role on the very popular television dramedy *Veronica Mars,* which was followed by work on the soap opera *General Hospital.* After that he was booked on *Prom Queen,* a new web series that was being produced by former Disney executive Michael Eisner. It was 2007, web series were still new, and Eisner was putting a million dollars into the project. AB was still was very green in the industry, which he freely admits, and barely knew what he was doing, yet he was excited. "I didn't know what really acting was. I didn't know what the business was about. I thought you just read some lines, you go on set, and if you're great, they like you, they'll hire you. That's how I always thought it would be. I never knew about playing a character, and being in the moment, hitting this mark, and hitting this comedic timing. I knew nothing about that, even though I booked a role."

Still, he was finding more roles, and after that he booked an episode of *Everybody Hates Chris*. Then, according to AB, "it got kind of weird." He wasn't castable for certain things, he said, and he had to prove that he was one thing or another. "Being told that you're not enough of anything makes you either want to fight against it and prove yourself, or makes you go into a little hole. It kind of did both," he said. "I still have this trouble of not being Black enough." I asked him for clarification, and he told me it varies every year. In his twenties (he's in his thirties now), it meant not being "urban" or "street" enough, as they were looking for people to work on shows like *Lincoln Heights* and parodies of *Save the Last Dance*. Now, he said, he's "too good looking." "The pretty boy look is totally gone. They look for regular people, whatever that means, guys that people can relate to. How can people not relate to me? I make people laugh. I'm funny, I smile, I'm a nice guy, right? I cook, is that relatable? I don't know."

Men are often left out of conversations about colorism, but AB seems to understand how his career has benefited or suffered because of it. Colorism—discrimination against those with darker skin—is not a thing of the past. Actresses Keke Palmer and Lupita Nyong'o have both talked about wishing they had lighter skin in the past, while mixed-race actress Zendaya Coleman said her skin sometimes privileges her. "Can I honestly say that I've had to face the same racism and struggles as a woman with darker skin? No, I cannot."[7]

AB admits that being biracial can give him an advantage sometimes. He is cast in racially ambiguous roles more easily than other dark-skinned actors, though it's usually not as an Asian character, since he said he doesn't often "read" as Filipino. It seems a real point of contention for him, since he wholeheartedly embraces his Asian heritage as much as his Black lineage. He said he usually gets called for African American roles because of his skin color. It's likely to happen even more now because he shaved his head and grew a beard, though he seems to long to be able to play roles that reflect the whole of his identity. Still, White casting offices see him as Black, "period. No matter what." When he works for productions being run by "Black Hollywood," he said they often don't see him as presenting fully as a Black man. He recalled wanting to go out for the Fox drama *Empire*, but his rep told him he wasn't "Black enough." "It really hurt."

His first solution has been "to be undeniably talented so they don't see color. They don't see you as a man. They don't see you as a woman. They see you as just a talent." That's easier said than done. As he points out, "Most roles are already written for White people period. End of story. They don't see that struggle. They might have a struggle because they might not be tall, or their eyes might not be blue, or something like that, to match a brother/sister role. They don't have a problem when I have to change the color of my skin, or I can't get a role based on the color of my skin, or I'm not able to do it because of the color of my skin."

His other solution is one that millennials are hearing across the board from executives, other Black actors, and casting agents alike. Create your own content. If you can't get an HBO deal with a page-long pitch and no real characters like Lena Dunham, then creating a web series may be a way to gain visibility. But AB said it must be something unique and different because a lot of web series are feeling the same. He pointed to a new popular web series called *Giants* (it's produced by Issa Rae and Jussie Smollett from *Empire*) that airs on Rae's web channel. It's a coming-of-age story about Black millennials dealing with "adulting," sexuality, and mental health. It's "amazing" with a compelling storyline, he said, because it's "bigger than just being Black or White." He believes that people of color have to think smarter and outside the box. "We're just as smart and able bodied, just like everybody else. We can be the next Spielberg; we can be the next James Cameron; we can be the next whoever we want to be. We, as a people, we need to collectively come together and make smarter material."

AB decided to turn some of his frustrations with the industry into something positive. So he created a web series called *Venice Boulevard*, a show about three guys trying to make it in Hollywood. It grew a cult following, and AB liked producing so much that in addition to acting, he decided to jump into more content creation. Most recently, he starred in another web show he wrote and produced, *My So-Called Co Star Life*. The scenario sounds vaguely like his own life. "I play a guy named Will Smith who's not Black enough to be in the industry. He tries to use the celebrity name to get things in life, but it just doesn't pan out that way."

A VETERAN BLACK CASTING DIRECTOR SAID SHE WAS SURPRISED at the outward displays of stereotyping that I heard from some people—one woman said she was told her backside would look too big on camera and was constantly being asked if her hair was real—though she admitted that the industry has the same amount of racism that the real world does. She said in some ways while race played a role, the industry was just "the industry."

Even Black folk who have "made it" have complicated relationships with Hollywood. In *Harper's Bazaar*, *Being Mary Jane* actress Gabrielle Union talked about working in the industry as "being hyper-visible or invisible." "When do you stand up and point out every micro-aggression, and when do you stand down so you're not the angry Black person all the time? It's tiring. It feels like another job that you're not getting paid for—that is all encompassing." Actor Anthony Mackie said, "It's frustrating that the movies I want to make I haven't been able to make. Orlando Bloom was given 15 opportunities after 'Lord of the Rings.' Black men are given no opportunities." Zoe Saldana, a Black Latinx, said of her roles in films like *Avatar* and *Guardians of the Galaxy Vol. 2*, "[Playing a science fiction character] makes me feel superhuman because, obviously, it's been brought to my attention continuously since I was born that I'm not a conventional person because of the color of my skin or my gender or my cultural background," she told the *Daily Telegraph*.[8]

No matter how much people love the industry, and no matter how many successes they have, it can take its toll. And sometimes all you need is humor. Ben[9] knows this well. A Compton native, he started out on a set managing a coffee shop. He managed to work his way up and started acting, while still holding onto a day job. He had landed a small role in a star-studded film, when he said a producer propositioned him on set. "This gentleman, he was very, very specific about what he wanted to have happen, yeah, and I very respectfully, at least I thought, let him know that that's not what I'm about and he needs to go elsewhere. He didn't take that too well." After that, Ben said, things began to change, and he believed he was blacklisted from some films. "After that I got a phone call to do some ADR [automated dialogue replacement] work on the same movie, and he was there. He was like, 'Yeah, I just didn't like the way you said those lines, so we're just going to have you redo them.' So long story short, he made sure that they sound so bad in the dub that he said we're just going to have to gut the thing all together." Ben was stunned. This was before #MeToo, before other Black actors like Terry Crews were speaking about improper sexual conduct and abuse. "I didn't report it, I didn't say anything about it, and I feel like it's because me growing up African American in the hood, you don't snitch. I was like, you know what, that's his thing, that's his hang up, whatever. He'll get his in the end." In hindsight, Ben said he wishes he had done things differently and took care of himself more.

He fell into a deep depression after that. He couldn't believe one guy could show up and just tear away his hard work. He lost his "heart" for the industry for about a year and left Hollywood. He started working at a charter school and was doing well, but he just wasn't fully feeling satisfied. Entertainment was his love and passion, and without it he felt a void. Finally, Ben worked his way back. He was worried about the producer, but he made his peace with it, told himself that this guy could only control a limited number of movies, and he began working again. Slowly. He mainly did voice-overs at first, but he soon crept back into acting. Before long he realized he had another dream: comedy. So he signed up for classes at West Los Angeles College and had a ball. He realized he had a talent for storytelling. He booked his first performance at the Comedy Store two years ago on his birthday. He bombed. But his spirit was warm. His soul, it seemed, had been fed. "I loved that feeling. It was just something about failing so terribly, but still being alive and it was like, well, I wanna see if I can fail a lot less next time."

He's still working in the industry. He's a day-to-day substitute teacher and a driver for Lyft while he works on perfecting his craft. He realizes he has to play the game a little to make things happen, especially as a Black comedian. "You wanna talk about what's going on at your job, but they're like, wait, well don't forget about all the Black stuff, cuz you're Black. You gotta talk about being poor, and you gotta talk about your loud, drunk uncle. Or you gotta talk about your stint with selling drugs and playing sports." Ben said some of that stuff is *in* his comedy, but it's more than that. Sometimes he wants to talk about everyday stuff, like the people who steal his yogurt from the fridge at work. I chuckled—he's funny in a sort of Seinfeldian way. He said he's learned how to balance it, how to draw the crowd in and make them see him as a person with regular office issues, not just a Black man.

Knowing yourself is important, he says, especially for a young Black comedian. "Do not do comedy for other people. Do comedy for yourself. Talk about what's funny to you, because no matter what, somebody is interested in your comedy, in your story. Like, if your comedy is about you growin' up whitewashed in a suburban community, don't try to talk about how hard it was for you in the streets. It's not who you are. Never, never, never try to be something you're not on stage, because people can tell when you're B.S.-ing. You have to be authentically you."

In comedy, as in the rest of the entertainment industry in LA, you have to find a way to make people relate to you. Then you will find that sweet spot. "People, they love listening to painful stories, because everybody can relate to pain. So just tell your story, and don't give up so easily. Because there's gonna be people out there that's gonna do what they feel is necessary for you to quit. You can slow down; just don't give up."

∾∾

When it comes to pursuing your dreams, Hollywood is one of the toughest industries to break into, and often your successes and failures are on full display. For Black millennials, who don't get the same opportunity to break in, who have to be twice as good when they do get in, whose successes according to the veteran casting director may come later than their peers', and who often never make the same as their counterparts (the Forbes top 30 paid actors and actresses in Hollywood included a range of White millennials like Mila Kunis, Jennifer Lawrence, Emma Watson, and Emma Stone; no young Blacks were listed),[10] and who constantly face things like colorism, stereotypes, and tokenism, it seems admirable that any of them would want to go to Hollywood. But rather than evoking despair, like in many other stories in this book, Black millennials here and those who have become successful in Hollywood are a testament to the Black spirit, to overcoming in the face of adversity, finding another way to make your voice heard. One artist, Shamir, has proved that even when you make it and are successful, you still have to fight hard to be your authentic self.

After spending time with a bunch of dedicated artists who were loving the warm and sunny Hollywood lifestyle, despite its obstacles, I was almost ready to pack my bags and move there myself. But then I met a singer who didn't love it so much. Shamir had just moved from Los Angeles to Philadelphia because he was tired of the music industry and was ready for freedom and some room to just be his true self away from the glitz and glam. Ben was managing to be himself in Los Angeles, but while Shamir loved his work, he saw how easily he could lose himself there. Shamir had experienced the quick rise to fame, and all the pitfalls that came with it, and found that shooting to the top wasn't as glamorous as he thought. Many times young Blacks in particular aren't given space to be who they really are, to showcase the diversity of the Black experience and themselves, but people like Shamir are trying to change that.

Shamir is an artist from Las Vegas who found fame at the age of nineteen, right out of high school, as a solo pop artist. He's primarily a musician, but he's a millennial through and through, so he has a plethora of side hustles. He recently finished acting in an episode of the Netflix show *Dear White People,* and he also loves to do stand-up comedy. Right now, the twenty-two-year-old is focused on his second album, *Hope,* which he released on his own through Soundcloud, after being frustrated with record labels boxing him in as a Black queer pop artist. It's a totally different sound from his previous album, which was electronic and pop-oriented. *Hope* is more low-fi, which he said is truer to his authentic self, though he was worried that no one wanted to hear it.

The album came out of a "very desperate place" for him. He was working with a bunch of big-name producers in Los Angeles and got some demos together, but something was off. He just wasn't feeling it. It felt too polished, too clean, not quite who he was. Lo-fi means nonstudio recordings, home recordings, an homage to just one's voice and the beats. It's meant to focus solely on the music, the lyrics, the writing, while embracing the unpolished edges. "I wanted my music to be still accessible and pop music, but also at the same time have a very rough quality about it."

After he figured this all out and began to embrace this new idea, he decided that he couldn't finish any of his current work. His heart just wasn't in it. So Shamir told his manager that he didn't want to release any of his recordings, picked up his things, and headed to Philadelphia to work on a new album. He started a new album with a friend of his, but the friend insisted that it be cleaned up, and once again he protested. Frustrated, he started working on a project all on his own. He wrote and recorded most of the songs for *Hope* over the course of one weekend. He recorded it on his phone and his four track, mastered it on Sunday, and released it on Monday. "At that time I thought that it was going to end my career. I honestly did, and I was okay with that prospect because I was like, I don't want to do music if I have to continue to be something I'm not."

People didn't know, however, that Shamir had been in a rock band and electronic music was just an experiment for him. "I was like, 'Oh, I want to see if I can do electronic pop music, and dance music, and see if I can do it well.' I didn't think that that being my first introduction for the world would actually box me into the thing. I was just nineteen.

I was just young." Initially he was happy that he got to write his own album. But it was hard for him to evolve and explore other styles of music because he was working with a straight White male producer who was into house. "A lot of people just were like, 'Oh, Shamir's queer and Black—of course he wants to do house music,' and little did they know that I played guitar."

The media, he said, created a narrative about him, and it was one he didn't necessarily embrace. Articles often labelled him "post-gender." He was called a "post-gender, androgyne angel of a millennial" by the *Guardian*. The *Advocate* asked if he was the "Post-Gender Pop Star for Our Time?" and *Vulture* cited his "Post-Gender, Post-Genre Charm" in the headline of a story about him.[11] It frustrated him because it was a word that never came out of his mouth. "I remember vividly being on the BBC World News and having this staunch British man sit in front of me, and he was like, "So, you're post-gender. What does that mean?" My only response was, 'I don't know because I didn't make that term up.'" He also got asked why he didn't do more drag ("just because I paint my nails I'm a drag queen?"). He had to explain to people repeatedly, "I'm queer and I'm a musician, but I'm not a queer musician. . . . People are their art form first, and then they happen to be queer. . . . I'm a musician who happens to be queer." While he was battling questions of one aspect of his identity, he decided that he needed to be truer to who he was. He was tired of making music with a computer, with things being in "sequence." He'd taught himself how to play multiple instruments and felt it was time to put that work to use.

There's a history of older executives managing younger artists in the music industry. They determine what the "market" wants; they define the audiences. Shamir thinks that model is behind the times. Now, if you have a computer, you can access recording tools. Young people are taking cues from successful artists like Chance the Rapper, who has never been signed to a label. They can truly have an independent voice. "A lot of people will compromise, or everyone will always say, 'sell your soul.' They will sell their soul for a check. Which is something that I refuse to [do]." Shamir knows that artists have always battled for more control, but said it's so different now because you can still remain relevant without a label. "The artist can keep going because they have the internet, they have their fans, and they're more tethered to their fans. I released *Hope* with no PR. *Hope* got all that attention by itself because my fans were like, 'Yo, Shamir just released an album after two years. We're going to listen to it.'"

Shamir's confidence comes, he said, from being "always unapologetically" himself. Some people may have thought he was weird or different, but mainly they respected his uniqueness. He realized that even in high school, when he was up against the senior class president for a "best dressed" contest. His opponent, he said, looked like a Banana Republic model, while he came to school in rags or a dashiki, with "weird" hair. "That just showed me that people are hungry for something unique and something different, and everyone's tired of seeing the same things over and over and over again. I think that's what helped me in the music industry too. I think that's what helped me stay myself within this industry that's trying to box me."

It seems to have worked for him. He has another album coming out in a few months with a new label, and they're giving him the control he wants over his music and his sound. "I think the only way [for] Black millennials, and even just millennials in general, to get better, or be able to do what they want, [is] to show people that their talent is never going to be taken away, and that you own your talent. You need to be precious with it."

He's excited. "I've already reached my American Dream. It feels beautiful because I'm only twenty-two, and I have this amazing career where I can do music, and I can act, and I've been writing. I have this career that feels boundless now. . . . It can only go up from there. I know there's still a lot of other things that I want to do, but they don't feel out of reach. Especially after releasing the album by myself, it's almost like I can literally do whatever I want now."

MILLENNIAL MOMENT: **RUSSIAN ROULETTE**

Blacks are only 12 percent of the US population but account for 44 percent of new HIV diagnoses, people living with HIV, and those with AIDS. Of the HIV diagnoses in 2015, 11 percent were Black women—the majority among women overall. Black women are diagnosed with HIV at a rate sixteen times higher than that of White women.[12]

M, AGE 30, ATLANTA

A young lady had on a T-shirt. It said, "I have HIV." It freaked me out. I asked her, did she really have HIV? She told me no. She told me to read the back of the shirt. It said, "If only it was just that easy to tell. Get tested." It prompted me that I hadn't been tested because I couldn't afford the school insurance, which was $400 a month.

I told my doctor I wanted to be tested for everything. Her immediate thing was "Why? Are you showing any symptoms?" I was like, "No. This girl freaked me out with a T-shirt."

Two weeks later, they kept asking me to come into the office. I'm thinking that they're going to tell me I have HPV, that they want to do a biopsy because I have cancer. Instead they told me I had HIV. I broke down. I was like, "Y'all got the wrong blood. Y'all need go to back and check the labs again. They mixed up the labs." It was traumatic; it was awful. It was scary. It was like experiencing death in the moment. Everybody's telling you you're going to live, but in your mind, you only got about six months because they really don't know.

I didn't know anything other than what the books taught you in school, which is you get HIV, there's medicine out there for it. You get AIDS, and you die. I knew that you couldn't get it from kissing or eating off spoons, but it didn't make sense to me because I believed in the myths as well. I cried every day.

I went back to the doctor in two weeks, and they told me that I was pregnant.

I didn't want the possibility of a baby being born HIV positive. I contemplated getting an abortion. I disclosed to my [boyfriend] about my status as soon as I found out, but we kept arguing because I wanted him to go get tested. He just would not go for whatever reason. He finally went. The test results he said came back negative, but I don't believe it. That's just my personal opinion. The person I was with for four years on and off [before], he still won't go get tested to this day.

[My boyfriend], I think, was suffering from depression, and I received an immense lack of support from him. It was just awful. He still wanted to have unprotected sex. It didn't make sense to me. I barely wanted him to touch me. I just started becoming disgusted by him. The smell of him, looking at him. It was so sad. I was so mean, but he wasn't giving me the emotional support, the babying that I was looking for.

I trusted my doctor a lot. She told me that in her twenty-five years of practicing, she has never delivered one HIV positive baby and she didn't intend to, so I needed to get it together. She went as far as praying for me while we were in the office. I don't remember not crying or throwing up during my visits. I would be there for hours.

I know that they had me under suicidal watch. I was having suicidal thoughts. I just couldn't figure out how to do it. I was smart enough not to tell no therapist or anybody. I would have days or periods where I just felt that way.

Every person I told about my status kept crying like they were going to a funeral. I had to pick people up off the floor. Even my pastor at the time was just like thinking death immediately. I had people tell me to pray over a bottle of olive oil. I started doing that too, and then I was like, "This don't make sense." HIV is no different than cancer. That's how I see it. Just the way that it attacks the body is different. One is contagious, and one is not.

Initially my son, he didn't want to be around me. He said he wouldn't hug me, touch me, kiss me anymore. He was only seven years old. He knew nothing about HIV. I told him he couldn't get it like that. I explained the bodily fluids that he could get it from. After that, he was like, "Well, I guess I'll still hug you, kiss you, and love you." That was really traumatic and hurtful at first.

My mom was very supportive from day one. It has helped us get closer. Everyone is supportive in their own way, but nobody really talks about my status. It's like my participation in things like the national campaigns. If people happen to see it and they know my mother, they would say, "Hey I saw M on CNN," or "I saw her on YouTube. Why you never said anything?" She's like, "Why would I say anything? She's living her life, and I'm living mine, and I don't think about it."

I think that's where some of the issue may be. People are just living their lives, and it's becoming more of a chronic illness instead of a terminal illness. That makes it difficult to even say there's a dire need for HIV/AIDS awareness, when you don't see people dropping like flies anymore.

My daughter was born HIV negative in 2011. I felt good; I felt liberated.

~

I RECENTLY QUIT MY JOB AS A PHARMACY TECHNICIAN OF ELEVEN years. Right now I'm doing Lyft and Uber to hold me over while I write my book and get ready to complete my paperwork for my nonprofit organization. I quit my job because I caught the flu, and my new manager was unaware of my HIV status. I had just started taking HIV meds three months before because I had been off for a year and a half. Instead of her checking on me, she threatened to terminate me because I didn't complete some computer work in time.

I had been a little complacent about doing computer work anyway because I had dropped my hours down even lower to keep my health insurance. I kept asking them, "Can you can give me full-time benefits with day shift and no weekends? I'm a single parent. I need to be at home with my children." They wouldn't give it to me. I was just fed up. I felt like I worked for a company where I count medications [in the pharmacy department], the same medicine that I take that's $3,000 a month, but this company won't pay me more than $1,000 a month to cover my quality of life, just to be able to get to and from work and my bills.

When Obamacare came around, and I reached out, I received about thirty-plus phone calls in one day. That was really frustrating. My medicine at the time was about $3,000 a month without health insurance, so I knew that there would be a deductible or out-of-pocket expense. I asked specifically what the prescription coverage copay amount would be, and they said 30 percent of whatever the cost of the drug is. Thirty percent of $3,000 is 900 bucks, which is my total monthly income.

I just stopped taking my medication. The children remained getting Medicaid. I would go get my labs done through the health department. I would use my income taxes to basically live off of that, and I had student loans before that, so it would just be one of the two. I did that for a year and a half. Then I would do little odd-end things. I would barter to do someone's hair in exchange for them to put a little money on my bill or do hair in exchange for a son's haircut and then my speaking engagements.

I had to question the whole hypocritical side of it. I'm encouraging people to take medicine, but I wasn't taking mines at the time. There were some other programs out there, but the fear of just having to fight for it—I just started shutting down without realizing it.

I finally tested lab results, and it showed that I was detectable again. My viral load had spiked. It took almost two years when I was off the meds. A lot of times people tell you, "Eat healthy, take meds, drink alkaline water, and do all these holistic things," and those things are helpful, but it don't really fight off the virus. That's why they say life expectancy without HIV meds could be about ten to fifteen years. That's it. It's like a Russian roulette type thing. You have to want to live in order to live with HIV. You have to want to live with it.

My goal is to get a job that will pay me a salary that will afford me health care benefits. I receive Medicaid. If I make over $400 a month, I no longer qualify for Medicaid. Lyft does [give you health insurance], but I think you have to be doing it full-time. By the time I try to do it full-time, I am exhausted physically. It's like if I want to shoot myself in the foot or the head. If I want to shoot myself in the head, I need to go ahead and tell them that I make a certain amount of money, so I no longer qualify. If I want to shoot myself in the foot, I make only a certain amount to make it work and manage it as best possible.

God has been taking care of me. I never have money, but I always have everything that I need. I just pray to God that nothing shows up where it's like, "Hey you've been getting over on the government. You owe us." That would be awful.

Being a spiritual person, having faith in God or the universe, helps me a lot, but it's more frustrating than anything else to continue seeing and hearing about the many, many women that are still being diagnosed. The lack of education, the lack of awareness that is out here is even more frustrating.

When people pass away from complications of HIV and AIDS, they don't talk about the HIV/AIDS part; they just talk about the complications. It was a lung failure. It was kidney failure. It was pneumonia, but they never say it was the HIV that caused it. We don't talk about the lack of support and the lack of love around it. There are people out there who know how to love and love hard, to give the support around people living with HIV and AIDS. However, the stigma is still very strong and very hurtful. It is still very traumatizing. For instance, I lost a hair client. After I disclosed to him, he cried about it, and he told me that he couldn't let me do his hair again.

I put myself in a position and a mind frame that if God took away my children, my mother, my grandmother, and all of my friends, what would I have left? I would have nothing left but God, and I would still have to choose to live. Either I was going to stay sad living and accept misery around me, or I was going to move on and continue finding the best way to live. I still have moments where I get sad. I still have moments where I still get depressed, but I do know how to put myself in a place where I will have joy.

chapter eight

STILL IN LOVE

MY DAD IS A PIECE OF TRASH. I RELISH BEING ABLE TO WRITE THOSE WORDS. I haven't seen him since I was eleven when he came to visit me after a five-year absence bearing pizza and the pretense of being a loving father. I was angry then. I desperately wanted a dad. I still do in my thirties. During that last meeting, he seemed to be frustrated with my indignant attitude, which was really a mix of annoyance and sadness that he wasn't in my life. After he left, I sat in my basement, my belly full of pizza and filled with rage, wondering what I did to make a father want to abandon his child and hoping—praying—that things would change in the future. They didn't. In fact they got worse, and after he got wind of my very vocal lamentations, he never bothered to try to have a relationship with me again. He never even talked to me again. Even though he vanished from my life after that day, I searched for him, mourned his disappearance for years. I still wonder on occasion what it would be like to have a dad tell me about boys. Or how much fun it would have been to hang out on his boat, since I, too, love the water. I still wonder how many more vacations we could have taken if he was around, or at least had bothered to send a child support check.

Or even if my dreams would have been different, given his influence as an immigrant from the former British colony of Guyana. My life turned out fine, and the game of "what if" has pretty much faded, though one question remains: Would I have given up on love so early on? Or at the very least had some marginal faith in relationships when I was younger?

I'm part of the population that grew up in a single-parent household. My parents were never married, and though my mom had a long-term partner for over twenty-five years, I wasn't surrounded by romantic love. I never gleaned from my mom that being in love was essential to breathing, but my grandparents were another story. My grandfather George, whom I called Poppy, met my grandmother Evelyn after journeying up to New York from Miami after World War II. He fell in love, and their destiny was settled. It was as simple as that. I can't imagine George without Evelyn or Evelyn without George. They shared cleaning and cooking responsibilities, laughter and tears. One of my earliest memories was when my grandmother, who had diabetes, passed out while doing some gardening. I never saw my Grandpa run so quickly. I was only seven or eight, but I remember the look of worry in his eyes that caused his whole face to wrinkle with pain. I saw that same look after she died a few years later. I was standing behind him as, grief stricken, he grabbed her body from the casket and held her. He was inconsolable. He didn't want to let her go, and he clung to her blue funeral gown for what felt like hours until someone had to pull him away. I was young, and the message to me was clear as I watched his brown face touch her skin: love was simply a necessity.

A few years later and a bit broken, Poppy remarried, and a little bit of my fairytale died. He married a nice enough woman, who was devoted to him and took care of him, but it wasn't that same love I remembered. That ride-or-die love. After he passed on some years later (in my mind, of an ailing heart), we learned a secret that Poppy had kept for his entire life. He was married before my grandmother. I was in shock. And once again, my idea of love faded a little bit more.

I went through high school thinking love wasn't real or at least didn't apply to my life. I wasn't particularly inundated with requests for companionship anyway, so maybe it was particularly easy to blow the whole idea off. I was a little chubby and very insecure, and I liked to wear plastic barrettes in my hair—the kind that punctuate the ends of the braids that little Black girls wear. It wasn't until I had a mono-like illness my senior year, dropped over twenty pounds, and threw in a weave track and some French tips that dudes all of a sudden seemed to take interest in me. I didn't really care. I knew I was a straight, cis woman, but I didn't really like men. I thought they were good for money and sex and not much more, though I didn't really benefit from many of those spoils either. I certainly didn't have any men dicking me down or throwing out Benjamins en masse on dates. Instead, I had experienced a different type of love in my life. It was the love of my mom and my great-aunt and the community of Black women, many single, who surrounded us and took care of each other. It was a steady and unwavering love, unlike that of the men who were always on the margins of these women's lives, and that was the love I came to depend on. Women were the shining stars in my life, and the men, it seemed, always played a secondary role. Women were fierce, independent, hard-working, and feminist (without having to announce it, display it, or safety-pin it). They made clear all too often that marriage and "happily ever after" was for White girls.

Looking back, I'm sad that I never swooned over guys in high school, that I never dreamed of having some Cinderella-like fantasy first date. I'm sad that my first kiss was in some gross, dimly lit teen club that was raided by the police just minutes later. I'm heartbroken I can't even remember my first date. And I'm even more disappointed that the first time I had sex, I was wearing giant turquoise granny panties, because I just didn't care that much and didn't know to cherish it. But such is life.

My experiences of young love are probably no less traumatic than others my age and perhaps not so sad. I did manage to fall in love more than once. I managed to have that same feeling I associate with my grandfather, and learned to absorb the highs and lows of love and everything that comes with it. In fact, I've even realized that now, like my nine-year-old self, I'm somewhat of a hopeless romantic. And that gives me pure joy and giggles. I have allowed myself to fantasize. And that was hard. I had to fight for that dream. I had to work through a lot of tears, pain, and loneliness to get here.

~

THE YEAR I TURNED THIRTY, AN AGE WHERE YOU ARE EXPECTED to start to make more "adult" decisions about your future, a document called "The Marriage Vow: A Declaration of Dependence Upon Marriage and Family" was beginning to circulate. It was a political pronouncement written by a Bob Vander Plaats, a conservative leader in Iowa and signed by Republican presidential candidates Michele Bachmann and Rick Santorum to show support for a heterosexual definition of marriage. At the top of the document were a set of preambles, starting with the romantic lives of Black folk. The statement accused Black people of having their love lives more together during bondage than today. "Slavery had a disastrous impact on African-American families," the document stated, "yet sadly a child born into slavery in 1860 was more likely to be raised by his mother and father in a two-parent household than was an African-American baby born after the election of the USA's first African-American President."[1] The statement was outrageous, but it wasn't exactly surprising. The all-too-familiar point had been made once again: our bodies and love lives were open to debate. The language about slavery was eventually removed from the statement, but the damage was already done.

Black Americans are used to having our love lives examined, policed, and criticized by everyone—politicians, pundits, our mamas, the government, and even ordinary citizens. I often try to tune it out, but it's hard. And it's relentless. The very next year, as I continued to fret about my love life, another book came out, *Is Marriage for White People? How the African American Marriage Decline Affects Everyone*, this time by Black law professor Ralph Richard Banks. He was trying to understand why Black people weren't marrying as much as their White counterparts. At the same time people kept touting an OkCupid study that showed Black women aren't as beloved online as their White counterparts.[2] Even people who seemingly had no stake in these matters at all—like comedian Steve Harvey—weighed in on what was wrong with Black women and their love lives. I took it all personally during those years, way more than I should have, letting their words, studies, and alleged expertise about Black love infiltrate my life and, more importantly, my heart.

Black people have never truly been in control of our love. It was always understood as someone else's to regulate, stigmatize, criticize, and legitimize. Our love, the love that we nourish and foster, when it looks different from their love, the love of White folk, is mocked and called unfit. This is the furthest from the truth. Family relationships have always been valued in the Black community; love has always been important to us, as well as our ancestors, and we've fought, rebelled, and bled because of it. Since the time of slavery, Black love has been shaped by the White power structure. It has been regulated, stigmatized, criticized, and used as a method of control.

According to scholar Tera Hunter, enslaved couples weren't always allowed to legally marry, because marriage inherently implied that the right gave couples control over "women's sexuality and labor" and parental rights to children, which would have been antithetical to the capitalistic enterprise of slavery, which necessitated that White plantation owners have full control over Black bodies. Slaves were also seen as not having the morality to "respect and honor" marriage. This, of course, couldn't be further from the truth. Scholar Katherine M. Franke has found that many enslaved people lived as husband and wife, which was formalized through celebrations like jumping over a broom or having a "scripture wedding" or a big banquet. She also found that aside from monogamous commitments, enslaved people were open to a range of relationships like "sweethearting" and living together. They also produced children through various arrangements.[3]

One slave, Henry Box Brown, was heartbroken about the loss of his family and decided to escape. In about 1836, when Brown was in his twenties, he fell in love with another enslaved woman, Nancy, who lived on the adjacent plantation from his in Louisa County, Virginia. They both asked their owners if they could marry, though it would still technically be illegal, and the owners consented, in addition to promising they wouldn't sell Nancy. But after twelve years of marriage, when Nancy was pregnant with their fourth child, Henry learned that she was being sold to a plantation in North Carolina. As he watched his wife and children walk away, he vowed to escape, which he did by "mailing" himself to freedom. In his autobiography after his escape from slavery, Henry wrote, "It is a horrible idea, but it is no less true, that no slave husband has any certainty whatever of being able to retain his wife a single hour; neither has any wife any more certainty of her husband: their fondest affection may be utterly disregarded, and their devoted attachment cruelly ignored at any moment a brutal slave-holder may think fit."[4]

During the Civil War, fugitive slaves were finally allowed to legally marry in services officiated by Union soldiers. They would receive an official government document. Officers were overwhelmed with requests for marriage. But once again, it wasn't a simple benefit of emancipation; it was part of a larger effort at regulation, promoting the idea that slaves still needed to be civilized. As one abolitionist noted, "[Marriage] is the great lever by which [the freed men and women] are to be lifted up and prepared for a state of civilization." With Victorian-era ideology now mainstream, Blacks after the war became penalized for not becoming legally maried because legal mariage became a sign of respectability and righteousness. As Hunter has argued, it also shifted the onus of control and caretaking from the slave owner to families, and in particular the husband, and released the state from any responsibility.

Still, marriage rights as a pathway to true citizenship was a narrative that even Blacks sometimes bought into. In 1866, after the state of Virginia became the first in the country to recognize Black marriage via the Cohabitation Act, a Black corporal explained to a gathering, "The marriage covenant is at the foundation of all our rights. In slavery we could not have legalized marriage: now we have it . . . and we shall be established as a people." People were drawn to marriage because it also signified some theoretical parity to Whites. One hundred years later, in 1950, 65 percent of Black men age fourteen and over were married, and 63 percent of Black women were married—rates comparable if slightly lower than that of Whites. Just ten years later, that number had dropped a bit for Black folks, to 64 percent of Black men and 60 percent of Black women. (White marriage rates remained roughly constant).[5]

By 1965, however, one Department of Labor policy analyst in the Johnson administration believed the tide had changed. In the infamous report *The Negro Family: The Case for National Action*, known more colloquially as the Moynihan Report, Daniel Patrick Moynihan said that a changing Black family structure, which included higher rates of nonmarriage, divorce, and female-dominated households, was responsible for a "tangle of pathology" in the Black community. He believed this affected school dropout rates, unemployment, fatherlessness, and criminal convictions. He also claimed that it had led to a "startling increase" in Black families dependent on welfare. The White family structure was also changing, he said, but not at the same rates. He attributed these differences to slavery and racial oppression of Black folk in America. "The Negro community has been forced into a matriarchal structure which, because it is too out of line with the rest of the American society, seriously retards the progress of the group as a whole, and imposes a crushing burden on the Negro male and, in consequence, on a great many Negro women as well." Critics like William Ryan charged him with "blaming the victim," and civil rights activist James Farmer, a cofounder of the Congress of Racial Equality, said the report was "a massive academic cop-out for the White conscience."

Yet the report still looms in the public debate, particularly when it comes to the Black family structure and sexuality. There was Ronald Reagan's fictional "welfare queen," which many heavily read as a lazy stereotype of an "oversexed" Black woman. Numerous stories on Black out-of-wedlock births were published with headlines like "The True Black Tragedy: Illegitimacy Rate of Nearly 75%." And even in 2017, it was revealed that one official in the Department of Homeland Security had previously criticized the status of Blacks in America on a radio show, saying, "It's an indictment of America's Black community that has turned America's major cities into slums because of laziness, drug use, and sexual promiscuity."[6]

To this day, marriage rates remain vastly different for Blacks than for their White counterparts, which has meant endless opportunities for Black love and marriage to be dissected. In 2016, 32 percent of Black people age fourteen and older were married, compared to 49 percent for all Americans. In study after study, married, two-parent families are seen as the key to upward mobility, as those households tend to earn more money, have higher levels of education, and have more free time to spend with their children. A report by the Brookings Institution noted, "Children of married parents have better life outcomes, in terms of education, health, and income—in large part because they have more resources available to them." Yet, marriage may not even be that much of an advantage for African Americans, particularly for Black women, because of assortative mating, in which a person marries someone with the same educational status. Since Black women go to school at higher rates than Black men, and also tend to interracially date less, our dating pool is smaller. On top of that, there's a lack of availability of Black men, particularly because of mass incarceration, so we don't participate in assortative mating the same way as our White counterparts.[7]

And while there are figures that media loves to hype—for example: 73 percent of births in 2010 were to unmarried Black women—there is less reporting on how those numbers actually may be wrong. In 2015 Charles Blow worked to change attitudes in a column headlined, "Black Dads Are Doing Best of All," citing a number of works that dispel the myth of absent Black fathers. In fact, he noted, the research points to just the opposite: when it comes to having relationships with their children, Black fathers tend to do better than other groups. He cites author Josh Levs, who points out in his book *All In* that despite the pervasive myth that Black dads are largely absent, what many reports get wrong is that most Black fathers live with their children but just aren't married.

MARITAL STATUS OF MILLENNIALS

MARITAL STATUS OF MILLENNIALS (AGE 18–34)	WHITE	BLACK	HISPANIC	ASIAN
Married	29%	14%	28%	33%
Widowed	0.1%	0.2%	0.2%	0.1%
Divorced	4%	2%	3%	2%
Separated	1%	2%	2%	1%
Never married	66%	82%	67%	64%
TOTAL	100%	100%	100%	100%

Source: US Census Bureau, 2016 American Community Survey data, from Steven Ruggles, Katie Genadek, Ronald Goeken, Josiah Grover, and Matthew Sobek, Integrated Public Use Microdata Series: Version 7.0 (dataset), Minneapolis: University of Minnesota, 2017, doi.org/10.18128/D010.V7.

Moreover, he refers to a CDC study that shows that Black dads who live with their children—about 2.5 million—are as involved as or more involved than their White and Latinx counterparts, meaning they diaper, feed, dress, and read to their kid on a daily basis.[8]

Still, the conversation around marriage and sexuality continues, and millennials haven't emerged unscathed. Probably unsurprisingly, similar patterns have emerged for the group: 77 percent of Black millennials are single, a higher share than for White millennials, 58 percent of whom are single, and Hispanic millennials, 61 percent of whom are single. Black millennial families headed by a married couple tend to have higher incomes (considering family size) than nonmarried millennial households. The majority of Black millennial families do not have children, but more Black millennial families have children than their

White counterparts. And the ones with children, statistics show, are more likely to be poor.

~

Love is hard for everyone. But for young Black people in America, it seems damn near impossible. Is it that surprising when we lack the love of our society? We are raised in a society that teaches us to hate ourselves, our bodies, our features, and to hate each other. We are taught that our hair is inappropriate and our skin is too dark. And then we are condemned when we learn to experience love in other ways. Because the history of our love and marriage is different, perhaps our experiences with love are also unique.

In a *Huffington Post* article, millennial journalist Ernest Owens makes a plea to his peers to not kill Black relationships. "Black love might look very different from how our grandparents had it, but it still deserves to exist." Relationship expert Tony Gaskins agrees that Black millennials have a rough time with marriage, part by design and part, he believes, because of the influence of hip-hop. "In older generations there were a lot more marriages. It was known that you are to get married. It's just been a breakdown slowly over time, every decade. It's just more and more of a trickle down effect from, especially in the Black experience, whether it's Jim Crow or Willie Lynch. Those things that were put in place to corrode the fabric of the Black race. It's working more and more every decade. The effects are becoming more and more severe." However, he told me that he believes the marriage issue is a "one-sided" goal that is more about Black women than Black men. "The women see it and hope for it and want it. I feel like marriage, no matter what generation it is, has always given men a little bit more of cold feet than women." He believes new ideas about relationships are making women settle for relationships they don't actually want. "Men didn't feel like they had the leeway to do what they want, and to just override the system. Now it's like a man knows he just can hit the override button and this woman goes from, 'Oh, I want to marry him, to 'Marriage is overrated. As long as we have love it doesn't matter. I don't need a lifetime commitment because we have real love and I know it's going to last.'"[9]

While one may agree or disagree with Gaskins's assessment of Black love, the state of love in the Black community is constantly up for debate, and it seems that there *is* a different dynamic going on with young Black people. While White millennials, too, are increasingly not marrying, they are shacking up more, raising kids together, without the legal recognition of marriage. As expert April Masini, told online magazine *Bustle*, "Millennials aren't big on tradition." "They prefer hanging out to dating, renting to buying and living together to marriage. It's not that they don't want a commitment—they do. They are having meaningful relationships and there have been studies that show they're actually having less sex at their age than prior generations—so it's not they want freedom to sleep around. They just don't want to get married." Yet while White millennials are experimenting with ideas around marriage, open relationships, sexuality, and identity, it's not framed as something *pathological*, but instead as something liberating, or for women, feminist. Black people, especially Black women, have long been raising kids alone or foregoing the formal institutions of marriage, but now that middle-class and wealthy White people are doing it, it's recast as "trendy" and "empowering." Relationship and family dynamics are different in the Black community—which is far more conservative than mainstream coverage often acknowledges—and we're overdue for an honest conversation about how Black millennials are building families.

The double standard has hit home for me in new ways as I face my aging ovaries and start thinking about things like egg freezing, something largely seen as a tool for rich White women, not allegedly "baby mama"–oriented Black women. I spoke with Monica Simpson, the executive director of SisterSong, a reproductive justice organization for people of color. She shared similar fears with me as we talked about the stigma and pressure that young Black women face. "A lot of us come from single-parent homes, so we know how hard that was," said Monica. "We saw how our mothers or fathers or guardians struggled to take care of us. I come from that generation. I did come from a single-parent home, and it's like nope, I don't want that. At all. So I'm going to make sure my career is tight, that I'm getting the education that I need, in whatever form that looks like, so I'm able to get the job that, you know, would allow me to provide for myself and said family if I so chose." It's different, she said, for young White women who chose to go at it alone. "They wear it as a badge of honor: 'I'm raising this baby alone.'" She pauses to explain: "But you also are White and you have access and privilege that we never ever will have, period. I have Black women who decide to be single moms, but they know they can't create a blog and say 'I'm getting ready to be a single mom as a Black woman.' That's nothing new for us, and it's nothing we can wear as a badge of honor because we've been stigmatized for that, we've been demonized for that, we've been looked down upon for that."

There is story after story about how the millennial generation is redefining love—living together more, having partnerships—when in reality they are doing the same things that Black folks have been doing for decades, except now without the Moynihan-like stigma. So I decided to talk to a range of Black millennials about their thoughts on love, marriage, relationships, and everything else in between.

~

On a rainy day in Mississippi, three Black women sit down to have a conversation. Two are in love, one with someone she doesn't think loves her back and the other, despite having a boyfriend and three kids, questions whether she even knows what love was. All three have experienced hurt, and all wonder what love means to the Black women of this new generation, when social media, Botox, and *Real Housewives* influence love lives as much as Barack and Michelle. I don't think any of us know where the conversation is going, and by the end I am shocked about the pain that has been spilled, surprised by the frankness of our talk. We are all on the older side of the millennial generation, and we have all endured a lifetime of loss and love. It would be simplistic to say the conversation is merely about relationships, but it never strays from love, in its various iterations and crazy curves.

Unlike many of the millennials I've met—especially on the coasts—Theresa, an administrative professional, and Trina, a freelance business consultant, are far more "adult." Both have college degrees and multiple children, some in their teens, and they've both been in long-term relationships. They have families.

The first thing I learn about Theresa's husband of twelve years is that he's a "doody head." Theresa's been in love with this doody head for nearly eighteen years. They met at community college during her freshman year, when she was still a young single mom, and they started a friendship that soon began to develop into a romantic relationship. Things got serious quickly, and she ended up pregnant with a baby girl. They soon married. When he graduated, he decided that he wanted to move to Jackson to get his master's degree and become a teacher. Theresa was supportive and joined him there soon after. She got a job at Victoria's Secret while going to school. She got pregnant again, but this time she had complications, so she quit her studies. Things were going well between them, he was a teacher working three jobs, and though things were busy, they were making it work. At some point, Theresa decided to stay at home to take care of the kids. After she gave birth to her fourth child, a son, they decided after three months at home, she would put him in day care and go back to work. Work was not easy to find, she said, because she had been out of the job market for so long, but she pushed through and became a substitute teacher.

They were both tired all the time, and things in their marriage weren't going so well. They began to talk about splitting up. Looking back, she said, she thinks the financial strain of his growing family hit her husband hard, and he didn't want to admit he was overwhelmed. But with the help of her church, they pulled through and stuck it out together. The kids didn't even know what was going on, and the relationship was saved for a while. He was working long hours, and Theresa spent a lot of time by herself and with the kids.

Theresa didn't want to be a burden on anybody, so she kept to herself and didn't socialize much. When she got a good-paying job at a university with great benefits and a good retirement plan, it was the opportunity she had long desired and was finally happy with her career. But a few months after she started, things began to change. She noticed her husband going out more than usual. At first, he told her that he was studying for some tests at the library. He always stayed in school trying to get certifications, so she didn't think much of it. One day when he told her he was at the library, she had a sinking suspicion that he might not be telling the truth. Since she worked on the same campus where he was studying, she decided to take a drive to see if he was really there. She didn't see his car and wondered where he was. She had been feeling particularly lonely at the time but was committed to keeping her family together. "I haven't had a social life in years. I don't go nowhere. I don't do anything. Work, home, kids. I was content because I love him, and when you are in love, you don't care about nobody, you don't care about no club, you don't care about no friends, you don't care about going out to eat with nobody."

Trina, another mom of three, looks across at Theresa in disbelief as Theresa proclaims her love for the doody head. "Maybe I just ain't never been in love," she said.

"I'm still in love," Theresa said. "He's not, but I am."

"You believe that?" Trina said, skeptical of the story.

"Either that or he's on some drugs," Theresa mutters back. "Or he got somebody else."

"I don't know how it would feel for somebody to say, 'I'm not in love with you anymore,'" Trina said, seemingly still in doubt.

"Oh, it's the worst feeling," Theresa replied.

She later confronted her husband, and he claimed that he was at the sports bar, but she didn't believe him. Things got worse, and now her husband has increased his nightly jaunts. He'll leave the house at six or seven, stay out for an hour or two, or not come home at all and not bother to answer her calls or texts. Her kids, especially the oldest, who are now twenty and seventeen, have noticed and have said things to him about it, but he doesn't respond. It's gotten to the point, Theresa thinks, where he just wants to come and go as he pleases.

Theresa finally admits to Trina and me that he wants a divorce, but she does not. After eighteen years she feels she has invested too much in the relationship, so if anything, he will have to fight for it: "I feel like I gave this marriage . . . if anything happens, I deserve . . . you know what I'm saying. Whether it's being selfish, I don't know. I really don't care, to be honest with you, but to make sure that there's still stability with the kids." Trina tries to convince Theresa that if it's all in writing, she will get what she deserves, but then Theresa tells us the thing that seems to be the most painful. "I believe in marriage. I don't believe in divorce—that's just my background from the Bible. Some people believe that they can divorce. Some women divorce their husbands and still think that they can go get married and God is going to be okay with that. I'm not sure about other people's faith; I know within my faith, I don't feel that God will be okay. Unless, well, technically, if your husband divorces you. I feel like at a point, it will be okay, God may say, 'Okay, you could still move forward and marry again.' But if you're trying to divorce your husband as a wife and you leave him, my faith and what I've been taught and raised is like, 'Okay, you go marry again, you know that ain't right.'"

Theresa's pretty face is filled with pain, and it's hard to listen to her struggle with a relationship she deeply cares about. It's clear she doesn't talk about these burdens she's been carrying very often, and as she tears up, a relief, too, seems to settle in. As we sit and watch the downpour flood the street, I ask if marriage is something that we still need to have. I look over at Theresa, but Trina jumps in first. "I don't have a desire to be married right now. Don't get me wrong. I used to. I wanted the picket fence, the kids, the dog, the cat. . . . It's just feelings are too finicky. People are like emojis. You can tap and change easily. I don't have the time or the faith to put into you for you to come home one day and be like, 'You know what? I ain't in love with you no more,'" she said, referring to Theresa's plight.

Trina says right now Black culture is saturated with images of the "sidechick" via shows like *Being Mary Jane* and *Scandal*. It's just adding to the complexity of Black relationships, particularly relationships with Black men, that she thinks are already challenging enough. Given a choice, Trina would happily "play her part." "I wanna be submissive to you, but you gotta give me something to be submissive for." For example, she tells us, she was dating a guy—courting, she amends—and her car got a flat tire. He had no clue how to change a tire, so she had to get out—in her "pretty blue dress"—and change a tire. She was pissed. "At that point in time, I said, 'Baby, is this really what you want? Is this really what you want out of your man?' She admits that her dad, who used to get up on Sunday mornings to cook, made her independent, which she cherishes, but she draws the line at changing a tire.

Trina is used to being surrounded by strong women. Her mom, the story goes, had to jump out of a two-story window while carrying two-week-old Trina in one hand and her sister in the other in order to get away from her abusive biological father. Still, she managed to find love again twice, and Trina had two great stepdads growing up. Her mom is still married to one of them.

As a single mom, Trina understands wanting to be in a couple, because being a single parent is tough. She said a lot of Black millennial women deal with their own wounds by babying their children. "They treat their kids like they're a micro-sized version of the man that they want or the man that just left them." She's worried about the relationship two of her kids have with their dad and hopes that things may change. She'll never forget how, two years after her ex walked out of their lives, she received a call from her kids' school, saying her son and daughter were having a breakdown at the "Doughnuts for Dads" event because they didn't have anyone there. She got on the phone, and her church members came through, and soon the kids were surrounded by men. Still, the experience seems to have shaken her up.

Dating with kids, Trina said, can be both hard and horrible. "Men think you're out looking for a baby daddy. They see [me] as if I got food stamps, Medicaid, I stay in a HUD house, and I sell my kids for tax money." She said men never think that she is college educated and has her own business. I ask what her response is to those who ask why she would decide to have three kids. She said the answer is quite simple. Her first two were accidents. She got pregnant on Depo-Provera, and then the second time while using condoms and the pill. She's not sure why those methods failed. Her third baby was planned out and discussed, but what she didn't plan for was for the father to be shot and killed by the time her child turned three.

Trina understands why people would question her, and admits she is actually one of those people who sees a young women with six kids and says to herself, "Damn. Like six, baby?" But she urges people to try to see the complexity of Black women. "Some people want big families like that. Let's just be honest. Some people do it for the system. Some people. Black women especially, they do it cause they don't want to be lonely. Myself, I didn't do that. The first two were surprises, and the last one was planned. So, for the people who be like, 'You could have had an abortion.' Well I could have had Cheerios this morning. I just made the decision to have Fruit Loops."

Trina has been seeing a man for over a year, though she wonders how long it will last. A friend of hers recently asked if she would consider marriage, and she genuinely was baffled. "It was a real life question, and I said, 'Mmm . . . I don't know. I don't think I would.' She's like, 'Well, if you won't marry him, why are you dating him?'" She doesn't have an answer for that either.

Still, Trina seems to like this dude more than she'll admit outright. He seems to respect her for who she is. She's particularly happy that he likes her natural hair—he is one of the few—and loves her dark skin.

Theresa, who has been quiet for a while, jumps back into the beauty conversation to talk about the pressures she is beginning to feel over her weight. Both women might be deemed "overweight." Theresa is smaller than Trina, but she is starting to think that maybe her husband stopped coming home because she has gained about twenty or thirty pounds. Trina asks Theresa if her husband is still sexually attracted to her, and Theresa said she doesn't know, but doesn't think that's it. Trina asks about drugs again.

"Please don't tell me my husband's on drugs," Theresa responds, clearly stressed.

Trina tells the story of when she dated a man on drugs. She says she fell into it because of the pressure to be in a relationship as a single mom. Black people, she says, want to see a family unit, and she was trying to live up to that Barack and Michelle ideal. But things started going missing from her apartment. He would be gone for extended amounts of time, and his mood shifted. He was either extra happy or nonchalant and the in-betweens were non-existent. It went from that, Trina says, to him being gone on extended binges, but she didn't give up because she believed that she could fix him. More things went missing. Things she didn't care about, like an old digital camera, or her car would be parked in a different place than she parked it, and he would claim he didn't do it. She started to fall apart. Some days she would be on the floor crying after he disappeared on a binge, not knowing whether he was dead or in jail. Eventually she had to let him go, but it was hard because as a Black woman she couldn't have a total meltdown.

"I'm not allowed to because I can't break. I've got three kids that's always watching. We can't break. We've got capes on our back. We always got to be superman," Trina says. More than that, she says she can't really think about her own dreams. "I don't have an American Dream anymore because it's like society has played me. I feel like society has played me and degraded me and beaten me and underprivileged me so much that I don't seen an American Dream. Every day is a struggle to get to the next day. My dream is to be able to see my kids successful. See my kids not locked up or the police done killed them. When I chose to become a mother, I had to forego my dreams so that they could have one. So I don't have an American Dream. I have [my kids'] dream. My dream is obsolete. It is just making sure that they are in a situation that they can achieve what they need to achieve. It's beyond 'never get married.' Beyond 'forever a single mom.' It is what it is."

The air feels heavy, and I can't decide if it feels cathartic or toxic, and Trina brings up, again, the unresolved question of Theresa's marriage woes. After hours of conversation, Theresa still doesn't know what to do. "So my question is, do I give up?" she asks us.

Trina answers the question bluntly, "The thing with love is, only you know when you've had enough. Can't nobody answer that question for you. Because everybody breaking point ain't the same. Like, I used to be so impatient, if you left the cap off the toothpaste, that was a deal breaker. Now it's like, Okay, let me give you the opportunity. Because we keep falling in love with personalities rather than characteristics. You keep falling in love with the previews, and you ain't watch the whole damn movie."

"Girl, look," Theresa said, "I thought I was falling in love with the movie."

"Uh-uh. You was still in the previews. Look what happened to Jack and Rose in *Titanic*. Everybody thought it was going to be all fruits and vegetables and just love on a stick, and she froze his ass like a popsicle."

A few months later I saw a registry for Theresa and her husband on the website The Bump. They're having a new baby, due in July 2018.

Much of the relationship conversations about Black people center around Black women, but young millennial Black men are also working to figure things out in a society that too often seems to discard their stories of love in favor of ones solely about sex. I met Richard, a vivacious young man who is dressed impeccably, at lunchtime in the financial district. He greeted me with a warm smile, and as we talked over two salads, I learned that Richard is honest in a way that so many folk aren't about how love, wealth, race, and class affect relationships in New York City.

Richard has loved before. He has loved past the hurt, past the pain, past the point of happiness. He's tried to fix the men he was with. Stayed through the rough times. Dealt with addiction. Had his body violently attacked. Cleaned up his apartment after it was destroyed. Called the police. Yet if you ask him if he's ever really been *in* love, silence ensues. He's loved hard, he said, because that's what he thought you were supposed to do, but when he really thought about being in love, he realized, to his surprise, that it's never happened to him. "That's hard to say out loud because obviously that hurts in some respect the people that I've been with. Everybody wants to feel wanted, especially when you're young. You want to feel desirable, you want to feel wanted, and so to do those things you need to check these boxes. What we're not told as young, gay Black men—because we're not conditioned in any kind of way, shape, or form in society—is that not everyone is for you, and you're not going to be for everyone, so just get comfortable with being who you are and accepting who is drawn to that." It's a lesson that Richard had to learn by himself, and it has helped him deal with clashes over his sexuality with his über Catholic mother.

As a teeneager, he wasn't worried about being gay, but after he told his mom, she apparently was. She would throw holy water on him and put books on his bed about conversion therapy, but she also constantly let him know he was loved. Her actions "irked" him, but he was comforted because he knew he had her love and also his own. "I just woke up around the age of fifteen and was like, well, if I don't love me, who else is going to love me?" At the time, he didn't have any role models in his hometown of Miami who could help him navigate the murky waters of sexuality in the nineties. But when he watched Karamo come out on MTV's *The Real World*, it helped him find solace in who he was. He came out to a friend the next day. Soon after meeting another young

Black gay male while working at Abercrombie, he found a whole community of gay men to hang out with. In eleventh grade he started dating ("I found all the little gay Black boys in my neighborhood and the next thing you know I was their boyfriend," he said, laughing), but for him dating wasn't sexual (he wouldn't lose his virginity until nineteen)—it was about crushes, romance, and most of all, finding the love of his life.

Richard headed to Morehouse College for his undergraduate degree and soon had to deal with another part of his identity, which in the end seems like would be a bigger struggle than his sexuality: his class status. Morehouse was the first time Richard was around people with money, and he became hyper-aware of his position in the working class. He would lie and tell people that his mother was a doctor when she really was a nurse. "I was ashamed of coming from this working-class family and what that meant." His concerns around class soon began to mesh with his romantic desires. He wondered how he was going to provide for the future family he longed for and how he could make his dreams a reality. Deciding he needed more stability and financial freedom, he joined the military.

Life in the military was hard. It was hard, he said, just because being in the military is strenuous and emotionally "challenging and traumatic" for anyone, but especially he said, as a Haitian Black boy from Miami who had to go back in the closet, a place he hadn't been in for years. It began to take a toll on him, he said, when everyone was using derogatory language, like "faggot." It wasn't necessarily that they were directing those slurs toward him, but it was hard for him not to push back.

He stayed in the closet for over a year and a half and fell into a deep depression. Suicidal thoughts flooded his mind. While he was stationed in Germany, he decided he couldn't take it anymore and came out to his supervisors. "Don't Ask Don't Tell" was still the policy of the US Armed Services, but instead of shunning him, his bosses became protective of him. A year and a half later he went to Afghanistan, and the policy was overturned on his birthday. He was hopeful that young people in the future would never have to hide who they were again; it had totally exhausted him.

When he returned from Afghanistan, he moved to New York City and nine months later was in a relationship after running into an old friend. The guy was cute, had amazing energy, and had a good job. Everything happened so fast, but Richard was convinced he had found true love. Six months later, all of that changed when he realized his dude was addicted to cocaine. His man had been turned on to the habit by a celebrity, and he would go on binges for days, disappearing and spending all of the money he was making. Richard was frustrated but remained committed to making things work, because he thought that when you're in love, you stick it out. And so he stuck it out. Even after this man was violent with him. Even after he got arrested for attacking him and destroying his apartment.

But, Richard discovered, it wasn't just the drugs that had intoxicated his partner, but also the wealthy lifestyle. He came from a poor family, Richard said, and didn't even finish high school, but had learned how to mask it very well. He was very refined, very well dressed, presenting as though he was from a "segment of society he wasn't from." In retrospect, Richard began to think about not just the addiction issues but also class. He said this guy lacked a sort of intellectual curiosity—not that Richard thought a degree was necessary to be an intellectual, but it seemed to him that something was missing, so after three years he called it quits.

Richard, now a strategist for a nonprofit, continued to think about how class affected his dating life and posted a question on Facebook asking his peers about their experiences. The answers he found were interesting. One person said they didn't date people who weren't upper-middle-class because it just didn't work. Richard then realized he only dated people who had poor or working-class roots. His next boyfriend, also grew up poor. He was from Compton; his parents were drug addicts, so he lived with his grandmother. Unlike Richard's former beau, this guy put himself through college and then got a full ride to Columbia for a master's degree in social work. Richard was impressed by him, but found that money had affected him a different way: rather than spend it, his man would always "put off happiness and joy" for an unknown future when he was making more money.

Richard was frustrated by that attitude too. He was making "good money" and was happy to be the provider, yet his man was consumed by the struggle for money. He thinks people who are working-class just "show up" differently in relationships. "Escaping poverty becomes the central aim, and everything that you're doing in some way is married to the fact that you want to escape poverty. Your choices in love, your choices in career, even how you show up, even how you spend money, how you invest in money, a lot of it tends to be this superficial 'I'm building a life around me that is reinforcing in my mind that I'm not poor.'" He said that a lot of the money that people are living on is borrowed in some way, whether it's credit or student debt, but it's just smoke and mirrors. "We've been able to ascend, but now we're in all this fucking debt for the rest of our lives because we were conditioned to think that we needed to achieve some semblance of middle-class life," he said with a sigh. "Half these gay men that are out here, especially young ones, they're either so caught up with wanting to become wealthy, so they're in fashion, they're working to put on that they come from a certain lifestyle, they live a certain lifestyle, and it's all really just a ploy so they could be with rich men." He knows it's all bullshit, but admitted it still bothers him. It's especially hard in New York City. The pressure is on, and wealthy is the "bare minimum" here, whereas in places like Tallahassee people are just trying to be middle-class.

At twenty-nine, Richard feels as if he has dated "all" of the Black guys in New York, at least all the twenty-year-olds, so his next plan is to date some older men, maybe even consider dating a White man, "if he understood the world deeply." But he's skeptical. "I don't know what the dick taste like—I don't know, girl. Generally I like to date people who are African American. I really like dating people who are Caribbean background because there's this shared cultural heritage, but they tend to be crazy, and I'm just not sure if that's a good balance because I'm already crazy, so I'm probably just going to stick to the African Americans."

As a Black man, he said, there's another worry on his mind. HIV. He's encouraged that young Black gay men are talking about the virus and things like PrEP, since according to the CDC, one in two Black gay and bisexual men will receive a diagnosis in their lifetime, but he knows there is greater nuance needed in the conversation.[10] "Our survival in a lot of ways is necessitated by the fact that we need to be aware of what's happening. It's not because we're being more hypersexual than any other race, it's because we tend to just have sex with each other and sometimes that sex is unprotected." Plus, he said, he thinks young Black boys tend to have sex before they are taught about safer sex practices. He is HIV negative but also understands the root of unrestrained desire, especially as a youth. When he was younger, he too felt that way when he was first starting to have sex. He didn't think about putting a condom on: "I was thinking about feeling connected to somebody and feeling wanted by someone." But early on he contracted a sexually transmitted infection, and he got scared. He never bottomed (let someone penetrate him) again. He's ready to stop being paranoid and be a bit more open to sexual experiences that he may be missing out on as a top. "I want to see at least what the dick do and see if I like the dick, I don't know, because I might not. I've been pretty content just being a top." He thinks bottoms are at more risk for HIV, but said conversations about position and versatility and what that means emotionally and how it's tied to relationships aren't always conversations young Black millennials are having.

AFTER HAVING BEEN IN TWO RELATIONSHIPS FOR NEARLY THREE years each, Richard is trying to figure out what is next for him. It's been six years of pouring his heart and soul into other people and into his relationships, and he's tired and on his "selfish shit" now, figuring out his own thing. "I was literally just texting my homegirl. She's talking about how niggas ain't shit or whatever, and I was like, 'Well, everyone is broken. You just have to find someone whose pain isn't toxic.' All my exes have been broken, every single one of them. Every single nigga that I fucked in the last six months has been broken in some way or another, including the one that I slept with last night," he said. "I could just tell in his eyes he was damaged, but finding the balance between them not being toxic for you, I think so many of us get so consumed because life is fucking hard."

He's feeling hopeful. He recently met a guy he is slightly enamored with. "He's the first time that I felt so comfortable with somebody that I was like, I could fall in love with them, and it changed my life. He doesn't live here, he just gave me a lot of advice in the month that we spent together, and it changed my view on life in so many different ways, and I think for the better."

He's also still trying to evaluate his ideas around relationships and money. "There's still a part of me that wants to be wealthy. I don't think that's ever going to go away because I like kale salad with squash in it, but not even wealthy to where I need to have golden toilets. I want to be comfortable, and I want to be able to provide and create, and then also provide for the people that I love around me. I'd love to say I have a partner one day. I want that. I think right now having been three weeks out of my relationship, I really need to focus on me and my issues and explore sexually a little bit, and really figure out what makes Richie happy." He's honest that the quest for happiness that so many people make fun of millennials for may never be a reality. "I don't ever know if I'm going to be at a place where I'm like, I'm so content. I don't know if I'm built for that, but I will say that a lot of this work is for me to get to a healthy place, so I can have a healthy coupling with someone else. I ain't trying to be alone."

A 2016 STUDY FROM GLAAD FOUND THAT 20 PERCENT OF MILlennials eighteen to thirty-four identified as LGBTQ, the highest of any generation. Another 12 percent of millennials in that same report also said they identify as transgender or gender nonconforming. The study also noticed that terminology used to describe sexuality and gender identity differed between generations, with older groups more likely to use terms like "gay/lesbian" and "man/woman" more than their millennial counterparts, who are embracing terms like queer, pansexual, genderqueer, gender fluid, and bigender.

During many interviews for this project, I noticed a number of young Black people identifying as queer—a term that means someone doesn't totally identify as heterosexual, but it can also be nuanced and political—and who were frustrated at misconceptions about their experiences. Some said being Black and queer, in a space where so much focus of the LGBTQ community is still on gay men, especially gay White men, can be difficult. Even in places perceived as liberal like New York or California, they still talked about anxiety and isolation, especially when it comes to dating. While there is an emerging movement to profile Black queer love more publicly, like Instagram favorites Dominic Spence and Nick Gilyard (@dom_and_nick), many say it's not enough. Writer Hari went to a university in New York thinking they would find solace in the queer community only to find that they too were marginalized by a marginalized group.

∽∽

It was never acknowledged that there was something happening between Hari and their best friend. They both knew it, but neither spoke about it or ever attempted to act on it. The two had known each other since meeting in choir in high school, but it wasn't until the summer after graduation that things changed. Hari, who identifies using they/them and sometimes he/him pronouns, had spent the night at their friend's house, and the two got drunk together. When their friend beckoned them over to lie on the floor with him and watch a movie, Hari somehow knew. They didn't do anything that night but remained side by side as their feelings hung in the air. Something had changed. Hari was terrified, and the next morning they got up and ran home. Hari couldn't stop thinking about that night, wondering if it was best to pretend it all away. But they soon realized they couldn't. And they didn't care. They were no longer afraid.

Up until that point Hari had created a perfect little invisible world where they carved a space for themselves, away from everyone else. It was a safe space, Hari said, a space where many young Black people linger in, hidden from the public, but one that no one really talks about. "We know that we can't love like White people, because we have a lot of other structures in place that would harm us if we walked around as carefree as White men do."

But on that day Hari wasn't scared. They said, "Fuck it," and approached their friend about the unspoken secret that lay between them.

They started dating that day.

Hari grew up in Cleveland, Ohio, one of seventeen brothers and sisters. Their mother was one of the first Black Hare Krishnas in the country—that's how they got their Hindu name—and their dad is Muslim—that's how they got their Arabic last name. Their mom and dad each had kids before, but Hari was the first they had together. Their mom home-schooled Hari and their siblings and also worked as a marriage and family counselor, while their dad did the same. Much of their journey Hari said was less about sexuality and more about overcoming their parents' idea of masculinity. Fortunately, Hari has a lot of feminist older sisters who challenged their dad's ideas of what men and women do, and though Hari felt comfortable fighting against that, things were still hard.

One memory that particularly stands out is when during elementary school Hari danced with a friend of theirs. The young boy told his mother that Hari had been grinding on him, and she called up Hari's parents. In retrospect, Hari said they probably shouldn't have been grinding on the guy, but it also seemed like it was about more than just dancing with another dude. It was about not conforming to a certain version of masculinity. Their father was "livid." It was one of the few times

Hari was ever whopped as a child, but in that moment Hari also clearly remembers feeling that they didn't do anything seriously wrong. They knew the situation was wrong and that they weren't the problem. But Hari was a child, so they couldn't do much about it. As a teenager Hari was a bit more rebellious and got away with more, which they believe was because they were smart and doing well academically. They were a part of a gifted and talented program and for a while heeded those messages that they were special in some ways. "I bought into all these of ideas of academic achievement, and what it meant about worth, that I definitely don't subscribe to now." They "learned" that they needed to be "saved" from their life in East Cleveland, that they had to overcome and be "better" than their peers, and their community was temporarily built around that. Toward Hari's junior and senior year their politics started changing. Hari decided the program was bullshit, and they had a kind of epiphany. They realized that "you can't be saved from this shit until all of this stuff comes tumbling down." Hari became more involved with the queer community, but not intentionally. They weren't particularly trying to do queer activities, they said, and they weren't part of any queer organizations, but many of the activities they were involved in then, including choir, had a queer contingent, and Hari made many queer friends.

Hari opted to go to New York University for college and was excited to go to a school that is known to be super queer. Hari was looking forward to being part of a community there. In some ways, college was great for Hari, but they also realized they weren't experiencing queerness in quite the same way as the school's predominantly White students. NYU is only 3 percent Black, and Hari struggled to connect. They met another Black queer student, and while they had a lot of other queer White friends, they hung tight because they realized that there was something different they shared. Sometime around junior year, Hari realized that they could expand their reach beyond campus, and that maybe some Black queer folk would understand their plight more. "I was separating Blackness and queerness for so long that I wasn't even prepared for how much like home it would feel like to find a community where there were

Black queer people who understand that there are racist sexuals, and also queer-antagonistic sexuals. Understand that those things don't just add onto each other, but morph into a weird specific thing that only queer Black people experience. Homophobia and racism do all of this weird shit to queer Black folks."

As Hari was beginning to hit their stride in New York, things got harder back home. Their relationship with their best friend, who was still in Cleveland, ended. And then Hari's parents found out about their relationship with the friend. Hari had written their parents a long letter about the feelings they had around their sexuality. It was all "clichéd shit," they said. Hari's parents took a few days to respond, which Hari wasn't shocked about. Hari anticipated that their mother would be more understanding than their father, since when they were growing up it was Dad who had done the gender policing, not Mom. Yet after the letter, the opposite occurred. Their mother kept sending them scripture verses. Hari would send some back. The Hare Krishna religion doesn't have a clear position on sexuality, and there are some scriptures that seem supportive of queerness, Hari said. Their mom read it differently. She wouldn't relent and refused to help pay for school. Hari's dad, meanwhile, didn't talk to them for a few months, but when he finally did, he was most upset that Hari had written a letter instead of telling them in person about their sexuality. Hari and their father talked about it, and their father seemed to understand. Now Hari has a stronger bond with their father. Hari's relationship with their mom is okay, they said, but things aren't quite the same.

Still, once Hari had come out to their parents, they felt like their journey could continue, "full speed ahead." (Hari doesn't care for the term "coming out." Hari explains, "For me, my sexuality and gender journey has always been a journey. It's always been fluid and in motion. Today, even last year, I felt I identified in different ways. That's why I don't really like the term 'coming out.' It's like, coming out of where into what?") Hari soon met someone new. It was their first adult relationship and challenged the way Hari thought about gender. Their partner, they said, was willing to test the boundaries of gender and play around with it. It was new to Hari, who had grown up thinking in terms of masculinity, but it helped them break those notions. It was good for them, and though the couple broke up after two years, Hari said they now understand their fluidity in different ways. Hari now identifies as queer, but not really as a man.

Hari said lately they are actually trying to identify less, but queer seems to be the concept that they most closely identify with. I ask Hari to explain his understanding of the word. "Queer theory is rooted in the idea of existing in the not yet here. Your state of being can be an ideation, and not necessarily a reality, or reality as we conceive of realities. When it comes to sexuality, it translates generally as—because reality is so structured by heteronormative ideas—anything that's outside of the heteronormative concepts." And then I had a sort of "aha" moment, as Hari summed up so succinctly what so many people seemed to be trying to say about their lives. "I use nonbinaries, but at the same time I think that Black people already do that in so many ways. I think we're already denied a normative existence, or divided. Because Black could be the umbrella term that doesn't restrict people in this way."

MILLENNIAL MOMENT: **CATCH-22**

RAQUEL, AGE 25, OAKLAND

Relationships are just as important as they've always been. I think that there's more room for variation on what that relationship can look like nowadays. In a lot of ways it's more difficult than it's ever been because people can be more specific about qualities that they want. I feel like in the older generation, people weren't as picky, or they fell in love and didn't wonder as much about what else was out there, or what other ways could this relationship look like. I think it's a catch-22. There are more avenues and more ways to meet people, but people are becoming very much pinpointed or specific in what they're trying to find.

As a trans person, or as a trans woman, it's difficult to assess if it's easier now to date and to be in a relationship. There's more people who understand what being trans means and are open to dating trans people, but on the other hand I know that with that visibility also comes a lot of danger. We're seeing more reporting on trans women, particularly Black and Latinx trans women who are being murdered by their partners. Visibility has helped in some ways, but also hindered in other ways.

In some ways it is difficult to be a Black woman and date because of the ways in which we've been painted in media for centuries and the ways in which our bodies have been commodified, even by our own men. You think about pop culture, the emphasis on our asses and our bodies, and whether we're thick, and whether we're the right kind of thick. There are all of these expectations as a Black woman that you're expected to live up to in terms of desirability. That doesn't even take into account color, right? And how there's so much value in being a light-skinned woman versus being a dark-skinned woman.

I try to be very sensitive when I say this, but as a Black woman who very much appreciates dating Black men, it is difficult particularly as a Black transgender woman to find Black men who are open to understand my identity, or won't just write me off because I'm transgender.

I think a lot of it is because being Black in the United States, we have a very complex relationship to gender and sexuality, and in many ways the expectations of gender are harder on Black people. Black women, we often have to compete with images that try to strip us of our womanhood. The same thing goes for Black men, as they feel that they are competing with a society that doesn't really value their manhood. Sometimes that idea is very essentialist or problematic, but I think that there is an underlying truth to the fact that we are dealing with distorted images of ourselves. So when we date somebody, it often reflects more on us about our worth, our value to society and the rest of our culture in a way that I don't think it affects White people or people of a different race.

I think for Black men in particular, there is more of an incentive to date a woman who is not Black. If you want to think about the racial totem pole in the United States, being Black is pretty much on the bottom rung, and so the incentive socially to date a woman who is not Black is much higher for Black men than it is for men of other races. A lot of times if a woman is of a race that's not Black, or she's not dark-skinned, then she's seen as a trophy, right? She's seen as the fair maiden of the fairy tale. But if you're a Black woman, I think there's less of an incentive. I think it doesn't help that we have so many successful, prominent Black public figures who are men who don't date Black women and unabashedly share that publicly.

Going to interracial dating, I think the problem isn't in somebody dating somebody of another race, the problem is in someone not being able to critically think about these preferences in society and what they mean. I do think that we will continue to see more and more people dating regardless of race. I think that race will continue to be less of a determining factor in people's dating preferences. Just like I think gender will continue to be increasingly less of a preference probably for some people.

I think we have to look at cis-genders sometimes when we have this conversation, but women are given less room to think deeper about what a desirable partner is to them. So there's more room for men to have their pick of the litter because of the patriarchy. Women have historically been told who they were going to be with or who they should be with and that has unfortunately continued to be the case.

The average White person in America just has a completely different experience than the average Black person in America. The Black community has dealt with so much, well, continues to deal with so much trauma, just from generations of attacks against our families, and against our bodies, and against our future. So just thinking about how much of our population is locked up in prisons away from their families, right? Thinking about not having access to adequate jobs and adequate wages and adequate health care, all of these play a part in how healthy our relationships can be. I think that's playing a part in why we're not seeing the same numbers of marriage.

I think it is a part of the American Dream, but I think the American reality is that marriage, the idea that you will only be married once, needs to fade away. I think that because marriage has continued to be held on such a high pedestal, people feel rushed into it a lot of the time. A lot of times people make the decision to get married simply to be married, simply to blend in and feed into what they've always been told they were supposed to do.

I couldn't imagine having married someone before this point in my life, because I am so different than who I was even a year ago. I feel like if I had settled down before now, it would have stifled me and kept me from growing in the way that I needed to grow. In my head I like to think that maybe I'll meet someone and settle down around thirty, maybe a little after thirty, but for me it's not a guiding force in my life. I feel like the most important thing is to find a relationship that is fulfilling, and one that inspires me to be better, but one that also honors the person that I already am.

chapter nine

BREATHE

JASMINE IS ALL ALONE. THE CAMERAS ARE GONE, THE NATIONAL LEADERSHIP won't answer her calls, and most urgently, she's just been fired from her job and is wondering what she is going to do for money. It's a far cry from two years ago, when we first talked and she was enthralled by the passion of activism, frustrated with the system, and nonplussed about her felony charge because she believed the movement was going to change things. Today Jasmine's beyond that. She's weary, and worried about the cost of being such a visible organizer, and she wonders if any of it mattered. She was content doing activism in her hometown of Pasadena, content battling police officers she had known for years. All that changed after she was arrested for "felony lynching," a dated name for an obstruction of arrest. The media swarmed, and the public, outraged that a Black activist had been arrested for lynching, swarmed around her, and she shot to notoriety. Suddenly, she said, she had a documentary team paying for housing and filming her story, national leaders of Black Lives Matter calling and vowing to "take care of her," and a feeling that she was making a difference. She had problems, sure, but it felt as if change was near.

Nearly a year later, after she was convicted and served time, Jasmine is no longer the vivacious activist I first met. She's pissed at Black Lives Matter and is unclear about their direction, she's broke and depending on her girlfriend for money, she has no idea what the filmmaker is going to do with his project, and overall she's searching for answers in a world that is unable to give her any.

Jasmine is experiencing the other side of activism, the other side of wokeness that isn't as cute as a Pepsi ad. It's the side of activism that you usually hear about in passing years later or in some memoir of an activist reflecting on their radical days. It's the part that no one wants to capture on Instagram. The Angela without the high fist or perfect hair. It's not exciting or sexy. It's often depressing, and it's experienced by people still doing the work. And that's exactly what Jasmine is doing. Helping out the kids in her neighborhood and attending city council meetings. It's what seems to sustain her and the only bright spot as she struggles to figure out her next move.

Jasmine had a "wild childhood," as she calls it. She was out in the streets from a young age, gangbanging. Her mom was on and off drugs, and her dad wasn't in the picture. So instead her community, her hood, raised her. It's almost ironic, she said, because like with Jaleesa in the South Bronx, the gang members were the ones who made her stay in school. They told her explicitly not to come around until school was over. "What you hear on TV and what they put out there is cliché, it's a lie, it's a fabrication, because my hood is what taught me love, what taught me loyalty, and what taught me how to be there for somebody unconditionally, no matter what, you know? They're the ones that taught me that we come with flaws, you know what I mean? Flaws and all, we're still flawless." They would help her when she needed it and give her food when she was hungry, but things are different now. She said kids today have it harder than she did. They're suffering from depression and anxiety and have fewer places to turn for help. "Depleted and they haven't even touched life yet." She can relate. For much of her childhood, she said, her mom dealt with addiction, and even when her mom stopped using, she had to work hard to make up for those lost years. "I got to see what it meant for a Black woman to be resilient and persistent, but the lack of nurturing, there was lack of nurturing. That was kind of hard, as a child, growing up, you know what I mean? Constantly watching your own back, that was a lot for me as a kid." On the outside, to the public, she said, her childhood looked "awesome." She played violin and trumpet, went to math field days and participated in spelling bees, that *Leave It to Beaver* type stuff that America thinks is quintessential to growing up. Her mom tried, but inside her house was chaos, and they ended up living with someone who molested her. She pushed on, and things got better when she reconnected with her older brother around the age of fourteen. They had been separated when her mom was working out her issues, and he returned as head of the household. He was more than a big brother, she said; he was her shield. "When my brother was around, [no one was able] to touch me. My brother was protecting me, and my brother didn't even know—he was like my Superman." Life for her had begun to feel calm. Safe even.

And then he was murdered.

Once again the chaos returned, and Jasmine just didn't understand life and didn't really care to. She decided she had no reason to live. She felt dead on the inside. Never-ending days filled with depression lingered as a continuous mourning consumed her life. "I just wanted to go all gas, no brakes down the wrong road." It was 2002, and she was nineteen-years-old, a time when her life should have been just beginning, but she was doing drugs and everything possible to kill herself. She was, as she put it, wandering down a self-destructive road, and there was no one there to pull her to safety. "Every Black man in my life, he either left or he was murdered. When my brother passed away, I was asking God, 'Why?' I was mad at every Black man. I didn't understand what was going on. I was lost." Her mom had changed, too, since her brother's murder, though Jasmine understood why. "I know she loves all of us, but ever since my brother was murdered, it was like she didn't know how to be a mom anymore. The warmth, it goes somewhere. You as child, you start trying to protect your mama. You start trying to be the parent. Then I was parenting myself basically." Without anyone to help, she did what many unsupported young people do: she turned to the streets.

One person who did help her out was Wilson Pierre. They were best friends, and they'd talk about any and everything. He particularly liked to discuss what it meant to be Black in America, and he introduced her to a range of books about Black folk. Back then, Jasmine didn't really think about her identity much. She didn't know what it meant to be a Black person in America and didn't care much about it. But her time with Wilson helped change that. They'd do things like read *The 48 Laws of Power* (which according to Wikipedia is popular with celebrities and prison inmates), books by the Black Panthers, and biographies of Huey Newton. Wilson was like the activist Tookie Williams in her community, and everyone would go to him. But, she said, laughing, he was a big mama's boy who just "loved to love." She was beginning to think about the world in new ways, and so was he. The last time she spoke to him, they stayed up until seven am in the morning, and he talked about how he was living not just for himself, but also for his child. He told her that he no longer wanted to be "Connie J. Rock," his hood persona; he wanted more. "He was like, 'I can't be the Rock no more—I've got to be Wilson.'" They looked at each other, realizing there might be a brighter future ahead, and started crying. Then he, too, was taken away from her. Murdered.

Jasmine said he was killed by someone at a party as he was trying to protect his child's mother from someone who was out to get her. "My best friend died for his kid's mother. That's genuine love." The *Los Angeles Times* described Wilson's death as an "incident" that was thought to be "gang-related."[1] "You could call Wilson no matter what you were going through, and he would come. I just thought right now, that's who I want to be." Jasmine was fighting tears, but quickly lost that battle and immediately began to apologize for her tears, though I understood their presence. She was mourning an end, but it was also the beginning of something new, a transformation, though she didn't know it at the time.

She wanted to do something different from being on the streets, but she just wasn't sure what. She remembered Wilson telling her that she needed to be a preacher because she had a "big-ass mouth." Plus, she was just sitting back watching her friends die, collecting obituaries. She knew there had to be more, and one day, she thought maybe doing some work trying to help other people would be a good idea. In the past she had seen some campaigns to fight Proposition 8, an initiative that would deny same-sex couples the right to marry and thought that LGBTQ issues might be a good place to start. So she decided to join one of the organizations that was fighting the legislation. They seemed to be visibly doing good work in communities, hers included. She identified as a lesbian and knew what that struggle was about, not that she was ever really in the closet ("I told my mom, 'I'm coming out the closet,' and she said, with a laugh, 'What closet?'"). They were fighting for marriage rights, and she wanted to get married someday, so she thought it was a good fit. She was hired as a fundraiser/activist, but Jasmine's hopes were soon dashed when she realized there was racism in the White LGBTQ world. "I'm like okay, this is cool because I'm like a voice for the voiceless. Then I realized these LGBTQ places, they don't care about Black lesbians and gays." "I thought they genuinely cared about changing hearts and minds about the Black and Brown community, about the way they felt towards the LGBTQ community. I thought we were going to get the tools we needed to have those conversations with our people, and no. It was like convincing people to raise money, and that's it. They would go to the Black and Brown community and have us pander. They just wanted to raise money—it wasn't at all what I thought it was."

Around the same time Ferguson was beginning to explode over the death of eighteen-year-old Michael Brown, who according to the police officer who shot him was some sort of superhuman monster. Jasmine was mad about the whole thing, and her rage built even more was she watched a video of a seven-year-old girl getting milk poured on her face to counter the effects of tear gas. Jasmine was pacing back and forth, looking at this image, trying to figure out what to do, when a woman she worked with called her and asked if she wanted to go to Ferguson. Patrisse Cullors had sent a call encouraging allies to come to the village. Jasmine was scared, and her family was worried about her safety if she went. But when she saw the Bloods and the Crips making peace to fight for Michael Brown, she said, "Fuck this, I'm going."

When she got to Missouri, she noticed how things were so much different than in California. The racism at home was generally more covert. It could be something as banal as a person crossing to the other side of the street when they saw her walking with a group of friends, or someone clutching their purse for dear life on an elevator ride, little things that she barely paid attention to. Ferguson was another story: from the jump people looked at her and her group as if they had a target on their foreheads. People didn't even bother to try to repress their racist thoughts. At one point, she said, she even heard a White person ask his grandson if he had counted "all of them." She glared at him and said, "We're not cattle, Black sheep. We're people."

In the days after Mike Brown's death, she said there was this indescribable feeling, a stillness in the air, but the love from the Black community helped lift the dark clouds that hung over the city. The love was everywhere. Like the one time she was walking around the neighborhood looking for some weed, and some cats on the corner were surprised that she came to Missouri all the way from the West Coast.

He said, "You all came all the way from Cali for us? You all came all the way out here to be with us?"

"Yeah," she replied.

"Keep looking forward, because I got your back," the stranger told her.

It was an endearing moment—and a testament to how lonely, isolated, and unloved so many Black folk feel. But she was shocked even more so, because they were coming from opposite ends of the spectrum. "His rag was blue and mine's was red," she told me. "He loved me just for that, you know? Just for coming out there and flying out there because we was concerned. He couldn't believe that; he was in awe." She was shocked at the amount of trauma Black people face, but more so shocked that the man she talked to was in such awe that the community had his back. That he didn't believe they were there just for him.

She had other moments like that, like the time she was so frustrated about what was happening she was about to topple over with grief. She had just come to the church where organizers were meeting after walking on the street where Mike Brown was killed. She was huffing and puffing from the anger she felt in the community, and she just didn't know what to do. As she stood shaking, Melina Abdullah, an activist who has been a mentor to her, walked over and said one word: "Cry."

Jasmine was confused and didn't know what the fuck that meant. But she was also breaking down, and the tears just began to flow like never before. Crying, she said, like a little kid who has just gotten a beating. "We cried together—we got to really cry together. I've never cried before, really. Before Ferguson I never got to cry; I never got to breathe," she said. On the streets, crying was a form of powerlessness, and she was never allowed to be vulnerable. "I wanted to cry, but I couldn't. I had pent-up aggression. In my community crying is a form of weakness." Once she started, though, she couldn't stop. "It was like a cry from deep down inside my soul. It felt so good to cry, and I felt released—I felt cleansed." Then Abdullah took her in the back room and told her to take off her shoes. They sat down meditation style, and she offered another command. "Breathe."

Jasmine listened. She breathed in, she exhaled, she breathed in, she exhaled, and there was a clarity she said she never felt before. She realized that all the anxiety she had was the same feeling that a lot of people in the Black community have, and she had finally found a way to cope. Something that made her relax. In and out. In and out. She didn't know that breathing would help until that moment. "Right there was my eye opener, because I noticed a lot of us in my community, we have anxiety a lot, and I didn't know what the fuck it was called. I didn't know it was called anxiety. I didn't know what the feeling I've been feeling all my life was called, and I didn't know that it's a process, that we could eliminate the feeling by just breathing. I didn't know that I wasn't breathing."

It was there at that church where she was introduced to Black Lives Matter. It taught her, in so many ways, how to breathe. Looking back, she realized she had never even given herself permission to really feel the air inside her, and among those tears somehow clarity began to emerge for the first time, and she realized she had to join the movement. She never wanted to lose these folks, these Black Lives Matter people, these people whose arms felt like home.

She started going to meetings that week.

YOUNG BLACK PEOPLE HAVE OFTEN BEEN ACCUSED OF BEING apolitical, uninterested, and lazy, but statistics show they're anything but. In fact, young Black millennials are some of the most politically active people and have shown up to vote at rates higher than any other racial and ethnic groups in 2008 and 2012, partially inspired by the campaign of Obama. Researchers say that it wasn't the youth who got Barack Obama elected president; it was *youth of color*—though the narrative sometimes suggests otherwise. According to research by the Black Youth Project, while 58.7 percent of youth overall voted for Obama, there was a significant difference across racial groups. 95.8 percent of Black millennials supported Obama, and 76.3 percent of Latinxs. But only 44.7 percent of White millennials supported Obama. It makes sense: 37.1 percent of White millennials support the Democratic Party, and 36.7 support the Republican Party, meaning that while the story is often that young people are more loyal to the Democratic Party, there's a racial component that we can't ignore.[2] This doesn't mean Black millennials are completely committed to the Democratic Party: during the last presidential election in 2016 we proved that we're not solely in line with our parents' generation. We did not unanimously support the mainstream Democratic contender Hillary Clinton, instead supporting Bernie Sanders 44 to 32 percent in the primary contests, according to a GenForward Survey.[3]

More than just parties, we seem to be divided on the issues we're concerned about as young people. Overall millennials are concerned with the economy, terrorism, and debt, in that order; when you look at these issues by race, things change. The main issues that White millennials are concerned about are debt, the economy, and terrorism. Black millennials, on the other hand, are first concerned with race issues, gun control, and the economy. Latinxs were also first concerned with racial issues followed by the economy and terrorism, while Asian millennials were concerned with the economy, terrorism, and gun control, according to a report, *Millennials Deconstructed,* from the University of Texas.[4]

Millennials are now the largest voting bloc by generation, yet election participation by young Black people has waned in recent years. In 2016 Black millennials' turnout decreased to 49.4 percent, down from 55 percent in the last presidential election. In turn, White millennial turnout actually increased. There's the obvious excuse that without a Black man on the ticket, Blacks lost enthusiasm, but most young people say it's more complicated than that. Some blame Russian suppression. After all, it was found that Russians were specifically targeting young Black activists with messages discouraging them from voting. Others say they were influenced by Colin Kaepernick's comments about not being registered to vote. Others noted that they are just tired of being ignored, with some being frustrated specifically with the Democratic Party and others just annoyed with the system overall. An NBC/*Wall Street Journal* poll of Black millennials in Pennsylvania, a key battleground state Trump won by 44,000 votes, found that young Blacks were discouraged by the electoral process. They said they felt "outnumbered" and that their votes "don't really count."[5]

Recently, as part of a broader backlash against the Trump presidency, it seems that young Black people are becoming engaged again, though many don't seem particularly committed to doing so through traditional party leaders. Instead of continuing to give their support for established, especially White, candidates, they are running for office themselves, attending political meetings, volunteering time, and creating their own political PACS. Collective PAC, which is dedicated to electing people of color, is one such group, as is Woke Vote, which helped engage Black millennials in a special election in Alabama for Attorney General Jeff Sessions's seat, which Democrat Doug Jones won, a victory attributed especially to Black women. In short, Black millennials are doing what young Blacks have done in the past: putting in the work on the ground, often behind the scenes and out of the gaze of the media or most of the public.

Thanks to social media, activists can be both hyper-visible to the public, mini-celebrities even, but also hidden, and it's no different for Black millennials. Several young Black Americans told me of the stress they have encountered because of their activism. For some this has meant surviving on little money and battling stress and depression, like Jasmine, while for others it's meant death. A report in the *New York Times* found that in the last few years at least five activists who came to national notoriety during the Black Lives Matter Movement have died, though the causes of death vary from suicide to natural causes to homicide. Erica Garner, the daughter of Eric Garner, became an outspoken activist after the death of her father, who infamously was shown on video muttering the words, "I can't breathe" to cops who had put him in a chokehold during an arrest for selling loose cigarettes. She told a talk show host in 2016 that the pressures of activism were getting to her. "I'm struggling right now with the stress and everything," she said. "Because this thing, it beats you down. The system beats you down." A few months later, she was dead.

NO ONE UNDERSTANDS THIS ALL MORE THAN JASMINE. IN 2014, Black Lives Matter's organizing and direct action were two of the most visible forms of political expression we saw Black millennials participate in. Black Lives Matter was the rallying cry for many in our generation, and the technique of direction action attracted many young people to take to the streets. Jasmine organized with all the passion she had. Marches, phone calls, city council meetings—she did it all. Going to Beverly Hills on Rodeo Drive and inside the restaurants just to remind people that Black lives matter or to say the names of the young people who had been killed. They were doing everything they could to disrupt the status quo and mobilize folks, and it was working. She even did things like jump on cars, which remained debatable even among fellow activists, differences she attributed to a class divide and respectability politics. She was doing so much that she wouldn't even tell me all the details of her work so as to not incriminate herself. But it was all action. "Action, action, action," she said.

At the same time her activism was increasing, she began racking up arrests, which had an impact on her employment, even though she wasn't convicted for anything. The reasons for her unemployment vary. She got fired from one job when she got a charge for terroristic threats. She hadn't been found guilty, but they fired her anyway, despite her attempts to get Human Resources involved. When she got another job, at a non-profit that raises money for political issues, after two weeks she was told they would no longer need her services. She believes it was retaliation for handing out a Black Lives Matter flyer the week before. "People don't agree with Black Lives Matter—it's like those 'all lives matter' people. I believe it was some racism that happened, some prejudice that went on. It made me feel like just thrown away. Used up, objectified again. And I just don't understand why." But her activism had become a life-or-death issue for Jasmine, and despite the fact that within a few short years she'd get fourteen charges, she believed deeply in her cause, though she found it ironic that when she was out in the streets, her slate was clean. "When I was gangbanging, I like to tell people I never caught a charge. I never caught a case. I was so under the radar. But now that I'm standing up for my people, I have fourteen different charges. Terrorist threats, criminal threats, assault, battery, all types of things, right?"

But it wasn't until her arrest for lynching that those things really changed. Jasmine was arrested in August 2015 for attempting to "unlawfully remove a suspect from police custody," a charge that in California used to be known as "felony lynching." She was with a group of people who were leaving a peaceful rally protesting the shooting of an unarmed Black man by police in Pasadena. After the rally she saw officers detain a woman who was arguing with a restaurant owner, and Jasmine said she went to fight for the woman. Police officers had another opinion, and they charged her with inciting a riot, child endangerment, and lynching.

The California law was created in 1933 as a response to the actions of a vigilante mob that seized and hanged two White men who confessed to killing the twenty-two-year-old son of a store owner. The law was designed to make it a crime to remove someone from police custody. The term "lynching" covers any extrajudicial punishment by—in the words of the 1933 law—"means of riot," but the term has historically referred most often to hangings of Blacks by mobs of Whites. In 2015, California governor Jerry Brown removed the words "lynching" from the state penal code after another Black Lives Matter activist was arrested under the law to much protest, but the crime is still deemed a felony charge. The ridiculous name of the law garnered a lot of media attention, and Jasmine immediately rose to national attention, being hailed as one of the first political prisoners of the Black Lives Matter movement. She also, in true millennial fashion, became a hashtag. The #FreeJasmine campaign caused folks to take to the streets and protest and also inspired a Color of Change campaign to release Jasmine. It garnered 89,000 petition signatures.

Jasmine was terrified in jail and frustrated by the lynching charge. "Once I found out what lynching was and why it was created, I was feeling like I was mad, and I was appalled. I was like damn, I was a Black person trying to save a Black person. It was kind of ironic." But more than anything she thought she was going to be killed and was worried every time the jail door closed. She was so low that she thought about committing suicide. The only thing that stopped her, she said, was a letter from Redel

Jones's husband. Redel Jones was a thirty-year-old Black woman who was killed by a Los Angeles Police officer in 2015 for allegedly charging at police with a knife. Her husband thanked Jasmine for her work protesting the department and told her how much his family was grateful and understood the sacrifices she was making for his family and his late wife. At that moment, Jasmine knew she had to choose life, and she hung on for three long months. It was still overwhelming. She'd never had a record before and didn't receive counseling to help her deal, but she somehow made it through. Months later, she said, she is still trying to "process" it all emotionally, but she's struggling, and her support system, she said, has all but abandoned her.

Money was tight, but initially she had a place to live. A filmmaker wanted to make a documentary about her and paid for an apartment for her to live in. But the space was ransacked a couple of times, and she didn't feel safe there anymore. She said she asked Black Lives Matter leaders to help, but all she heard was silence. "My apartment had gotten ran into. I'm assuming it's the police. I'm like, 'Hey you guys, please get me out of here.' And no one even helped me. Nobody even helped get a new lock on my door." She ended up moving in with her girlfriend and her girlfriend's parents.

On a spring day in 2017, I spoke to Jasmine again, and she seemed particularly down. She had just been fired from a job after five months as a fundraiser. It was the first job she'd had in years. According to Jasmine she didn't meet her weekly $100 quota and was worried about the repercussions. Panicked, she knew she wouldn't raise the money in time, so she donated $45 dollars herself. It was against protocol, and her boss fired her. She wrote Human Resources to plead her case, hoping that she would get a call back, but she sounded doubtful they would help. She needed the job more than ever, because she said she had to do so much on her own. She thought that there would be more help, but it wasn't coming through. She was clearly in a bad situation with the national Black Lives Matter network, on a personal level, as she told me that they had promised they would help and support her when she called.

"I didn't receive a call back. I want to know why," she said, frustrated. But mainly, she wanted to know why they pushed for her story to become national news. "Why did you all even put me on blast like this, to the point where everybody knows me, as far as the mayor, all the police in the world?," she wanted to ask them. She said they could have just left her alone, and she would have handled it with the people she knows, "her police" in Pasadena. (A former representative with Black Lives Matter said at the time, "The organization exhausted every resource we had to meet Jasmine's immediate needs, including legal support and media outreach." Another current representative of the group concurred.)

But she also seemed worried about the political future of the movement. She said she saw a "shift" between the college-educated folks and the hood folks, and a lot of opportunists in the leadership. She's also troubled by a statement from Alicia Garza, one of the movement's cofounders, that said the movement was moving more toward changing policy and away from protest in the age of Trump. "What people are seeing is that there are less demonstrations," Garza told the *Washington Post*. "A lot of that is that people are channeling their energy into organizing locally, recognizing that in Trump's America, our communities are under direct attack."

Jasmine had a visceral reaction to the statement. "The only time they pay attention is when we're out in their face. When we're up in their face and we don't disappear. When they have to see young Black people crying, when they have to see us angry and fierce, and they're on their toes, and they don't know what to do because of our anger. That is our power. What Alicia did was she, man, she Martin Luther King'd us. She Martin Luther King'd us real quick, and made us look like we're subtle and subdued like good little Black kids should be, right? And I don't agree with that. She spoke out of turn; she did not speak for all of us," Jasmine said. "We have to push it in their faces, because other than that they're going to forget about it."

She told me it's not about "reproducing" the system but dismantling capitalism, and she said that doesn't mean going to Congress. Moreover, she said, she can't even vote now because she's a felon. "It's different shit that we've got to teach ourselves, and voting, it's not going to do shit. Not to me. We had the biggest turnout for Obama, and you all see where that got us. I don't trust these people. Once you take that oath you are no longer on our side, you are taking the oath on behalf of the serpent, and I can't get down with that."

Instead of dwelling on the negative, Jasmine is going to focus her energy working with BLM Pasadena, especially the youth group that is part of the local chapter. She calls the seventeen kids in it her "little family" and works on teaching them things like breathing and organizes activities to help them stay off the street, since the funding has been cut for many of the after-school programs. "I tutor the kids daily; I ask them have they eaten today; we sit down and talk about school. We talk about what's going on in their lives. For some crazy reason now they're starting to—sex questions are coming up. So we've been having deep conversations." She even has started taking them to the city council meetings on Mondays. At the last one, she told me proudly, the group did some civil disobedience. "That was awesome. I cried afterward." She's also been planning trips. The previous week they had raised money to go to a trampoline park. She's working on getting the kids involved in photography and doing a play. I asked her about her own needs. She brushed the question off, saying that people help her get by, especially her girlfriend. In the end, Jasmine seemed pretty positive about the movement, telling me about how community folk were thanking her for doing the work, and teaching them their rights and supporting the kids. "Folks are waking up. So hell yeah, it's worth it." She thinks that the hood people, the folks she calls the "lumpen," are ready to take back their communities and thinks they will do so soon.

Jasmine seemed less positive about her own future. In fact, she thinks the future is so bleak that she has begun planning her own funeral. She and her girlfriend had been followed the previous day—her chest tightened up just talking about it—and she felt as if she were a walking death wish. She was convinced the police were going to kill her because of her activism and work with children, just as they did the Black Panthers, and she's stressed out about the deaths of a number of Black activists, especially in Ferguson, where three activists have been found dead from gunshot wounds in cars.[6]

For now, though, she refuses to shy away from controversy. "People are scared to be the oddball. I'll go to city council meetings—I've been doing this every Monday for the last two years. I'll go there, and I'll step out on stage. I'll stop the meeting. I'll go post up signs everywhere," she said. She's mad that people aren't out there protecting each other more. She gets down a lot, but what helps her through is a quote from the Black Panther Assata Shakur: "It is our duty to fight for our freedom. It is our duty to win. We must love each other and support each other. We have nothing to lose but our chains."[7] For Jasmine, it's more than an affirmation; it's words to live by. I was silent for a few moments, unsure of what to say, and just then, Jasmine's optimism popped back up. "I'm ready to live. I'm not doing it to die. I'm doing this to live, because like I told you before, if I don't do it, we're going to die. I'm doing this to live."

~

There is a pressure among Black millennials to be "woke" in a certain way, to believe in the same progressive causes, to be active on Twitter, and on the streets, some say, but that's not reflective of the diversity of thought in the Black community. It's a pressure people like Dominique say is unfair. She thinks she is woke, proud of her heritage, and just as down as her peers, though her politics are very different from the Black millennial activists people tend to think of.

As a young teenager growing up in Compton, Dominique loved to argue. She thinks she got it from listening to talk radio shows with her dad. She wasn't interested in whatever George W. Bush was doing or the daily drama in the House and Senate, but she loved to hear the arguments and copied their style, often making speeches at church or in front of her friends just for fun. When she began attending high school, she decided that her love of fiery conversation would be a great fit for the debate team. At first she was afraid that no one would listen to what she had to say, but as she got deeper into it, she realized the power her voice had. She was getting her thoughts out there about any and every hot political issue that was happening at the time—euthanasia, same-sex marriage, the Iraq War, making what she said was the traditional liberal argument for each topic. But when she started traveling with the team, meeting other young debaters, things started to change. Sometime after attending the Junior Statesmen of America Conference, she realized that while she still loved the idea of debate, she wasn't feeling connected to the words she was saying. The philosophy just didn't make sense. "I was a Democrat. I followed my family. I was liberal. I believed in social justice. I did Black student union and everything. I was into it." After attending more Junior Statesmen conferences, meeting new people, and hearing about various political views, she realized she was more conservative than liberal. "It was as simple as that for me. It wasn't anything deeper than that, until people started putting different connotations on it."

Dominique wasn't just a Republican; by her own admission she was a radical right-winger. She didn't support marriage equality or abortion and was staunchly for gun rights. And no one could tell her otherwise. "I agreed with what they were saying about people needing to be responsible for their money and creating budgets for themselves." Her friends and classmates at her high school didn't seem to care much and supported and accepted her views. Some, she said, even agreed with her, and everyone was respectful. Most just wanted to hear her opinion. However, her parents were another story. Her mom was completely taken aback, but not angry. She told her she didn't know if she could fully get behind her politics but would support her nonetheless. Her dad took the news harder. Once she told him that her days as a liberal were over, he had to have a serious sit-down with her. "It was like I was coming out to him, out of the closet or something." He was upset, but also had questions. First he asked her, "So, why are you a conservative?"

She replied with a stock answer: "Well, I don't believe in gay marriage. I don't believe in abortion. I think that people need to get off welfare and start working and stop living off the government."

"But, Dominique," he protested.

Worried, she asked him if he was disappointed and if she had failed him. He told her he wasn't disappointed, just that he was worried about what she was getting into being a Black conservative. She brushed off his reaction; he was just being dramatic, she told herself. That all changed when she started college.

Dominique is a conservative, and she also considers herself Republican, a position that isn't super popular with African Americans, considering 88 percent of Black voters supported Hillary Clinton in 2016. Yet Black Republicans are nothing new. While most Black people aligned themselves with the Democratic Party in 1936 as a response to Franklin Roosevelt's New Deal, and even more so after President Lyndon B. Johnson signed into law the Civil Rights Act and Voting Rights Act, a small number of Blacks remained dedicated to the Republican Party. In the early twenty-first century, the party reached its peak support from Blacks: in 2004, 11 percent voted for George W. Bush, perhaps not a surprise since we also saw the simultaneous rise of prominent Black Republicans like Condoleezza Rice, Colin Powell, and Michael Steele. In the last presidential election, 8 percent of Blacks voted for Donald Trump. According to CNN's analysis of polling data, 9 percent of young Black adults ages eighteen to twenty-nine—millenials—voted for Donald Trump, 85 percent voted for Hillary, and 6 percent for other candidates. (Voters ages thirty to forty-four weren't that different.) By the same token, 47 percent of Whites ages eighteen to twenty-nine voted for Trump.

Still, there seems to be a growing and vocal number of Black voters who are fed up with the Democratic Party and the assumed loyalty that Black people are supposed to have to it. If it's any indication, Howard University, often considered one of the premiere HBCUs in the country, just reignited its Black Republican chapter, though according to a report in *Spin*, only four Black Republican chapters exist out of the 105 HBCUs in the country.[8]

Dominique doesn't quite understand the disconnect. She argues that Black people, historically, are very conservative. They believe in being frugal, not having debt, and are highly religious. Many of these values, she said, she learned not from the party platform but from her parents. For example, her mom is good with her money: she had six other kids to raise along with Dominique, and she had split from their father. Dominique remembers her mom recalling her own childhood, and Dominique's grandmother, too, was frugal as well as a single parent herself. They would eat spaghetti dinners every night, and share clothes and beds. Dominique's dad, as a landlord, is also good with money. He taught her how to count when she was three years old and later how to budget. She believes people today are taking advantage of the government help that's out there and teaching their children to live off it, too. "It's okay, if you need it. That's what it's there for, but you don't abuse the system, and you don't just take people's tax dollars, just because you don't want to work. I've seen it in my own family, from distant relatives and cousins, and such. I've seen them be on welfare, because it's just easier for them, and say they're in between jobs, or something. They don't hurt from it; it's really the kids that hurt from it, because they see that. They think it's a good example, but it's not really a good example."

Dominique started getting involved in political organizing in college. She joined a group called Turning Point USA, a nonprofit that talks to college youth about fiscal responsibility and free markets. She began tabling for the group as a student in college, while she was working on an associate's degree. When she decided to transfer to another institution, she started a chapter there too. The chapter didn't grow much, but she began touring other campuses in California, like UCLA, UC Irvine, and Santa Monica College and hearing stories of frustrated millenials looking for a better way. Eventually she became a student director for the group and she saw just what it meant to be a young Black Republican in America today. She particularly saw it when she went to table for

Turning Point when there would be a conservative speaker on campus. There were always protesters, she said, often hundreds, from groups like Black Lives Matter, Latinx Student Unions, LGBTQ groups, and "people that are for social justice." It was a hard environment to be around as a young Black woman. "They think that you hate yourself, because you root for a conservative speaker." "They talk about tolerance, tolerance, tolerance, but they're not very tolerant towards us. They won't let us speak most of the time."

It can be hard for her to be taken seriously as a young Black woman who is proud of her Black identity on the right. "I was a Black woman before I was a Black woman conservative. I will always be that." And she admits that racism is alive and prevalent today. "I'm not going to just act like there's not a problem between police and Black people, and Black people getting shot and killed and murdered. I'm not just going to take a backseat and be like, 'They should have followed the rules. They should not have been looking suspicious, or in the hood.'" She said there are times her conservative counterparts will offer "excuses" for the police for what they did, and it's wrong. "You don't just shoot somebody just because you're suspicious of their activity and what they're doing. They don't have a gun on them—if they're pulling out something out of their pocket, you just don't know. You can't—this could be somebody's husband or wife, mom or dad, or child, or something. You cannot just react so fast like that."

She understands that sometimes these folks at the receiving end of police brutality get a bad rep, and they don't deserve to be killed and murdered. She also thinks that Black Lives Matter actually has a "really good point." However, she doesn't like what the group has turned into. She thinks it's become too radicalized. "I think what people have turned Black Lives Matter into, and it's not just regular people like you and me, but it's really these angry thugs that are mad at cops, these gang members, and I know some because I've seen some in the flesh. Some of them have attacked me at conservative events on campuses. You look back, and you see that they have had arrest records, and they were part of gang activity, and they're taking over Black Lives Matter, which it should not be that way. It started off as a social justice kind of thing, now it's more radicalized." Right now, she said, she just can't get behind them. And she wants them to address Black-on-Black violence more, a criticism that Black conservatives often repeat.

Her twenty-five-year-old cousin, for example, just got shot recently while playing basketball at a park in Compton. He's not in a gang, and he was going to California State University, Northridge. He's okay now, and staying with his mom in another area, but she said, it's hard to figure out ways to make it better without having these hard conversations about violence in the Black community. She said it's time for people to make the effort, and to start taking responsibility and teaching their children "respect and values."

She's on social media, writing, and doing television, and she has embraced the "Black conservative" label. But it has been a struggle. "Some Black people want you to fight for Black issues, especially my family." Her family supports her but thinks that she is fighting for "the White side," something she vehemently disagrees with. "Now, you get that label, so it's hard. You want to support your Black community, and you try to do that, but at the end of the day, sometimes that conservative label will overshadow that." She's been called names like Coconut and Uncle Tom, told she can't think for herself and that she's not "woke" enough, but she's learned to brush it all off.

Things became even more intense after she appeared on Fox News during a millennial town hall. She was on a panel with Donald Trump Jr. and Eric Trump about what conservative students have to go through on campus. She didn't know the Trumps were going to be on until that day, and she was freaked out and excited. She held her own and talked about the adversity she faced, and the things that were going on at her school. "I've never done anything like this before. It was just really big for me." People started recognizing her more. She's happy that she's a recognizable voice in the conservative community and that she can be a voice for Black conservatives—something she knows is rare.

She's part of a small network of Black conservative men and women, all of whom she said are "cool," and she is overjoyed when she meets people who share her experience. Like eighteen-year-old Leonard Robinson, whom she is very close with. He is gay and Black and Republican, and talks about how passionate people who fall outside of the norm have to be. "Oftentimes, it's more rewarding to kind of go against the grain and really be different and really even have your ideas challenged. One thing I would say is people that are like me, which are not many, but those that are Black, gay, and Republican, or even Black and Republican, gay and Republican, oftentimes they are probably the most strongest supporters of their cause."

Dominique is still working on her degree, online now, because of her full-time activism, and she has ideas about where the conservative movement should go. She wants to see conservatives do more outreach in Black communities and sometimes take a more wholesome approach. She said the group often derides people for what's going on without giving them real solutions. "Conservatives sometimes bash minorities for their problems, but they don't look at how their city governments have been affecting them, school boards, and everything, because they were very corrupt in Compton, when I lived in Compton. School boards were super corrupt." That's something she feels she can address. "I was actually thinking of joining and running for school board in Compton," she told me, "because I did not like how they dealt with certain things in high school." She wants more conservatives to let the Black community know that they are on their side. "Right now, Black people do not trust conservatives. At all. If you talk to my family right now, they think Trump is a joke. Black people are fed up with Trump, and they are fed up with establishment government. They want somebody to actually reach out them and say, 'Hey, We feel you. We understand your struggles and we want to help you.'"

For now, she's going to continue to organize and see what this new administration will bring. She's a Trump supporter and has been for a while. He hasn't gone back on his word, she said, and is doing the things he said he would do, especially around illegal immigration and Obamacare, though she was not happy about the new health care legislation. She likes that he's holding his own. "I feel like he never really lost who he was. He never really lost that pledge. I think that makes him more human than politician, too. At his first address, he said so many things that people like Obama would never have said, and previous presidents would never have uttered in a speech before. He's just so bold. I admire that and I respect that." She doesn't agree with all the things he has said and done, but insists that no one is perfect. "I don't know if he's fully conservative, as he says he is. He wasn't always conservative. He was on *Oprah* before, I think in the '80s, saying that he was a Democrat, but people change. I changed. I was a Democrat." She said there's so much untapped potential in the Black community, particularly among Black millennials, that she hopes the Right will be able to mobilize. "There are so many Black students who are so worthy of being part of the conservative movement and being big-time leaders in the conservative movement, making good money and being in charge of a group of people, and being able to mobilize people and such. We haven't even tapped into that potential yet."

BLACK WOMEN LIKE JASMINE AND DOMINIQUE ARE FINALLY starting to realize their power as political actors. They are also starting to realize their potential for public office. In 2018, after Black women helped elect Democrat Doug Jones to the Senate in Alabama (98 percent voted for him) seventy Black women decided to run for various federal, state, and local seats in Alabama—a record number. And they're often doing so without the help of Democratic institutions. While there's great excitement about these women, Alabama seems to be just the beginning. According to a database of Black women running for office, blackwomeninpolitics.com, created by writer Luvvie Ajayi, over four hundred Black women are running for federal, state, and local office in 2018. It's about time. Black women have long been underrepresented in government. According to a recent report by the Higher Heights

Leadership Fund and the Center for American Women and Politics, despite the fact that Black women make up 7.3 percent of the population, they hold less than 5 percent of the seats at the federal, statewide executive, and state legislative levels.[9]

∽∽

As downtown Ferguson spilled over with rage on November 24, 2014, after the announcement that the police officer charged with shooting and killing Mike Brown wouldn't be indicted for a crime, Park sat trying to figure out what she wanted to do next. She was in Atlanta, just blocks from where Martin Luther King Jr. was buried, and knew that she needed to do something, though she wasn't sure what. Deciding that perhaps she could join some of the direct action protests that were happening, Park jumped in her car. She wasn't exactly sure where she was going, but at least she was driving somewhere. Out of her car window she saw protesters attempting to block the highway. She had been a part of protests like that before, but that moment, it didn't feel like the place for her to be, and she realized that she just wanted some time by herself. So she headed to the state capitol. It was nighttime, and the intersections were blocked off by cop cars with their blaring lights, shining on the building, perhaps trying to protect it, should the protesters head that way.

You couldn't access it, but as it shone in the night sky, Park was drawn to it, and she sat across the street, looking at the building. Alone, dressed in a skirt and heels, she sat, thinking about what was going on in the world around her. Suddenly the police started to honk at her and yelled at her to move away from the building. She didn't understand why. She was alone on public property, not inciting anything, not holding up a sign. Just sitting thinking about the world. She knew her rights; it was public property that she technically could be on since she is a resident of the state so she simply stayed. Tension was all around her, helicopters patrolled the air, groups were marching around the city, but she was surprised that the offices where the decisions are made were quiet and deserted. Aside from the officers, she was the only person there. "So I started to beam my eyes into the capitol building and see what was happening in there. I could picture maybe there's a few janitorial folks in there who are cleaning up. Maybe the air conditioner is running, even though no one's in there. Perhaps there's someone who has taken the secret passageway and left something in their office, and ran inside to get it and ran back out. But overall nothing was happening. I felt like that was where change needed to happen. We needed to see ourselves in those places of power and literally be on that same horizontal slate as the folks who were making these decisions."

The officers eventually left her alone, and she sat there for an hour envisioning herself working there for the first time. She had become more committed to social justice causes after someone wrote "Nigger" all over her door during her freshman year of college at Chapman University, and she felt little support from the community. When she graduated college (from another university) and began work at a feminist health center as a health advocate focusing on Black women, she continued to see disparities in the system and wanted to continue to fight for change. The next week she began to learn more about her state legislature. The next month she started to go to hearings, and after that she would pay attention to what was happening legislatively. She started talking to people, and her own state legislator, Simone Bell, became a mentor. When Bell decided to resign a few months later, she asked Park to run for her seat. "I had that very visceral moment where I realized no matter what, it would have to be me that was willing to make that change for our generation. And so I was willing to do it." Four elections later, after a runoff election in February 2016, Park won the seat, despite the perceived obstacles of being a young, Black, queer woman. At the time women made up 24.6 percent of the legislature (they made up 52 percent of the state), only three people were openly gay in the Georgia Senate, and no one identified as queer (she became the first). Park didn't have time to worry about the odds against her as she's been working hard since day one to make sure her community is being served. Her first order of business was to work on women's health needs based on her experience working at the women's health clinic.

Park said that the Southern political system only allows people horizontal mobility, which means that you can change jobs or move to a different social group, but "at the end of the day you'll still have that same status." And while there are big macroaggressions that she can talk about, she's more focused on microaggressions, something Black millennials have been particularly attuned to when racial issues don't always look as blatant as a cross burning in your yard.

Park came to politics during the time of Obama's ascendency, a time of "Democratic hope," she said, when she was a student at the University of North Carolina at Chapel Hill, but she said her story illustrates how even the most well intentioned young person can get cut out of the political system. First, as a college student, she couldn't donate money to candidates she supported because she was barely making money at her college job. Second, she missed out on an important election in North Carolina because she hadn't been able to move her voter registration from Georgia early enough. (Across the country, 72.9 percent of Black millennials said they were asked for voter identification ID at the polls, compared to 50.8 percent of their White counterparts.)[10] It frustrated her immensely. She thinks her experience is typical of where a lot of millennials are. "There's a certain piece of the system that cut us out because we are not privileged. But yet we still prevail because we know that there is something coming after us and with us that is powerful." She is excited about the different organizations that are helping people break barriers in running for office, as well as about the people—everyday citizens—who are becoming a part of the process, using their skills to help run campaigns and create policy.

Sometimes it's tough. For example, she tells me of a time when she was working on a piece of health care legislation, and one of her staff members reminded her that it had gendered language in it. So she went back to the legislative counsel to ask if there could be a gender-neutral version of the bill passed. "Because at the end of the day, if you're receiving services from a health clinic, you're a client, you're a patient, you're not necessarily a he or she at that point." Her colleagues opposed it. They told her that the language was trans inclusive. She pushed back: she said if someone, particularly at a health clinic, is transitioning, it doesn't mean that they conform to one gender at the time. It was an example of how she has to bring intersectionality to the capitol every single day.

Park thinks now the is the prime time for young folks to make sure their voices are heard. "I am not doing this to be haphazard, to start any coups or anything. I am trying to bring us into the political system because I am realizing that we are being cut out in so many different ways." She knows there is a narrative around millennials that we are frustrated, overqualified, and underemployed and that we throw tantrums when we don't get what we want or see things change fast enough. But she sees the opposite. She said she sees millennial Democrats and millennial Republicans working together to get solutions, not going toe to toe.

Yet despite her conciliatory political voice, there is still a rebellious quality to the young Democrat. She's an ally of Black Lives Matter and has had conversations with leadership of the movement. She said she does not plan to "distance" herself from the critical work they are doing. She also doesn't pledge allegiance to the flag every day after they pray. She said she considers it a Confederate flag. When I ask about the American Dream, she said that this generation is pushing back on some of the patriotism within it—like the flag—but there are other aspects that still are important to young Black millennials, things she wants to fight for as a politician. "There is a piece of home, or of having a place that we believe is important. That place should be a place where we are safe. Where we feel as though we can eventually have some vertical mobility, and that at the end of the day, without disregard for our history, we are able to avenge the wrongdoings of our nation."

Though their strategies and politics differ, Jasmine, Dominique, and Park are a part of a new group of young activists who are fighting, dying, and working to make the world a better place for the next generation. There may be frustrated days, weeks, even years, but none show any signs of slowing down anytime soon.

MILLENNIAL MOMENT: **THE DAY AFTER**

On November 9, 2016, the day after Donald Trump was elected president of the United States, I spoke to a group of young radical Black activists around the county, who like many of us were hungover from the night's dramatic end and trying to make sense of Trump's win and what it meant for the future.

Amir, Cofounder of the United Hood Movement: *I think the verdict was very much exactly what America represents. They have a perfect public figure now for the representation of this country. I have a lot of White friends, some that were literally in tears. I'm like, 'You do realize this country was built on killin' hella people and taking their land? You do understand that we are built on a really fucked up foundation?' So the fact that everyone was going in a frenzy and "I'm with her," whatever. To me I was very confused. This is more of a wakeup for White folks. We're going to continue to wake up to the same thing every day. This is a perfect, perfect realization of where we're at. There are a lot of people who are deeply distraught, deeply hurt, and I care for them. I care for their feelings on that. However, it doesn't stop our movement. It doesn't stop any type of organizing for Black people to get free. We've been organizing. We're gonna continue to organize.*

Akua, International Socialist Organization/Millions March NYC: *The expression that elected Trump was caused not just because of the economic crisis but also a racist backlash against the Black Lives movement. We've been seeing some of this. We had nine innocent Black people murdered* *in cold blood in South Carolina just a year ago. Black churches have been burned—this was before the elections were gaining momentum. So we've been battling the right-wing expression of this dissention for a bit.*

I think the politics of lesser-evilism and fear mongering really took over, especially after [Bernie] Sanders lost the nomination. Things didn't become about the politics that were being raised by Sanders—about Fight for Fifteen, ending the war, and health care—it became about Trump and then fighting Trump. The level of debate went down, and it became about two people yelling at each other about who's more corrupt as opposed to what's gonna happen, what you're gonna do for us, what you're gonna do for the majority of people.

Povi-Tamu, Organizer: *If we weren't clear before, then we should be clear now: the American Dream has never been for so many of us. With Trump's promises to "make America great again" and his promise to "renew the American Dream" in last night's victory speech, it's really clear that that dream is not a dream of freedom for Black folks, women, queer people, Muslim folks, undocumented folks, Latinx people, or disabled people or any of us who live at the intersections of those identities.*

Amir: *People are more distraught because people really believe in this voting system. They really believe in America. For folks like myself, and those who this will resonate with if they read it, we don't have that same type of faith in the electoral process. I don't believe this was a response to Obama. This America. This is the day to day of the business of America. Capitalism, misogyny, classism, racism, all the isms, hate. I believe it's a good thing he got elected because it will show those that are concerned, especially all the good White folk who believe that racism is over and all that, that shit is very fucked up, shit is very wrong here, and we have a lot of work to do. And all you so-called progressives—this is really the true America. This is how most of your peers feel that voted. I think this is a great thing for America. It just shows how much work we have to do.*

I think things can only get better, not worse, from here. I think it's only going to get better.

Akua: *They keep telling us the Democratic Party is the home to bring our demands and grievances, home for our movement, but they continue to betray us when it comes to actually doing something about it. I think we need to continue or build on the movement we've been building right now, the Black Lives Matter movement, the Dream activists, immigrant rights movement. We need to support the indigenous struggles, the climate justice struggle—that's where our power lies. It's not an easy path, but I think we need to have a long-term perspective on building this alternative, building these movements, and building a third-party alternative to the two-party system that represents these movements. I don't think electoral politics is where change primarily happens. I think it's what we're doing outside these spaces of power to make sure that they do represent us.*

Amir: *We're gonna have some people who are still going to be respectable. They're going to be afraid to say certain things during this time. You might see some activists who go totally underground. This might be a very dangerous time for people to be as open on Facebook and social media about their locations and their plans and what they're doing and what's next.*

Akua: *The Democrat[ic] Party said we owe him, him being Trump, an open mind. What they're saying is do not act up, do not get angry, do not protest. Let's make this peaceful. After months of saying this is the worst person ever and that we cannot vote for him, you're telling us to accept it and be peaceful and that he will unite us! They're so delusional.*

Povi-Tamu: *I'm focused on our dreams, what are we trying to build, what do we want to see, and organizing those dreams into being. The Trump win just solidifies that focus for me. It crystallizes our immediate need to come* *together and refuse electoral politics as usual and create our own solutions and answers and then fight like hell for them.*

Akua: *The right wing and the White supremacists are emboldened. It means that things are more precarious than in previous years. Over 45 percent of the population didn't vote. I don't think there are any shortcuts to the crises we are seeing today. We have to build an independent movement that represents oppressed people, working people, people of color, Black communities, LGBT communities, immigrants, et cetera.*

Amir: *We're past the complaining. We need to be more focused, more clear. We need to incorporate our elders and the youth—I'm talking seven, eight, nine, ten. They need to be a part of this movement as well as us millennials. I think us millennials are leading this. I like to believe that we could organize in a fashion with a focused agenda that can create real revolutionary change. I think we do need to advocate for more self-defense organizations so we aren't getting killed by the police. We have to understand that we can't wait for politicians. We can't wait for White folks. We can't wait for certain media. We have to find out what is our agenda, what are we doing, and follow suit. They're different types of Black folks, and we have to figure out whose principles align with what. Just because we're skinfolk doesn't mean we're kinfolk.*

Akua: *It's very clear for a lot of people in the Black Lives Matter movement what we need to do, what the task is, which is to continue to push and pressure and fight and make visible the vile anti-Black racism that continues to divide this country, continues to shape our life. I can't even predict where things will go. It's a very volatile period, but there's no alternative. I think the movement has been very clear during the election that we need to build our power. We need local campaigns; we need national coordination to get more organization—not just be responsive to killings, but also local campaigns that help channel our energy into concrete things that we can mobilize people around,* *get more people involved, and not just people in our circles—people outside of our circles. People are looking for places to get organized.*

Amir: *I'm trying not to live in worry or fear. I feel like that's also a part of White supremacy. I think that's why we're seeing such alarming rates of Black death on social media. I feel like that's all a part of their plan: keep us in fear. It's so easy to give into the fear, but to me it takes a little more courage to look at our resilience, to look at our strength and love. We are a very strong people. We're still here. Ain't nothing you can do.*

CONCLUSION

> The only way to deal with an unfree world is to become so absolutely free that your very existence is an act of rebellion.
>
> —ALBERT CAMUS

> Mask on, Fuck it, Mask off
>
> —FUTURE, "MASK OFF"

MY JOURNEY, THIS QUEST TO FIGURE OUT MY AMERICAN DREAM, ENDED UP like so many do: at the beginning. The beginning for me was not my beginning, but my family's. The folks who started it all, the ones who left the luscious green farms of Manning, South Carolina, for a dream up North that had not yet been realized. I didn't know much about Manning; they'd left that I-95 pit stop behind in the 1940s and never looked back. They never visited, never spoke of any cousins, never elaborated on their history there as children. Yet it was never forgotten, and it was always, at least in the mind of my great-aunt, whom I knew best, one simple thing. It was home. So four months after she died, and nearly a year after I began interviewing Black millennials about their American Dream, I went to Manning, determined to pick up the pieces of my family's past.

Early on a hazy Father's Day, I jumped on an Amtrak train to South Carolina. To be honest, I wasn't exactly feeling as if the whole dream thing was working out in New York. I'd paid off some extra bills and realized only days earlier that I'd spent some of my mortgage money. I had to swallow my pride and ask my mom for a quick loan. I was finishing up a part-time gig and trying to really think about the future. Aside from my relationship, which was going well, it was the first time in a number of years that I had no plan, no real dream or vision for the future. The dim goals I had felt so unattainable that I wasn't even sure they were real.

The trip was supposed to take twelve hours, and then I'd have to get a car and drive another hour to get to Manning. I expected to be tired or annoyed by the long journey, but I wasn't. I listened to the recordings of my interviews, replaying the many stories of Black millennials trying to figure out their dreams—from the dominatrix Miss V in Chicago teaching feminism to Michael in Ohio trying to pay off his student debt to Jaleesa in Los Angeles working for corporate America—and I thought about the questions I had originally set out to answer. What does upward mobility look like for Black millennials? Do Black millennials have their own version of the American Dream, and is it accessible for them? I'd gotten many answers, and while Black millennials—like many of their generation—push back on the white-picket-fence version of the Dream, many aspire to what the dream means at its core: freedom. Though many said that the conditions of American society today made the dream of moving on up inaccessible to them and their peers, they were all determined to push through and redefine whatever success meant to them. For people like Jasmine, it's mentoring young kids; for M, it's driving an Uber until she can raise money for an HIV awareness nonprofit she wants to start; and for some folks in Hollywood it's simply making good web series that reflect our experience.

A few said they were living their dream, like Shamir with his independently released album recorded in his bedroom, and in those moments I often smiled. Those were the exceptions, and they contrasted so much with what most young Black millennials told me: that the Dream wasn't for them, that they were left behind, that their lives were different from those of White Americans. It made me sad because all too many Black millennials think that the American Dream wasn't and isn't for them, and I had no real answers to counter their assessments.

This is in part a structural issue that can be fixed by some major changes in public policy. Universal health care is a good start, including expanded access for Black women, whose maternal mortality rates are three to four times higher than their White counterparts'. Affordable colleges (not just community colleges) for all students and more equitable hiring. The eradication of mandatory minimums and Gestapo-like policing policies. Better home loan access and more equitable neighborhoods. These are not new solutions; these problems were diagnosed decades, if not centuries, ago.

But it's more than just public policy that needs to change and a system that needs to be redesigned to make sure all Americans are truly equal; it's the attitude that this country has toward young Blacks particularly. It's a constant belief that we are less than, lazy, scary. And while I think of myself as an optimist—an anxious optimist, but an optimist nonetheless—I truly wonder if any of this will ever be different. There needs to be more than just empty platitudes of commitments to diversity and ever be different, but a real enforcement of these promises. As we can see in the past, only when America truly commits to racial equity, with the enforcement of the law, does real change happen.

We're at a dire moment that has only been highlighted by technology, which has allowed us to post videos and pictures of these moments, and made even clearer by a president and an administration that seem to care little about policies and practices that will benefit and protect people like me.

We're seeing Black men and women get killed, assaulted, and berated nearly every week, whether it's in their own backyard, at a Waffle House, or sitting down at a Starbucks. This needs to change, and it needs to happen now. This country needs to commit itself to making sure that young Black dreaming doesn't die. That young Black America is given the tools to dream and the opportunity to actually realize those dreams in a fair and equitable way. We, too, as young Black people have to push ourselves even harder, push ourselves to the limit, and continue to dare to dream—a radical act in itself when so much of society seems to encourage us to do anything but that. And maybe more of us, as so many have started to do, need to redefine what our dreams really are.

~~

WHEN I GOT TO MANNING, ONE OF THE FIRST PEOPLE I MET WAS Meesha, whom I mentioned in Chapter 1. When I looked at her golden brown skin and big brown eyes, I couldn't help but search for my grandmother's and aunt's faces in hers. Any little speck, any little feature that was similar. But I just wasn't sure. She shares the last name of my great-grandmother, the only connection I have, and the city was full of them. I'd never met a Black person with that name until I got to Manning.

Perhaps it was just Southern hospitality, but as I sat in Meesha's office talking with her, it felt familiar. It felt like home. She told me about her job; her two cute kids, their photo perched on her desk; and, probably most importantly, about her decision to stay. She has two master's degrees and, at thirty, is settled down with her two children. She seems to have everything figured out, a far cry from my single, freelance-laden patchwork of the American Dream.

She tells me about life growing up in Manning, about a segregated classroom and dating White boys, and it doesn't sound much different from my life. Sure, some things were foreign to me, like talk of the Klan, but far more interesting to me were her stories of her close-knit family.

She was particularly proud of her brother, who had just gotten an electrical engineering degree. On a recent visit to Chicago, a friend tried to get her to move there, and though she loved the midwestern city, she declined. She said, "No, I love my town. They need me. Probably not as much as I need them." It made me smile. And I got it.

After our conversation, I wandered around lost for a little bit, and two police officers, one Black and one White, helped me figure out where to find the proper office to look up my grandmother's records. I found the street where my great-aunt and grandmother's mother lived. The house was no longer there, but it seemed like a poor, rundown area of town, with falling-down houses and shacks near the address where they had lived. I wondered if their move North had been worth it. Even more, I wondered if I had followed in their upward trajectory. Had I achieved any real upward mobility? Had I achieved that dream of having your kids do better than you? Had I gotten closer to realizing the American Dream?

BACK IN NEW JERSEY, A FEW DAYS AFTER MY THIRTY-SIXTH birthday, I realized that I wasn't making it. Here I was, sitting in my great-aunt's house, still in Englewood, New Jersey, watching the next-door neighbors with the same views I'd been seeing for thirty-six years. I sat with a mountain of debt, an unfinished PhD, and an old Prius in the driveway. I didn't have that perfect chocolate family I dreamed of, and that so-called wonderful corporate job had eluded me.

But at the same time, maybe I had achieved some kind of millennial version of the dream. Defining my future and doing what I wanted, even if it wasn't so traditional. Sure, much of my dream is traditional. I still want to get married, have kids, buy another house, and finish my PhD, but I guess I've also learned that it's okay if my success story doesn't play out that way either. I'm stupidly, happily in love, adore my family and friends, and am grateful that while I am currently in overdraft, I've been able to get my voice and ideas out into the world with my writing, produce films I care about (something my mom was never able to do), and happy I can study what I want and say, "Fuck you," to respectability politics. I'm happy that Black girls can be nerds, that I can proudly say I love *The Sims*, *Archie Comics*, and Bon Jovi, and not shirk the way I used to, running to my room when the doorbell rang, turning down Z100 playing on the radio. Maybe that's progress; maybe that's a certain type of mobility—or at least freedom that we haven't always been afforded. Maybe that's what upward mobility is beginning to look like for Black millennials. Sure, it looks like social mobility; it looks like economic mobility; it looks like the things that social science tells us matter: marriage, jobs, homeownership, and education. They still matter to me, and if anything, they've left us full of hope but still further behind. Even so, we are seeing new and different kinds of mobility, in ways that perhaps can't be measured on charts. Maybe our mobility shouldn't always be measured like our White millennial peers'; maybe it's measured in joy and pleasure. If this country was never meant for us anyway, maybe we have to look beyond.

I WANTED THIS BOOK TO ANSWER THE QUESTION JAY-Z HAD asked back in 2002, when he remixed Biggie's classic "Juicy." I wanted to figure out if this was all a dream, if success was possible, but it feels that the current American nightmare, my current American nightmare, isn't helping to give me any clarity at all. Sure technology has helped—we have figured out a way to be visible in some spaces—but our humanity remains unseen. We've strategized and suffered, made careers out of what seemed to be nothing. When the media wasn't paying attention to us, we made our own shows. We stepped out on faith, we survived, and we endured. We've experienced pain, but we've also experienced joy. I could end with a bunch of policy proposals you've heard before.

I could throw in some so-called radical ones, like reparations, cures for Post-Traumatic Slave Syndrome, or simply burning the whole country down, as many seem to advocate today. Or I could, as we've done in the past, have faith that somehow this generation will figure it out, as Black folks have always had to do. Perhaps it doesn't matter whether our dreams are real or not. We'll claw our way to the top, despite being called monkeys, nappy-headed hos, gorillas, bitches, ungrateful and uppity Negroes, and we'll make it. Perhaps hip-hop has the answer to my question. If I look to our history, I see that we have always risen, always rocked it, and always done more with less. We're survivors like Beyoncé, fighters like Serena. Fly like Drake. And as Kendrick Lamar said, we gon' be alright.

ACKNOWLEDGMENTS

I COULDN'T HAVE WRITTEN THIS BOOK WITHOUT THE SUPPORT OF MANY, MANY people. To my wonderful researcher Artem Gulish, your help has been invaluable. Thank you for crunching all of the data in this book and being there to track down random facts day or night. To J. Mijin Cha for not only believing in this book from the beginning but starting as my first researcher despite your busy, busy, busy schedule and tons of degrees. To those who helped me find the voices of this generation that are all too often unheard: Michele Lent Hirsch, Donovan X. Ramsey, Alex Berke, Evita Robinson, Crystal Goode, William Turner, Nina Smith, the folks at the Young Invincibles, Mark Huelsman, Tanisha Colon-Bibb, Dona Tarectecan, Jenn Rolnick Borchetta, Camilo Ramirez, the Bronx Defenders, Valerie Rochester and the Black Women's Health Imperative, Ansel Augustine, Shanelle Matthews, Milan Griffin and the folks at HomeFree-USA, Dreux Dougall, Itohen Ihaza, Meesha Witherspoon, Nancy Cave and the staff of the Clarendon County Archives, Kimino Rutherford, Brit Schulte and the amazing people of Support Ho(s)e, Amanda Furdge, Children's Defense Fund Southern Regional Office,

Leonard Robinson, and everyone else who sent emails, DMs, and texts trying to help get these voices out.

To all the interviewees, even the ones I didn't use, your voices, your stories matter. I am eternally grateful.

To Heather McGhee, Tamara Draut, and my colleagues at Demos, thank you for your support. Robert Snyder, Ruth Feldstein, Sherri-Ann Butterfield, I owe you all for pushing my thinking on the Dream. Thanks to Laura Lomas for your kindness, talks in Cuba, and letting me use your home in Havana when I needed a break. To Ida Campbell for your continual support since I was a young intern in television. To Amy Eisman, my professor at American University, thank you for believing that I was a writer, even before I realized it. To Cliff Hahn, Winnie Guillaume, and Children's Express, which helped instill my love of journalism when I was still in middle school. Thanks to Rachel Dry for being an amazing editor. Marina Khidekel, thank you for publishing my first big magazine piece. Steve Coll, Andrew Martinez, Faith Smith, and the folks at the New America Foundation: this idea started because of you. Thanks to Susan Page Tillet, Kamala Tully, Peter Barnes, and the staff of the Mesa Refuge: I so needed that time in Point Reyes. I'm so grateful for the beautiful weeks I got to spend reading and writing there. Thanks to my writing cohort Christina Conklin and Jael Humphrey, who spent many nights listening to unpolished drafts. To my old colleagues who hired me from Fox News: Sally Roy, Judy Doctoroff-O'Neill, Diana Warner, and of course, Bill Moyers, who is still the best journalist and one of the best people I know. Thank you to my old Moyers crew, Lena Shemel, Alexis Pancrazi, Gina Kim, Ismael Gonzalez, Robert Booth, and Anthony Volastro: you make me want to stay in journalism forever. To Tom Casciato, Karim Hajj, Emir Lewis, and Bob Herbert: without our talks, this book would never have been completed.

To Gail Ross: the agent who found me, when I wasn't even thinking of ever writing a book—I owe you. To the Ross/Yoon team: thanks for you continual help and support. To the best publishing team especially Katy O'Donnell, an editor who doesn't mind midnight binge emails, thank you. To the rest of the Nation Books/Hachette team: Kristina Fazzalaro, Miguel

Cervantes, Clive Priddle, Kleaver Cruz (thank you for being the first Black millennial to read this, I am forever grateful), Collin Tracy, Beth Wright, Elisa Rivlin, and Taya Kitman, so many thanks. To the Nation Institute, thank you for walking the walk and helping writers like me support ourselves.

And thanks to the best group of friends one could have, despite my stress and anxiety. Liana and George Kamen, our group chats make the world not seem so bad. Caroline and Phillip Scott, you guys are my rock, even though we don't see each other much. Nikki Cannon, thank you for paying my way to the Yankees game, giving me tons of junk food, and your continued belief that the system does work. You're fighting the good fight. To Jeff Washington, whose friendship I will forever cherish. Meredith Davis, I simply wouldn't have survived this without you. Robin Davis and Traci Luthy, my girls for life. To Traci's son, Miles Luthy, for his many smiles (smiles!), for always making me laugh, and Steve Luthy. To Simone Weichschelbaum, for always having my back. To Elektra Gray, from your time as my boss to now as a very dear friend. Come back East! Vanessa McKelvey and Dana LaForey, I don't always get to see you a lot, but you both forever inspire me to be better and do more. To Crystal Belle-Apenteg for all your positivity and for pushing me even when I don't want to admit I am wrong. I am a better thinker because of you. To Kaia Shivers for your brilliance, knowledge, support, and determination. To David Beard for being there for me throughout the years. Jasmine Johnson, I couldn't live without your texts every day that show how ridiculous the world is. To new(er) friends: Emma and Jeff Frank and Cheryl Taylor, I'm so glad to have met you.

For my family: Jihan Quail, I love your excitement over this project. To my "cousin" Sonja Williams, I wouldn't have known how to write a book without you. Thank you for your guidance, love, and many edits! To my loving godparents, Lillian "Aunt Bee" and Al Crawford, for support and love when I need it. Aunt Bee, my heart is still broken that you've passed on. To James Washington, for your brilliance, your dedication to my mom, and unwavering love and support of me. I'm so sad you aren't here to read this. I miss you. Peter Evans and Louise Lamphere, I'm so happy to have your positivity, smarts, fearlessness, and love in my life. To Quyên Lamphere for challenging me about the world in the ways that only a sixth grader can on race, Trump, and everything in between while distracting me with a million riddles that I will never solve. Thanks for those laughs (Kawaii forever!). To my love, Peter Lamphere, who accepts me for who I am, pushes me and challenges me into understanding the world, and reminds me every day, even on those darkest days, that dreams can come true. This book wouldn't have been finished without you—from fact-checking in the early morning, to late-night edits, to reading citations because I didn't want to. I can't repay your for your dedication, kindness, and generosity. Our love has redefined what love means to me. Our love is a dream, and I can't wait to spend my life with you. I love you and thank you. To my mom, who is everything in this world to me and has provided me invaluable support, love, a healthy dose of criticism, and let me live rent free for months while I finished this book because she believed in me: I love you more than any words I could write.

And finally, to my ancestors, the Witherspoons in Manning whom I may never know, those in Guyana, and those close to my heart. To my grandfather George Allen and grandmother Evelyn Allen, who all passed on too young. Thank you for making me believe that the dream of America is possible. Thank you for your sacrifices, love, and compassion. For suffering through war, segregation, divorce, tragedy, disaster, white folk, and poverty, and still somehow making your dreams come true. And to my great aunt Dee, Esterlena Trammell, who died as I was writing this. Aunt Dee told me many times that I was the love of her life, and no phrase has ever meant more to me. Her quiet warmness and dignity showed me what true grace, compassion, and nonjudgmental love is. She always accepted me for who I was, and whether we were playing Barbies, watching our favorite soap (*General Hospital*), or taking trips to the mall, I learned not just what unconditional love is but that dreams may come true. Aunt Dee certainly remains the love of my life too, and I miss her everyday. In so many ways she is the American Dream come true, or at least she is my American Dream realized.

NOTES

INTRODUCTION

1. Scholar Walter Fisher believes that there are two parts to the American Dream, the moralistic version and the materialistic one, with neither one being better than the other. Walter R. Fisher, "Reaffirmation and Subversion of the American Dream," *Quarterly Journal of Speech* 59, no. 2 (2009): 160–167.

2. Jim Cullen, *The American Dream: A Short History of an Idea That Shaped a Nation* (New York: Oxford University Press, 2006); James Truslow Adams, *The Epic of America* (Boston: Little, Brown, 1931); James Truslow Adams, "What of 'The American Dream'?; A Historian Back from Abroad Finds Our Morale Regained but Fails to Discover a Return of That Philosophy Which, Based on Life's 'Real Values,' Would Restore Our Vision of Old," *New York Times*, May 14, 1933, nytimes.com/1933/05/14/archives/what-of-the-american-dream-a-historian-back-from-abroad-finds-our.html.

3. Samantha Smith, "Most Think the 'American Dream' Is Within Reach for Them," Pew Research Center, October 31, 2017, pewresearch.org/fact-tank/2017/10/31/most-think-the-american-dream-is-within-reach-for-them; Mark Robert Rank, Thomas A. Hirschl, and Kirk A. Foster, *Chasing the American Dream:*

Understanding What Shapes Our Fortunes (New York: Oxford University Press, 2016); American Dream statistics from Bridget Jameson Johnson, Pew Research Center, email correspondence with author, May 7, 2018.

4. Jim Cullen, author of *The American Dream*, said the American Dream may be thought of as "hokey" by some academic scholars, and that's why they don't want to study it.

5. See Cullen, *The American Dream*.

6. Martin Luther King Jr., "The American Dream," speech presented at Drew University, February 5, 1964, depts.drew.edu/lib/archives/online_exhibits/king/speech/theamericandream.pdf; James Baldwin, "The American Dream and the American Negro," *New York Times*, March 7, 1965, archive.nytimes.com/.nytimes.com/books/98/03/29/specials/baldwin-dream.html.

7. Joel Stein, "Millennials: The Me Me Me Generation," *Time*, May 9, 2013, time.com/247/millennials-the-me-me-me-generation.

8. Spencer Piston, "How Explicit Racial Prejudice Hurt Obama in the 2008 Election," *Political Behavior* 32 (2010): 431–451. In a piece for the *New Yorker* in 2017, Jia Tolentino wrote, "The type of millennial that much of the media flocks to—white, rich, thoughtlessly entitled—is largely unrepresentative of what is, in fact, a diverse and often downwardly mobile group."

9. "Millennials in Adulthood," Social & Demographic Trends Project, Pew Research Center, March 7, 2014, pewsocialtrends.org/2014/03/07/millennials-in-adulthood.

CHAPTER ONE: WE OUT

1. Marcy S. Sacks, *Before Harlem: The Black Experience in New York City Before World War I* (Philadelphia: University of Pennsylvania Press, 2013).

2. Isabel Wilkerson, *The Warmth of Other Suns: the Epic Story of America's Great Migration* (New York: Vintage Books, 2011).

3. US Census Bureau, "New York—Race and Hispanic Origin for Selected Large Cities and Other Places," July 13, 2005, census.gov/population//documentation/twps0076/NYtab.pdf; Rob Zellers, "'Duke': An Elegant Biography Reveals the Essential Ellington," *Pittsburgh Post-Gazette*, November 23, 2013, post-gazette.com/ae/book-reviews/2013/11/24/Duke-Ellington-didn-t-necessarily-want-to-be-known/stories/201311240042.

4. Bureau of Labor Statistics, Current Population Survey, 2008; Pamela Newkirk, "The Not-So-Great Migration," *Columbia Journalism Review* (May 2011), archives.cjr.org/feature/the_not-so-great_migration.php.

5. John King, "The Invisible Tax on Teachers of Color," *Washington Post*, May 15, 2016. Teachers of color leave the field 24 percent more often than their White peers, according to a 2005 study by Richard Ingersoll at the University of Pennsylvania. See also Melinda Burns, "Teachers of Color at Risk," *Pacific Standard*, December 5, 2010, psmag.com/education/minority-teachers-hard-to-get-and-hard-to-keep-25852; Emily Hanford, "A Fellowship of the Few: Black Male Teachers in America's Classrooms Are in Short Supply," APM Reports, August 28, 2017, apmreports.org/story/2017/08/28/black-male-teachers-fellowship.

6. Latinxs had a similar rate. (Asians, on the other hand, also had a positive net migration of 25 percent.) "New York City's Millennials in Recession and Recovery," 2018, Office of the New York City Comptroller Scott M. Stringer, comptroller.nyc.gov/reports/new-york-citys-millennials-in-recession-and-recovery; US Census Bureau, 2016 American Community Survey data, from Steven Ruggles, Katie Genadek, Ronald Goeken, Josiah Grover, and Matthew Sobek, Integrated Public Use Microdata Series: Version 7.0 (dataset), Minneapolis: University of Minnesota, 2017, doi.org/10.18128/D010.V7.0.

7. "New York City's Millennials in Recession and Recovery," 2018; US Census Bureau, 2016 American Community Survey data.

8. US Census Bureau, 2016 American Community Survey data. Forty-nine percent of Black millennial migrants from abroad live in the South, as do forty-nine percent of Hispanics, 33 percent of Whites, and 27 percent of Asians.

9. Carol B. Stack, *Call to Home: African Americans Reclaim the Rural South* (New York: Basic Books, 2003). More from my interview with Dr. Pendergrass: "With the reverse migration you have a similar dynamic happening, but some of the institutions have shifted, so people are in some ways following family patterns. They are moving to places where either their Southern-born family either came from those places, or they have family who were born in the North or the West who already moved, and they are going to move with them, so you have that dynamic. You have employers who are also moving to particular areas like Charlotte, which is a future financial center, or Atlanta, and they are transferring, especially Black middle-class people, to particular destinations in the South. You have the role of historically Black colleges, so you have African Americans who grow up in the North, and they decide they want to go to an HBCU, and so that means they usually have to go down South. If they go to a predominantly White institution, they are likely to stay in the North. . . . And then finally, Black media, I think, report certain cities as these kinds of up-and-coming places for Black people. Atlanta, for instance. . . . The people I interview, they literally say, 'I first thought about Charlotte when I read in *Black Enterprise* or when I read in *Essence* that it

was the top city for Black people.' So it's almost a parallel to kind of the *Chicago Defender* during the great migration, where people are reading in Black media outlets about these places that are good for Black people."

10. Kevin McGruder, "The New York Times Company," *New York Times*, July 26, 2013, opinionator.blogs.nytimes.com/author/kevin-mcgruder; Sacks, *Before Harlem*; Thomas Buckley, "Negro Segregation in the North: Barriers Relaxing, but Slowly," *New York Times*, June 2, 1963, nytimes.com/1963/06/02/archives/negro-segregation-in-the-north-barriers-relaxing-but-slowly-bias.html; Christina Viega, "New Analysis Shows New York State Has the Country's Most Segregated Schools," Chalkbeat, December 6, 2017, chalkbeat.org/posts/ny/2014/03/26/new-analysis-shows-new-york-state-has-the-countrys-most-segregated-schools.

11. The US Census Bureau classifies Washington, DC, Maryland, and Delaware as the South, though often people consider Dixie to be the eleven states that formed the Confederacy. Jenny Rogers, "Is the District of Columbia in or Part of 'the South'?," *Washington City Paper*, January 24, 2014, washingtoncitypaper.com/news/article/13045129/is-the-district-of-columbia-in-or-part-of-the.

12. US Census Bureau, 2016 American Community Survey data.

13. "Hate Map by State," Southern Poverty Law Center, splcenter.org/hate-map/by-state, accessed April 25, 2018; Brian Levin and Kevin Grisham, "Special Status Report: Hate Crime in the City of Los Angeles 2016," Center for the Study of Hate and Extremism, 2017, csbs.csusb.edu/sites/csusb_csbs/files/Los Angeles Hate Crime Special Status 2017 4417.pdf.

14. Mark Lee, "A Time to Act: Fatal Violence Against Transgender People in America 2017," November 2017, assets2.hrc.org/files/assets/resources/A_Time_To_Act_2017_REV3.pdf.

15. Nick Baumann, "This Study Said the South Is More Racist Than the North," *Mother Jones*, June 25, 2013, motherjones.com/politics/2013/06/south-more-racist-north; Christopher S. Elmendorf and Douglas M. Spencer, "The Geography of Racial Stereotyping: Evidence and Implications for VRA Preclearance After Shelby County," UC Davis Legal Studies Research Paper No. 339, July 29, 2013.

16. Joel Kotkin, "The Cities Where African-Americans Are Doing the Best Economically," *Forbes*, January 15, 2015, forbes.com/sites/joelkotkin/2015/01/15/the-cities-where-african-americans-are-doing-the-best-economically/#4de8c3a164f2; Kim Severson, "Atlanta Emerges as a Black Entertainment Mecca," *New York Times*, November 25, 2011, nytimes.com/2011/11/26/us/atlanta-emerges-as-a-center-of-black-entertainment.html.

17. Alan Berube and Natalie Holmes, "Some Cities Are Still More Unequal Than Others: An Update," Brookings, March 17, 2015, brookings.edu/research/some-cities-are-still-more-unequal-than-others-an-update; Phil W. Hudson, "Atlanta Fed Chief: Atlanta 'Still Among the Worst for Economic Mobility,'" *Atlanta Business Chronicle*, October 25, 2016, bizjournals.com/atlanta/news/2016/10/25/atlanta-fed-chief-atlanta-still-among-the-worst.html; US Census Bureau, 2016 American Community Survey data. For a large slice of the African American community, life in Atlanta can be tough. There are families stuck in concentrated poverty with few prospects of escape, students dropping out of high school at an alarming rate, teenagers entering adulthood without ever having a job, workers cut off from suburban employment centers because of inadequate public transit, low-income public housing residents dispersed into neighborhoods where support services are inadequate or nonexistent, health care for poor and uninsured families threatened by closure of the "safety net" hospital, neighborhoods targeted by predatory lenders, food deserts created by supermarket redlining, and land speculation and redevelopment projects that have spawned unchecked gentrification and displacement, potentially driving families from their homes and their neighborhoods. See Robert D. Bullard, Glenn S. Johnson, Angel O. Torres D., Glenn S. Johnson, and Angel O. Torres, "The State of Black Atlanta 2010," *Atlanta Tribune*, February 24, 2010, atlantatribune.com/2010/02/24/complete-report-the-state-of-Black-atlanta-2010. A separate report in the *Southern Spaces* journal confirmed that "Black Atlanta," while embracing a large Black middle class and having high rates of homeownership, remains segregated from their White counterparts, and their children remain in majority minority schools. See Karen Pooley, "Segregations New Geography: The Atlanta Metro Region, Race, and the Declining Prospects for Upward Mobility," *Southern Spaces*, April 15, 2015.

18. Median wages are for full-time and part-time workers. In the Northeast the median wage is $25,000—the highest. US Census Bureau, 2016 American Community Survey data.

19. Jed Lipinski, "Black Teens in New Orleans Four Times as Likely to Have PTSD, Survey Shows," NOLA.com, November 18. 2014, nola.com/education/index.ssf/2014/11/Black_adolescents_in_new_orlea.html.

CHAPTER TWO: DON'T DOUBLE DOWN ON STUPID

1. His name has been changed.

2. Lemony Snicket, *The Ersatz Elevator*, A Series of Unfortunate Events, Book 6 (New York: HarperCollins, 2001).

3. Matt Bruenig, "White High School Dropouts Have More Wealth Than Black and Hispanic College Graduates," *Demos*, September 23, 2014, demos.org/blog/9/23/14/White-high-school-dropouts-have-more-wealth-Black-and-hispanic-college-graduates; Signe-Mary McKernan, Caroline Ratcliffe, Eugene Steuerle, and Sisi Zhang, "Less Than Equal: Racial Disparities in Wealth Accumulation," Urban Institute, April 2013, urban.org/sites/default/files/publication/23536/412802-less-than-equal-racial-disparities-in-wealth-accumulation.pdf; Angela Hanks, Danyelle Solomon, and Christian E. Weller, "Systematic Inequality: How America's Structural Racism Helped Create the Black-White Wealth Gap," Center for American Progress, February 21, 2018, americanprogress.org/issues/race/reports/2018/02/21/447051/systematic-inequality.

4. The College Board, Trends in College Pricing 2016, Table 2.

5. Valerie Smith, "African Americans Are Paid Less Than Whites at Every Education Level," Economic Policy Institute, October 4, 2016, epi.org/publication/african-americans-are-paid-less-than-Whites-at-every-education-level. Blacks with a high school degree make $14.24 versus Blacks with a college education, who make $25.77 an hour, versus those with an advanced degree, who clock in at $33.51 an hour, the EPI study finds.

6. The housing bust, Emmons noted, may partially explain the differences. Blacks and Latinxs tend to have more of their assets invested in housing, and they also sometimes live in predominantly Black and Latinx neighborhoods, which have lower housing values than their White counterparts'. However, he said that neither housing nor the Recession is the whole story, especially when looking at the long term study. He believes that things such as workplace discrimination and the lack of Blacks and Latinxs in STEM fields also factor into the college effect. Aimee Picchi, "College Isn't Paying off for Many Minorities," CBS News, August 18, 2015, cbsnews.com/news/college-isnt-paying-off-for-many-minorities; William R. Emmons and Lowell R. Ricketts, "College Is Not Enough: Higher Education Does Not Eliminate Racial and Ethnic Wealth Gaps," Federal Reserve Bank of St. Louis Review, 2017, files.stlouisfed.org/files/htdocs/publications/review/2017-02-15/college-is-not-enough-higher-education-does-not-eliminate-racial-and-ethnic-wealth-gaps.pdf; Patricia Cohen, "Racial Wealth Gap Persists Despite Degree, Study Says," *New York Times*, August 17, 2015, nytimes.com/2015/08/17/business/racial-wealth-gap-persists-despite-degree-study-says.html. Data on Asians complicate the narrative: Asian college graduates also saw their net worth rise by 97 percent.

7. Maya Beasley, "There Is a Supply of Diverse Workers in Tech, So Why Is Silicon Valley So Lacking in Diversity?," Center for American Progress, March

29, 2017, americanprogress.org/issues/race/reports/2017/03/29/429424/supply-diverse-workers-tech-silicon-valley-lacking-diversity; Charles Mudede, "Why the Overrepresentation of Black Americans in Professional Sports Is Not a Good Thing," *Stranger*, September 25, 2017, thestranger.com/slog/2017/09/25/25432524/why-the-over-representation-of-Black-americans-in-professional-sports-is-not-a-good-thing; Tom Farrey, "The Gentrification of College Hoops," *Undefeated*, May 9, 2017, theundefeated.com/features/gentrification-of-ncaa-division-1-college-basketball.

8. "Frequently Asked Questions About the NCAA," NCAA.org, ncaa.org/about/frequently-asked-questions-about-ncaa, accessed April 12, 2018.

9. "Executive Summary: Survey of Young Americans' Attitudes Toward Politics and Public Service: 24th Edition," Harvard Institute of Politics at the Kennedy School, December 4, 2014, iop.harvard.edu/sites/default/files_new/Harvard_ExecSummaryFall2013.pdf; Anne Johnson, Tobin Van Ostern, and Abraham White, "The Student Debt Crisis," Center for American Progress, October 25, 2012, cdn.americanprogress.org/wp-content/uploads/2012/10/WhiteStudentDebt-3.pdf. According to the CAP study, 27 percent of Blacks with bachelor's degrees had more than $30,000 in student debt, compared to 16 percent of White graduates.

10. President Barack Obama, "Remarks by the President on the Economy in Osawatomie, Kansas," The White House, December 6, 2011, obamawhitehouse.archives.gov/the-press-office/2011/12/06/remarks-president-economy-osawatomie-kansas; President Barack Obama, "Weekly Address: A Student Aid Bill of Rights," The White House, March 14, 2015, obamawhitehouse.archives.gov/the-press-office/2015/03/14/weekly-address-student-aid-bill-rights; "Highest Educational Levels Reached by Adults in the U.S. Since 1940," US Census Bureau, March 30, 2017, census.gov/newsroom/press-releases/2017/cb17-51.html.

11. Ben Miller, "New Federal Data Show a Student Loan Crisis for African American Borrowers," Center for American Progress, October 16, 2017, americanprogress.org/issues/education-postsecondary/news/2017/10/16/440711/new-federal-data-show-student-loan-crisis-african-american-borrowers.

CHAPTER THREE: SURVIVAL

1. His name has been changed.

2. Emily Badger, Claire Cain Miller, Adam Pearce, and Kevin Quealy, "Extensive Data Shows Punishing Reach of Racism for Black Boys," *New York Times*,

March 19, 2018, nytimes.com/interactive/2018/03/19/upshot/race-class-white-and-black-men.html.

3. His name has been changed.

4. Anat Bracha and Mary A. Burke, "Informal Work in the United States: Evidence from Survey Responses," Federal Reserve Bank of Boston, December 2014, bostonfed.org/publications/current-policy-perspectives/2014/informal-work-in-the-united-states-evidence-from-survey-responses.aspx.

5. Austin Carr, "Report: Is Human Capital the New Venture Capital?," *Fast Company*, July 30, 2012, fastcompany.com/1677217/report-human-capital-new-venture-capital.

6. Asha DuMonthier, Chandra Childers, and Jessica Mili, "The Status of Black Women in the United States," Domestic Workers Alliance, 2017, domesticworkers.org/sites/default/files/SOBW_report2017_compressed.pdf. In 2016 Black women between twenty-five and thirty-four had an unemployment rate of 8.8 percent; in 2010, the year after the recession ended, White women's unemployment rate peaked at 7.7 percent. Chandra Childers and Gladys McLean, "Black and Hispanic Women Lag in Recovering from the Recession," Institute for Women's Policy Research, August 31, 2017, iwpr.org/publications/black-hispanic-women-lag-recovering-recession.

7. LaShawn Harris, *Sex Workers, Psychics, and Numbers Runners Black Women in New York City's Underground Economy* (Champaign: University of Illinois Press, 2016.

8. Allana Akhtar, "Cardi B: How the Rapper Escaped Poverty to Top Billboard," *Time*, September 27, 2017, time.com/money/4959065/how-cardi-b-escaped-poverty-to-become-the-first-female-rapper-in-19-years-to-top-the-charts; Rachel Shatto, "The Real Amber Rose," *Curve*, November 11, 2011, curvemag.com/Curve-Magazine/Web-Articles-2011/The-Real-Amber-Rose.

9. Her name has been changed.

10. Anthony Ponce, "Sheriff Gunning for Craigslist Hookers," NBC Chicago, March 6, 2009, nbcchicago.com/news/local/Craigslist-Sued-Sheriff-Tom-Dart-Prostitution-Sex.html; Aamer Madhani, "Supreme Court Declines Sheriff's Appeal in Backpage Sex Ads Fight," *USA Today*, October 3, 2016, usatoday.com/story/news/2016/10/03/supreme-court-declines-sheriffs-appeal-backpage-sex-ads-fight/91467380.

11. Howard N. Snyder, "Arrest in the United States, 1990–2010," Bureau of Justice Statistics, October 2012, bjs.gov/content/pub/pdf/aus9010.pdf.

12. Nita Bhalla, "Indian Sex Worker Groups Slam Global Conference on Abolition of Prostitution," Reuters, January 31, 2017, reuters.com/article/us-india

-trafficking-prostitution/indian-sex-worker-groups-slam-global-conference-on-abolition-of-prostitution-idUSKBN15F1WF; "Fact Sheet: Sex Work & Sex Assault," Sex Workers Outreach Project USA, March 2017, new.swopusa.org/wp-content/uploads/2017/03/Sexual-Assault-Sex-Workers-USA-Fact-Sheet-Two-Side-Hand-Out.pdf; "Behind Closed Doors: An Analysis of Indoor Sex Work in New York City," Global Network of Sex Work Projects, 2005, nswp.org/sites/nswp.org/files/BehindClosedDoors.pdf; Maggie McNeill, "Lies, Damned Lies and Sex Work Statistics," *Washington Post*, March 27, 2014, washingtonpost.com/news/the-watch/wp/2014/03/27/lies-damned-lies-and-sex-work-statistics/?utm_term=.dcbc57b0f80b.

13. Data from Stoptransmurders.org, accessed April 26, 2018; Christine Hauser, "Transgender Woman Shot Dead in Motel Is 7th Killed in U.S. This Year, Rights Advocates Say," *New York Times*, March 30, 2018, nytimes.com/2018/03/30/us/transgender-woman-killed-baton-rouge.html.

14. Sociologist Ronald Weitzer said sex work is actually more complex and nuanced than those frames. He acknowledges both exploitation and empowerment can play a part in the narrative of sex worker life, but "there is sufficient variation across time, place, and sector to demonstrate that prostitution cannot be reduced to one or the other. An alternative perspective, what I call the polymorphous paradigm, holds that there is a constellation of occupational arrangements, power relations, and worker experiences. Unlike the other two, this paradigm is sensitive to complexities and to the structural conditions shaping the uneven distribution of agency, subordination, and job satisfaction." Ronald Weitzer, "Sociology of Sex Work," *Annual Review of Sociology* 35 (2009): 213–234.

15. His name has been changed.

16. Mike Nolan, "Lawyer: Unprotected-Sex Dispute Led to Killing of Brother Rice Teacher," *Chicago Tribune*, January 14, 2016, chicagotribune.com/suburbs/daily-southtown/crime/ct-sta-brother-rice-murder-trial-st-0113-20160112-story.html.

17. Nolan, "Lawyer."

18. Rummana Hussain, "15 Years for Prostitute in Fatal Stabbing of Brother Rice Teacher," *Chicago Sun-Times*, March 24, 2016, chicago.suntimes.com/news/hooker-gets-15-years-for-stabbing-brother-rice-teacher-to-death; Erica Demarest, "Prostitute Who Killed Brother Rice Teacher Guilty of 2nd-Degree Murder," DNAinfo Chicago, January 14, 2016, dnainfo.com/chicago/20160114/mt-greenwood/case-of-prostitute-who-killed-brother-rice-teacher-could-go-jury-today.

19. Hussain, "15 Years for Prostitute"; Mike Nolan, "Defendant Doesn't Testify in Brother Rice Teacher Killing," *Chicago Tribune*, January 15, 2016,

chicagotribune.com/suburbs/daily-southtown/crime/ct-sta-brother-rice-murder-trial-st-0114-20160113-story.html.

20. Demarest, "Prostitute Who Killed Brother Rice Teacher Guilty."

21. "Prostitute Convicted of Second-Degree Murder for Stabbing Teacher," CBS Chicago, January 15, 2016, chicago.cbslocal.com/2016/01/15/prostitute-convicted-of-second-degree-murder-for-stabbing-teacher.

22. Hussain,"15 Years for Prostitute."

CHAPTER FOUR: BLUE COLLARS

1. Defining social class is tough. While many studies use income as a measurement, I think wealth is the more accurate measure. Because Black families, however, have had neither income nor wealth, often class is defined by aspiration or status. This project uses a combination of economics and aspiration.

2. In 2012, journalist Mary Curtis wrote an article about just that for the *Washington Post*. Mary C. Curtis, "Yes, You Can Be Black and Blue-collar, but the Media Gets It Wrong," She the People (blog), *Washington Post*, January 29, 2012, washingtonpost.com/blogs/she-the-people/post/yes-you-can-be-black-and-blue-collar-but-the-media-gets-it-wrong/2012/01/29/gIQATIBoaQ_blog.html.

3. "Today, Is the White Working Class in the US Being Ignored?," BBC Radio 4, April 27, 2017, bbc.co.uk/programmes/p0518by8; "The Struggling, Rural, White Communities That Feel Like Nobody Cares," *PBS NewsHour*, September 27, 2016, pbs.org/newshour/show/struggling-rural-white-communities-feel-like-nobody-one-cares; Rod Dreher, "Stop Demonizing the White Working Class," *American Conservative*, May 15, 2017, theamericanconservative.com/dreher/stop-demonizing-the-white-working-class; Wilson Paine, "Rural White Working Class Neglected," *Knoxville News-Sentinel*, August 13, 2016, archive.knoxnews.com/opinion/columnists/rural-white-working-class-neglected-39bae814-fea5-3b9f-e053-0100007fd7b1-390016081.html; Jefferson Cowie, "The Great White Nope," *Foreign Affairs* (November/December 2016), foreignaffairs.com/reviews/review-essay/2016-10-17/great-white-nope.

4. Tanzina Vega, "What About the Black Working Class?" CNNMoney, November 23, 2016, money.cnn.com/2016/11/23/news/economy/black-working-class-trump/index.html.

5. According to a report from Cherrie Bucknor at CEPR, "Black union workers on average earn 16.4 percent higher wages than non-union Black workers. Black union workers are also 17.4 percentage points more likely than non-union

Blacks to have employer-provided health insurance, and 18.3 percentage points more likely to have an employer-sponsored retirement plan." Cherrie Bucknor, "Black Workers, Unions, and Inequality," Center for Economic and Policy Research, August 2016, cepr.net/publications/reports/black-workers-unions-and-inequality. Max Ehrenfreund and Jeff Guo, "If You've Ever Described People as 'White Working Class,' Read This," *Washington Post*, November 23, 2016, washingtonpost.com/news/wonk/wp/2016/11/22/who-exactly-is-the-white-working-class-and-what-do-they-believe-good-questions.

6. US Census Bureau, 2016 American Community Survey data, from Steven Ruggles, Katie Genadek, Ronald Goeken, Josiah Grover, and Matthew Sobek, Integrated Public Use Microdata Series: Version 7.0 (dataset), Minneapolis: University of Minnesota, 2017, doi.org/10.18128/D010.V7.0.

7. Alex Rowell, "What Everyone Should Know About America's Diverse Working Class," Center for American Progress Action, December 11, 2017, americanprogressaction.org/issues/economy/reports/2017/12/11/169303/everyone-know-americas-diverse-working-class.

8. Rowell, "What Everyone Should Know"; Tanvi Misra, "Who Makes Up the Working Class, in 3 Graphs," *CityLab*, December 11, 2017, citylab.com/equity/2017/12/who-is-working-class-in-3-infographics/547559.

9. US Census Bureau, 2016 American Community Survey data.

10. Joe William Trotter, *Coal, Class, and Color: Blacks in Southern West Virginia: 1915–32* (Urbana: University of Illinois Press, 1990).

11. William Hobart Turner, *Blacks in Appalachia: Special Issue, Appalachian Heritage* (Berea, KY: Berea College, 1991).

12. Trotter, *Coal, Class, and Color*.

13. Joe William Trotter, "African-American Heritage," *West Virginia Encyclopedia*, October 19, 2010, wvencyclopedia.org/articles/27.

14. US Census Bureau, Current Population Survey, March Supplement, 2017.

15. Clifford Krauss, "Coal Miners Struggle to Survive in an Industry Battered by Layoffs and Bankruptcy," *New York Times*, July 17, 2015, nytimes.com/2015/07/18/business/energy-environment/coal-miners-struggle-to-survive-in-an-industry-battered-by-layoffs-and-bankruptcy.html; Eric Bowen et al., "An Economic Analysis of the Appalachian Coal Industry Ecosystem," Appalachian Regional Commission, January 2017, arc.gov/research/researchreportdetails.asp?REPORT_ID=141.

16. US Census Bureau, 2016 American Community Survey data.

17. Alan Flippen, "When Union Membership Was Rising," *New York Times*, May 29, 2014, nytimes.com/2014/05/30/upshot/union-membership-has-declined-since-the-1970s.html. It should also be noted that union membership is declining the most in Southern states—a region that has never been hospitable to organizing, but the region of the country where most Blacks live. Thomas C. Frohlich, "Cities with the Strongest Unions," *USA Today*, September 5, 2016, usatoday.com/story/money/business/2016/09/05/cities-strongest-unions/89343244.

18. "Projections of Industry Employment, 2016–26," Career Outlook, US Bureau of Labor Statistics, December 2017.

19. Noah Pransky, "Black Arrest Numbers Off-the-Charts in Tampa," WTSP via *Indianapolis Star*, May 6, 2015, indystar.com/story/news/investigations/2015/05/05/majority-of-tampa-arrests-are-black-people/26940149.

20. Gallup, "Labor Unions," Gallup.com, news.gallup.com/poll/12751/labor-unions.aspx, accessed April 26, 2018; Gallup, "In U.S., Majority Approves of Unions, but Say They'll Weaken," Gallup.com, August 30, 2013, news.gallup.com/poll/164186/majority-approves-unions-say-weaken.aspx; Shiva Maniam, "Most Americans See Labor Unions, Corporations Favorably," Pew Research Center, January 30, 2017, pewresearch.org/fact-tank/2017/01/30/most-americans-see-labor-unions-corporations-favorably; Eli Day, "The Economic Outlook for Millennials Is Bleak. Now They're Unionizing in Record Numbers," *Mother Jones*, February 9, 2018, motherjones.com/politics/2018/02/millennials-survived-the-financial-crisis-now-theyre-unionizing-in-record-numbers.

21. "Union Affiliation of Employed Wage and Salary Workers by Selected Characteristics," US Bureau of Labor Statistics, January 19, 2018, bls.gov/news.release/union2.t01.htm; Cherrie Bucknor, "Union Membership Byte 2017," Center for Economic and Policy Research, January 2017, cepr.net/images/stories/reports/union-byte-2017-01.pdf; John Schmitt, "Biggest Gains in Union Membership in 2017 Were for Younger Workers," Economic Policy Institute, January 25, 2018, epi.org/publication/biggest-gains-in-union-membership-in-2017-were-for-younger-workers.

22. Jonathan Timm, "Can Millennials Save Unions?" *Atlantic*, September 7, 2015, theatlantic.com/business/archive/2015/09/millennials-unions/401918; Dave Jamieson, "Union Behind the 'Fight For $15' Cuts Funding for Fast-Food Campaign," *Huffington Post*, April 3, 2018, huffingtonpost.com/entry/union-behind-the-fight-for-15-cuts-funding-for-fast-food-campaign_us_5abfe925e4b055e50ace1a2d.

23. Stuart Mora, email message to the author, April 17, 2018.

24. John Hawkins, "John Hawkins—5 Reasons Unions Are Bad for America," *Townhall,* March 8, 2011, townhall.com/columnists/johnhawkins/2011/03/08/5-reasons-unions-are-bad-for-america-n1180613.

25. Bruce Rauner, "It's Time We Say 'Enough,'" *Chicago Tribune,* September 12, 2012, articles.chicagotribune.com/2012-09-12/opinion/ct-perspec-0912-strike-20120912_1_cps-teachers-cps-schools-charter-school.

26. US Census Bureau and Bureau of Labor Statistics, Current Population Survey ASEC (March Supplement), 2017; Kimberly Brown and Marc Bayard, "And Still I Rise: Black Women Labor Leaders' Voices/Power/Promise," Institute for Policy Studies, 2015, and-still-i-rise.org/wp-content/uploads/2015/04/ASIR4_21.pdf.

27. Stuart Mora, email message to author, April 28, 2018. UNITE HERE!, it should be noted, has had victories organizing other industries in Indiana, like food service workers at several universities and public schools.

28. Josh Bivens and Lawrence Mishel, "Understanding the Historic Divergence Between Productivity and a Typical Worker's Pay: Why It Matters and Why It's Real," Economic Policy Institute, September 2, 2015, epi.org/publication/understanding-the-historic-divergence-between-productivity-and-a-typical-workers-pay-why-it-matters-and-why-its-real.

CHAPTER FIVE: PAINTED WALLS AND TEMPLES

1. Joseph T. Hallinan, *Going Up the River: Travels in a Prison Nation* (New York: Random House, 2003).

2. "Quarterly Residential Vacancies and Homeownership, Fourth Quarter 2017," Census.gov, January 30, 2018, census.gov/housing/hvs/files/currenthvspress.pdf.

3. Gurner's home purchase was made with a friend; they ended up profiting from it in a few months. After entering the real estate industry, Gurner reached out to his grandfather for a $34,000 loan to start a gym. He paid the loan back but said it had nothing to do with his real estate properties.

4. Kaitlin Pitsker, "Spending: Millennials Make the Leap to Home Ownership," *Chicago Tribune,* March 16, 2018, http://www.chicagotribune.com/business/sns-201802221507--tms--kplngmpctnkm-a20180316-20180316-story.html.

5. Derek Thompson, "Why Millennials Aren't Buying Houses," *Atlantic,* August 24, 2016.

6. "Meaning of 'The American Dream' Different for Minorities, Whites," Johns Hopkins University, April 9, 2014, releases.jhu.edu/2014/04/09/meaning-of-the-american-dream-different-for-minorities-whites.

7. Meredith Greif, "The Intersection of Homeownership, Race and Neighbourhood Context: Implications for Neighbourhood Satisfaction," *Urban Studies* 52, no. 1 (2015): 50–70.

8. "The Homestead Act of 1862," National Archives and Records Administration, October 3, 2016, https://.archives.gov/education/lessons/homestead-act; Robert B. Williams, *The Privileges of Wealth: Rising Inequality and the Growing Racial Divide* (London: Routledge, 2016).

9. "Exodusters," National Parks Service, US Department of the Interior, Accessed June 6, 2018, nps.gov/home/learn/historyculture/exodusters.htm.

10. The recent book by Maria Krysan and Kyle Crowder, *Cycle of Segregation: Social Processes and Residential Stratification* (New York: Russell Sage Foundation, 2017), points out that while Asian Americans and Hispanics have slowly started to integrate into White communities, African Americans have remained largely confined to their own communities, so much so that you can look at patterns of Black-White segregation in 1980 and predict the same patterns in 2010, meaning that little change has been made.

11. Linda Qui, "Sanders: African-Americans Lost Half Their Wealth Because of Wall Street Collapse," *Politifact*, February 11, 2016.

12. Emily Badger, "Why a Housing Scheme Founded in Racism Is Making a Resurgence Today," *Washington Post*, May 13. 2016, washingtonpost.com/news/wonk/wp/2016/05/13/why-a-housing-scheme-founded-in-racism-is-making-a-resurgence-today.

13. Andrew Billingsley, *Mighty like a River the Black Church and Social Reform* (New York: Oxford University Press, 2003); Henry Louis Gates, "The Truth Behind '40 Acres and a Mule,'" *Root*, January 7, 2013, theroot.com/the-truth-behind-40-acres-and-a-mule-1790894780.

14. Gates, "The Truth Behind '40 Acres and a Mule.'"

15. Anita Hill, *Reimagining Equality: Stories of Gender, Race, and Finding Home* (Boston: Beacon, 2011).

16. George Lipsitz, *The Possessive Investment in Whiteness: How White People Profit from Identity Politics* (Philadelphia: Temple University Press, 2006).

17. Wells Fargo, it should be noted, was sued by the Department of Justice in 2012 for discriminatory lending practices. The bank never agreed to wrongdoing, but agreed to pay $175 million in order to avoid further litigation. In 2017, Wells Fargo committed to helping increase Black homeownership, saying that it would lend at least $60 billion to Black borrowers over the next ten years. To assist with this initiative the bank is working with Black organizations around the country. HomeFree USA is one of them.

18. "President Hosts Conference on Minority Homeownership," National Archives and Records Administration, October 15, 2002, georgewbush-whitehouse.archives.gov/news/releases/2002/10/20021015-7.html.

19. Michael Fletcher, "The American Dream Shatters in Prince George's County," *Washington Post,* January 24, 2015, washingtonpost.com/sf/investigative/2015/01/24/the-american-dream-shatters-in-prince-georges-county.

20. Felipe Chacón, "Family Tradition: Kids Are More Likely to Own a Home If Their Parents Did," Trulia's Blog, August 10, 2010, trulia.com/blog/trends/family-tradition/.

21. "Quarterly Residential Vacancies and Homeownership, First Quarter 2018," Census.gov, 2018, census.gov/housing/hvs/files/currenthvspress.pdf.

22. Aaron Glantz, Emmanuel Martinez, and Jennifer Gollan, "8 Lenders That Aren't Serving People of Color for Home Loans," *Reveal,* February 15, 2018, revealnews.org/article/8-lenders-that-arent-serving-people-of-color-for-home-loans.

23. Jonathan Stempel, "Wells Fargo Loses Bid to End Philadelphia Predatory Lending Lawsuit," Thomson Reuters, January 16, 2018, reuters.com/article/wells-fargo-philadelphia/wells-fargo-loses-bid-to-end-philadelphia-predatory-lending-lawsuit-idUSL1N1PB19T.

24. Editorial Board, "Blacks Still Face a Red Line on Housing," *New York Times,* April 14, 2018, nytimes.com/2018/04/14/opinion/blacks-still-face-a-red-line-on-housing.html.

25. Jonathan Mahler and Steve Eder, "'No Vacancies' for Blacks: How Donald Trump Got His Start, and Was First Accused of Bias," *New York Times,* August 27, 2016, nytimes.com/2016/08/28/us/politics/donald-trump-housing-race.html.

26. Renae Merle, "Trump Administration Strips Consumer Watchdog Office of Enforcement Powers in Lending Discrimination Cases," *Washington Post,* February 1, 2018, washingtonpost.com/news/business/wp/2018/02/01/trump-administration-strips-consumer-watchdog-office-of-enforcement-powers-against-financial-firms-in-lending-discrimination-cases.

27. Anna Clark, "The Threat to Detroit's Rebound Isn't Crime or the Economy, It's the Mortgage Industry," *Next City,* December 7, 2015, nextcity.org/features/view/detroit-bankruptcy-revival-crime-economy-mortgage-loans-redlining; Kai, Ryssdal, "Barriers to Homeownership Still Exist for People of Color," Marketplace, February 15, 2018, marketplace.org/2018/02/15/world/barriers-homeownership-still-exist-people-color; Brentin Mock, "Remember Redlining? It's Alive and Evolving," *Atlantic,* October 8, 2015 theatlantic.com/politics/archive/2015/10/remember-redlining-its-alive-and-evolving/433065.

28. Noah Smith, "It Isn't Just Asian Immigrants Who Excel in the U.S.," Bloomberg, October 13, 2015, bloomberg.com/view/articles/2015-10-13/it-isn-t-just-asian-immigrants-who-excel-in-the-u-s-. See also: www.pewresearch.org/fact-tank/2018/01/21/key-facts-about-black-immigrants-in-the-U-S. Jan. 24, 2018, Monica Anderson and Gustavo Lopez, "Key Facts About Black Immigrants in the US"; and www.latimes.com/world/africa/la-fg-global-african-immigrants-explainer-20180112-story.html. Jan. 12, 2018, Ann M. Simmons, "African Immigrants Are More Educated Than Most, Including People Born in the US."

29. US Census Bureau, 2009–2016 American Community Survey data, from Steven Ruggles, Katie Genadek, Ronald Goeken, Josiah Grover, and Matthew Sobek, Integrated Public Use Microdata Series: Version 7.0 (dataset), Minneapolis: University of Minnesota, 2017, doi.org/10.18128/D010.V7.0,

CHAPTER SIX: LUCK

1. Mary Pattillo-McCoy, "Middle Class, Yet Black: A Review Essay," *African American Research Perspectives* 5, no. 1 (1999): 2–3; Henry Louis Gates, "Black America and the Class Divide," *New York Times*, February 1, 2016, nytimes.com/2016/02/07/education/edlife/black-america-and-the-class-divide.html.

2. Abigail Thernstrom, and Stephan Thernstrom, "Black Progress: How Far We've Come, and How Far We Have to Go," Brookings, July 28, 2016, brookings.edu/articles/Black-progress-how-far-weve-come-and-how-far-we-have-to-go.

3. Bart Landry, *The New Black Middle Class in the Twenty-First Century* (New Brunswick, NJ: Rutgers University Press, 2018); Sam Fulwood, "Blacks Find Bias Amid Affluence," *Los Angeles Times*, November 20, 1991, articles.latimes.com/1991-11-20/news/mn-180_1_middle-class-blacks; John Eligon and Robert Gebeloff, "Affluent and Black, and Still Trapped by Segregation," *New York Times*, August 20, 2016, nytimes.com/2016/08/21/us/milwaukee-segregation-wealthy-black-families.html.

4. E. Franklin Frazier, *Black Bourgeoisie* (New York: Free Press, 1957), 24–25.

5. Lyndon B. Johnson, "Radio and Television Remarks Upon Signing the Civil Rights Bill," July 2, 1964, The American Presidency Project, presidency.ucsb.edu/ws/?pid=26361.

6. Steven Brown, "The Stalled, Struggling Black Middle Class," Urban Institute, February 10, 2016, urban.org/urban-wire/stalled-struggling-Black-middle-class.

7. Bart Landry, *The New Black Middle Class in the Twenty-First Century* (New Brunswick, NJ: Rutgers University Press, 2018).

8. US Census Bureau, 2009–2016 American Community Survey data, from Steven Ruggles, Katie Genadek, Ronald Goeken, Josiah Grover, and Matthew Sobek, Integrated Public Use Microdata Series: Version 7.0 (dataset), Minneapolis: University of Minnesota, 2017, doi.org/10.18128/D010.V7.0.

9. Nancy DiTomaso, "How Social Networks Drive Black Unemployment," *New York Times*, May 5, 2013, opinionator.blogs.nytimes.com/2013/05/05/how-social-networks-drive-Black-unemployment.

10. Ellis Cose, *The Rage of a Privileged Class* (New York: HarperCollins, 1993).

11. "Look Different Bias Survey," DBR MTV Bias Survey Summary, April 2014, lookdifferent.org/about-us/research-studies/1-2014-mtv-david-binder-research-study.

12. The newspaper noted that when it comes to work ethic, 35 percent of White baby boomers, 32 percent of gen Xers, and an astonishing 31 percent of White millennials say Blacks are lazier and less hardworking than Whites. Twenty-three percent of White millennials and 24 percent of baby boomers say Blacks are less intelligent. Thirty-eight percent of White millennials also say Blacks are less well off because of intelligence. Scott Clement, "Millennials Are Just as Racist as Their Parents," *Washington Post*, April 7, 2015, washingtonpost.com/news/wonk/wp/2015/06/23/millennials-are-just-as-racist-as-their-parents.

13. Costas Cavounidis and Kevin Lang, "Discrimination and Worker Evaluation," NBER Working Paper Series, October 2015, nber.org/papers/w21612.

14. Adia Harvey Wingfield, *Changing Times for Black Professionals* (New York: Routledge, 2011).

15. Adia Harvey Wingfield, "Being Black—but Not Too Black—in the Workplace," *Atlantic*, October 14, 2015, theatlantic.com/business/archive/2015/10/being-black-work/409990. "Mammy" sacrifices her life for a White-run corporation. "Educated Bitches" are "merciless" in their pursuit of their goals—which are largely sexual. The Black Lady is someone whose sexuality is invisible or represented by a monogamous middle-class marriage, like the TV character Claire Huxtable in *The Cosby Show*. See Wingfield, *Changing Times*.

16. Dina Bass, "Everyone Knows Tech Workers Are Mostly White Men—Except Tech Workers," Bloomberg, March 22, 2017, bloomberg.com/news/articles/2017-03-22/everyone-knows-tech-workers-are-mostly-white-men-except-tech-workers.

17. His name has been changed.

18. His name has been changed.

CHAPTER SEVEN: FAME

1. Jean Bruce Poole and Tevvy Ball, *El Pueblo: The Historic Heart of Los Angeles* (Los Angeles: Getty Conservation Institute, 2002).

2. Stacy L. Smith, Marc Choueiti, and Katherine Pieper, "Inequality in 900 Popular Films," Annenberg Institute, July 2017, annenberg.usc.edu/sites/default/files/Dr_Stacy_L_Smith-Inequality_in_900_Popular_Films.pdf; Charlene Regester, "African American Extras in Hollywood During the 1920s and 1930s," *Film History* 9, no. 1 (1997): 95; Danielle Cadet, "The 'Straight Outta Compton' Casting Call Is So Offensive It Will Make Your Jaw Drop," *Huffington Post*, December 7, 2017, huffingtonpost.com/2014/07/17/straight-out-of-compton-casting-call_n_5597010.html.

3. Lacey Rose, "'Girls': Read Lena Dunham's Original Pitch for the Show," *Hollywood Reporter*, February 6, 2017, hollywoodreporter.com/live-feed/girls-read-lena-dunhams-original-pitch-show-972037.

4. Regester, "African American Extras."

5. Darnell Hunt and Ana-Christina Ramón, "2015 Hollywood Diversity Report: Flipping the Script," Ralph J. Bunche Center for African American Studies at UCLA, February 15, 2015, irle.ucla.edu/wp-content/uploads/2017/11/2015-Hollywood-Diversity-Report-2-25-15.pdf.

6. Margeaux Watson and Jennifer Armstrong, "Diversity: Why Is TV So White?," EW.com, June 13, 2008, ew.com/article/2008/06/13/diversity-why-tv-so-white.

7. Laurie Sandell, "Zendaya Explains the Real Reason She Came Back to Disney," *Cosmopolitan*, July 2, 2016, cosmopolitan.com/entertainment/news/a59215/zendaya-july-2016.

8. Rebecca Carroll, "Gabrielle Union: The Outspoken Actress Hollywood Has Been Waiting For," *Harper's Bazaar*, November 21, 2016, harpersbazaar.com/culture/features/a18822/gabrielle-union-interview; Steven Zeitchik, "Does Hollywood Discriminate Against Young Black Actors?," *Los Angeles Times*, March 4, 2011, latimesblogs.latimes.com/movies/2011/03/will-smith-black-actors-denzel-washington-anthony-mackie-discrimination/comments/page/4; Robert Piper, "Why Zoe Saldana Prefers Sci-fi to the Real World," *Daily Telegraph* (London), April 8, 2017, dailytelegraph.com.au/lifestyle/stellar/zoe-saldana-on-guardians-of-the-galaxy-2-i-love-defying-gravity/news-story/9e0953cf337b14ef20674a1d4e9263f5?nk=55975db845204f2ceca01c2ab3da685b-1524340786.

9. His name has been changed.

10. Natalie Robehmed, "Full List: The World's Highest-Paid Actors and Actresses 2017," *Forbes*, August 22, 2017, forbes.com/sites/natalierobehmed/2017/08/22/full-list-the-worlds-highest-paid-actors-and-actresses-2017/#567fc5903751.

11. Hermione Hoby, "Shamir: 'I Never Felt like a Boy or a Girl, That I Should Dress like This or That,'" *Guardian* (London), May 11, 2015, theguardian.com/music/2015/may/11/shamir-bailey-ratchet-on-the-regular; Gina Vivinetto, "Is Shamir the Post-Gender Pop Star for Our Time?" *Advocate*, May 14, 2015, advocate.com/arts-entertainment/music/2015/05/14/shamir-post-gender-pop-star-our-time; Lindsay Zoladz, "The Post-Gender, Post-Genre Charm of Indie Music's Newest Star," *Vulture*, April 23, 2015, vulture.com/2015/04/shamir-bailey-ratchet.html.

12. "HIV/AIDS," Centers for Disease Control and Prevention, April 25, 2018, cdc.gov/hiv/group/racialethnic/africanamericans/index.html; "HIV Among African Americans," Centers for Disease Control and Prevention, February 2017, cdc.gov/nchhstp/newsroom/docs/factsheets/cdc-hiv-aa-508.pdf.

CHAPTER EIGHT: STILL IN LOVE

1. Maggie Haberman, "Marriage Pledge Language Retracted," *Politico*, July 11, 2011, politico.com/story/2011/07/marriage-pledge-language-retracted-058631.

2. "Race and Attraction, 2009–2014," OkCupid Blog, September 10, 2014, theblog.okcupid.com/race-and-attraction-2009-2014-107dcbb4f060.

3. Tanisha C. Ford, "Black Marriage Unshackled: An Interview with Historian Tera W. Hunter," *Feminist Wire*, May 22, 2017, thefeministwire.com/2017/05/black-intimacy-nineteenth-century-conversation-historian-tera-w-hunter; Katherine M. Franke, "Becoming a Citizen: Reconstruction Era Regulation of African American Marriages," *Yale Journal of Law and the Humanities* 11, no. 2 (1999).

4. Henry Brown, *Narrative of the Life of Henry Box Brown* (New York: Dover Publications, 2015).

5. For the record, 69 percent of White men and 67 percent of White women were married in 1950. See Richard Morin, "A Crisis: Among Blacks, Major Changes in the Family Structure," *Washington Post*, March 25, 1997; US Census Bureau, 1950 and 1960 Decennial Census data, from Steven Ruggles, Katie Genadek, Ronald Goeken, Josiah Grover, and Matthew Sobek, Integrated Public Use Microdata Series: Version 7.0 (dataset), Minneapolis: University of Minnesota, 2017, doi.org/10.18128/D010.V7.0.

6. Walter E. Williams, "The True Black Tragedy: Illegitimacy Rate of Nearly 75%," *CNS News*, May 19, 2015, cnsnews.com/commentary/walter-e-williams/true-Black-tragedy-illegitimacy-rate-nearly-75; Andrew Kaczynski, "Homeland Security's Head of Community Outreach Once Said Blacks Turned Cities to 'Slums' with 'Laziness, Drug Use and Sexual Promiscuity,'" CNN, November 16, 2017, cnn.com/2017/11/16/politics/kfile-jamie-johnson-dhs/index.html.

7. Richard V. Reeves and Joanna Venator, "The Marriage Crisis Hurts Social Mobility," Brookings, July 29, 2016, brookings.edu/blog/social-mobility-memos/2013/10/03/the-marriage-crisis-hurts-social-mobility; Gillian B. White, "Marrying Your Peer, a Tougher Prospect for Black Women," *Atlantic*, April 28, 2015, theatlantic.com/business/archive/2015/04/marrying-your-peer-a-tougher-prospect-for-black-women/391586/.

8. Charles Blow, "Black Dads Are Doing Best of All," *New York Times*, June 8, 2015 nytimes.com/2015/06/08/opinion/charles-blow-black-dads-are-doing-the-best-of-all.html; Josh Levs, *All In: How Our Work-First Culture Fails Dads, Families, and Businesses—and How We Can Fix It Together* (New York: HarperOne, 2015); Jo Jones and William D Mosher, "Fathers' Involvement with Their Children: United States, 2006–2010," *National Health Statistics Report*, Centers for Disease Control and Prevention, December 20, 2013, cdc.gov/nchs/data/nhsr/nhsr071.pdf.

9. Ernest Owens, "Millennials, Let's Not Kill Black Love," *Huffington Post*, June 4, 2016, huffingtonpost.com/ernest-owens/millennials-lets-not-kill-black-love_b_7481586.html.

10. Centers for Disease Control and Prevention. 2017.

CHAPTER NINE: BREATHE

1. "Wilson Pierre, 22—The Homicide Report," *Los Angeles Times*, August 22, 2011, homicide.latimes.com/post/wilson-pierre.

2. Jon C. Rogowski and Cathy J. Cohen, "Black Millennials in America," Black Youth Project, October 27, 2015, blackyouthproject.com/wp-content/uploads/2015/11/BYP-millenials-report-10-27-15-FINAL.pdf.

3. "GenForward August 2016 Toplines," GenForward Survey, August 2016, genforwardsurvey.com/data.

4. Shannon Dunbar-Rubio, *Millennials Deconstructed*, October 2016, millennialsdeconstructed.com.

5. Jens Manuel Krogstad and Mark Hugo Lopez, "Black Voter Turnout Fell in 2016, Even as a Record Number of Americans Cast Ballots," Pew

Research Center, May 12, 2017, pewresearch.org/fact-tank/2017/05/12/black-voter-turnout-fell-in-2016-even-as-a-record-number-of-americans-cast-ballots; Matthew Mosk, Trish Turner, and Katherine Faulders, "Russian Influence Operation Attempted to Suppress Black Vote: Indictment," ABC News, February 18, 2018, abcnews.go.com/Politics/russian-influence-operation-attempted-suppress-black-vote-indictment/story?id=53185084; Mark Murray, "Focus Group: Dems 'Have a Lot of Work to Do' with Black Millennials," NBC News, September 28, 2017, nbcnews.com/politics/first-read/focus-group-reveals-democrats-have-lot-work-do-black-millennials-n805526.

6. Emily O'Hara, "Ferguson Protester Featured in Iconic Photo Found Dead," NBCNews, May 5, 2017, nbcnews.com/news/us-news/ferguson-protester-edward-crawford-subject-iconic-photo-found-dead-n755401.

7. Assata Shakur, *Assata: An Autobiography* (London: Zed Books, 1987).

8. Alec Tyson and Shiva Maniam, "Behind Trump's Victory: Divisions by Race, Gender, Education," Pew Research Center, November 9, 2016, pewresearch.org/fact-tank/2016/11/09/behind-trumps-victory-divisions-by-race-gender-education; Kari A. Frederickson, *The Dixiecrat Revolt and the End of the Solid South, 1932-1968* (Chapel Hill: University of North Carolina Press, 2001); "How Groups Voted in 2004," Roper Center, 2018, ropercenter.cornell.edu/polls/us-elections/how-groups-voted/how-groups-voted-2004; "Exit Polls," CNN, November 23, 2016, cnn.com/election/2016/results/exit-polls; Brian Josephs, "How Howard University's Republicans Plan to Coexist With Trump's White Right," *Spin*, January 31, 2017, spin.com/featured/young-african-american-gop-washington-dc.

9. Vanessa Williams, "Report: Black Women Underrepresented in Elected Offices, but Could Make Gains and History in 2018," *Washington Post*, March 5, 2018, washingtonpost.com/news/post-nation/wp/2018/03/05/black-women-looking-to-make-history-increase-their-numbers-in-elected-offices-in-2018; "Black Women Running for Office in the U.S.," Black Women in Politics, blackwomeninpolitics.com, accessed June 25, 2018; "Chisholm Effect: Black Women in America Politics 2018," Higher Heights Leadership Fund and Center for American Women and Politics, higherheightsleadershipfund.org/2018_report, accessed June 25, 2018.

10. Jon C. Rogowski and Cathy J. Cohen, "Black Millennials in America," Black Youth Project, University of Chicago, December 2015, blackyouthproject.com/wp-content/uploads/2015/11/BYP_ReportDesign04b_Dec03_HiRes.pdf.

INDEX

CREDIT: NINA SUBIN

Reniqua Allen is an Eisner Fellow at the Nation Institute and a former fellow at New America and Demos. She has written for the *New York Times, Washington Post, Guardian, Teen Vogue,* and more, and was a producer for WNYC, PBS, and MSNBC. Allen lives in the Bronx.